Five
Women
of Sennar

Second Edition

Five Women of Sennar

CULTURE & CHANGE IN CENTRAL SUDAN

Second Edition

Susan M. Kenyon

Butler University

WAVELAND

PRESS, INC.

Long Grove, Illinois

For information about this book, contact:
Waveland Press, Inc.
4180 IL Route 83, Suite 101
Long Grove, IL 60047-9580
(847) 634-0081
info@waveland.com
www.waveland.com

CONTENTS

ACKNOWLEDGEMENTS

This book is drawn from data collected in the town of Sennar during the period 1980 to 1985 and updated in 2000 and 2001. It consists primarily of interviews made with five Muslim women: Halima, Fatima, Zachara, Bitt al-Jamīl, and Naiema. In my introductory remarks, I have attempted to present their accounts in historical and ethnographic setting, but it is the women themselves who provide the real insight into contemporary Sudanese society. This is their book, and it could not have been undertaken without their cooperation and direction. For this second edition, the assistance of their families is also gratefully acknowledged.

As in all research, far more people contributed than is immediately evident. Besides the five who speak out in the following pages, many other women in Sennar and elsewhere in the Sudan have given of their time and hospitality over the years to help me with my inquiries. I am particularly indebted to Miriam Idris and her family for their support. Miriam's generous friendship has helped my research in countless ways as well as ensured that our stays in Sudan are memorable. In addition, Nur Esham Muhammad Ahmad, Asia Ibrahim, Miriam Omar, the late Suad al-Khoda, Nafisa Muhammad, Najat Abbas, Hannan Ahmad, Shemma

Muhammad, the late Bitt al-Imam, Fatima "Bitt al-Obeid," Allawīya Muhammad, Sharma Omar, Asma Hassan, the late Rabha Muhammad, the late Fatima "Abd al-Aziz," Zeinab Bushra, Zachara Aizadin, Fatima Kandi, Sittena Mohamad, Fatima Shateina, Ahlam Atabani, and Selma Ahmad al-Obeid, all contributed directly and in important ways to this project, and their assistance is gratefully acknowledged. Dina Omar Osman and Sara Zecki in Khartoum and Leila Mahmud of Nyala helped transcribe my earlier taped material, while Hanan Muhammad and Hiba Osman assisted with transcription in 2001. In doing this, they all went far beyond the job of simply translating interviews and provided me with a great deal of insight into general social and cultural issues in the Sudan.

In Khartoum, I benefited from discussions particularly with the late Muhammad Omar Beshir, Maureen Makki, Asha Musa El-Saeed and family, and Balghis Bedri. Ahmad El-Safi and the late Sharafeldin E. Abdelsalam shared with me their knowledge of traditional medicine and contemporary holy men. Martin Daly helped me locate some records at the Central Archives and the late R. C. Stevenson puzzled over some linguistic terms with me. Grace Khalifa and family were always ready with sustenance and encouragement. My thanks to each of them.

Continuation of my research in Sennar would not have been possible without the assistance of Dr. Ali Abdel Magid and his wife Sitt al-Jil, who facilitated our travel to Sudan and encouraged me to revise the text. Their friendship, now spanning more than twenty years, has helped broaden my view of Sudanese society and continues to provoke me to new interpretations of developments within Sudan. Dr. Suad M. Sulaiman sponsored my recent research and her ingenuity and commitment have provided a remarkable model for my research.

In Sennar I am indebted to the staff and their families of the Regional Veterinary Laboratory: Dr. Osman Asawi (director), Iman, Abdullah, Il Ham, Adil, Hanan, Agri, Iwen, Ishrara, Amal, and Hibat. They all not only provided my research assistants and I with a home base and hospitable extended family but also helped give our research credibility in Sennar itself.

Research in both 2000 and 2001 was facilitated by academic grants from Butler University. I am also grateful to Butler for academic (sabbatical) leave in 2001 and for professional support in writing up the results of this research. I particularly acknowledge the assistance of colleagues Paul Hanson, Erica Tucker, and Fred Yaniga at various stages of its completion. Through the years, my ideas have also been significantly shaped by discussions with Jeanette Dickerson Putman, Lesley A. Sharp, Rogaia Abu Sharaf, and Eriberto Lozada.

All or parts of this second edition were read by undergraduate students Kalil Dabagia (Butler University) and Sara Davidson (Purdue University). Their comments were both critical and insightful, alerting me particularly to issues that would confuse students. I thank them profoundly for the time and effort they put into this summer reading. Tom Curtin at Waveland Press has been unfailingly encouraging about this project and his patience particularly is acknowledged. He never once doubted that, despite my flagging energy from recurrent bouts of malaria, the revisions would finally be completed.

Finally, I should like to thank my family. Ali, Katie, and Christopher variously shared our experiences in the Sudan, our affection for its peoples, and ongoing conversations which have led to this revised edition. I am particularly grateful to Katie for her very thorough and thoughtful reading of the text. Although her memories of many of the events and people here have now faded, her interest has not, and her comments and support have been invaluable. Finally I acknowledge the contributions of my husband Simon, who has shared most of my research in Sudan and has helped support it in myriad ways. His perspectives on Sudanese society and culture, often very different from my own, have played a significant part in shaping my ideas and interpretations.

Note on Arabic Usage

In this edition, I have tried to keep Arabic terms to a minimum, many times using a less-than-exact English translation. When an Arabic term is found in the text, usually where no adequate translation is available, I have attempted to make it as simple and manageable as possible to the English reader, sometimes adopting a popular Anglicized form, including an Anglicized plural for the terms that resist translation. These are explained as they are introduced and in the glossary at the end of the volume. Local, colloquial variations in pronunciation and usage are preferred, such as *bitt* and *wad* (for the classical *bint* and *walad)*.

In order to make the text easily accessible to general readers I also sometimes use U.S. currency terms for Sudanese pounds (£S) and piastres (pennies). Readers should, of course, be aware that very few women in Sennar have access to U.S. dollars.

SMK

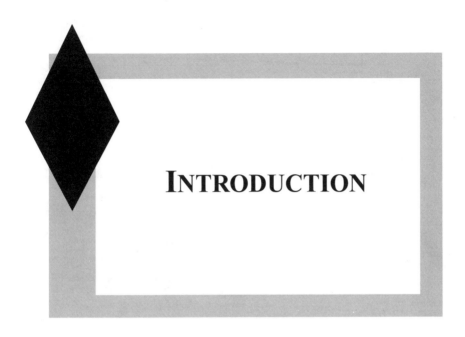

INTRODUCTION

The Republic of Sudan, usually known simply as Sudan, is the largest country in Africa. Yet it remains a relatively little-known place despite the range of disasters it has suffered in the last few decades and the reputation it has recently acquired, notably in the United States, as a leading terrorist state. Drought, followed by famine and large-scale internal migration, brought suffering to hundreds of thousands of people in the 1980s, while civil war has been tearing the country apart for at least half a century. This dire situation has been exacerbated by the introduction of Islamic law (Sharī'a) in 1983, and the policies of the present government, the National Islamic Front (NIF), which came to power in a military coup in Khartoum in 1989. The subsequent attempts to "Islamize" the country, for Muslims and non-Muslims alike, have increased internal tensions in Sudan, particularly between people in the northern and central regions and those from the south and west. Many Sudanese have fled abroad, from the south to escape the war, from the north to evade political and economic persecution. Meanwhile the government has aligned itself with other Middle Eastern and Far Eastern, particularly Muslim, nations, in ways that appear to threaten the interests of the West.

1

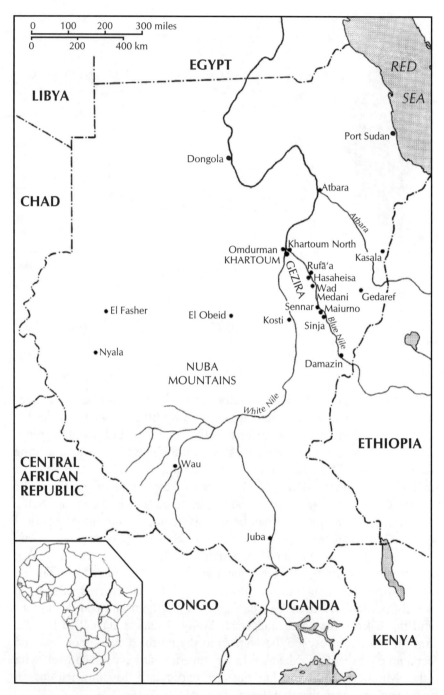

The Sudan and its neighbors

Yet for many Sudanese these events are neither new nor every-where so dramatic as the Western media projects. Famine, flooding, and drought have occurred before in the country's history. Just over a hun-dred years ago, during the Mahdīya (see chapter 1), there was an equally difficult period in which natural calamities were exacerbated by political uncertainty. Political problems, especially along the Sudan's vast bor-ders, have also occurred frequently, together with intertribal warfare. For many ordinary people in central Sudan recent events have not disrupted their way of life or been seen to mark any sharp changes in the way things were. Life just becomes increasingly harder and more expensive as basic necessities become luxuries and there seem to be more demands on less income or capital.

The crises of recent years, however, have brought changes, not always dramatic but essentially far-reaching. Large-scale population movements, economic transformations, political changes, and social unrest are all symptoms of underlying processes that have been affecting Sudanese society from within and without. Many people have moved to the cities and towns of northern and central Sudan, driven by war, environ-mental pressures, as well as their own desires for a better life for their fam-ilies. Here they find improved opportunities for employment, education, and health care, even though the rapid inflation of recent years has meant that in real terms it is ever more difficult to make ends meet. The shift towards a political form of Islam, begun in the early 1980s, was consoli-dated with the coup of 1989. The dominance of the political arm of the Muslim Brotherhood since that time has spread a form of Islamic correct-ness with impacts throughout society. Opposition to this correctness, or to the political hegemony enforcing it, continues to be closely monitored but has certainly not disappeared. Student unrest particularly reflects the diverse views of Sudan's heterogeneous society.

For Sudanese women especially times are changing as their lives become quite different from those of their mothers and their grandmoth-ers. Superficially, they like to reminisce, as do people everywhere, about the "good old days," when things were cheap and life was simple and pre-dictable. Women recognize, however, that the changes are not necessarily to their disadvantage. Many are enjoying increased opportunities for edu-cation and employment, for better health care and maternity choices, for easier travel and simpler communication. They feel their lives are better than their mothers'. Most important of all, they see improved prospects for their children, daughters as well as sons.

Women everywhere are becoming more independent and confident, even though they are aware there may be a cost. Independent women are not new in Sudan, as becomes clear from the following accounts of five older women from the town of Sennar, in central Sudan, but they are increasingly common in the country today. At all levels of society, women are assuming more responsibility for themselves and their families, as men are often absent, working elsewhere in the Sudan and the Middle East, or forced to migrate for political reasons. In the process, women are finding new sources of strength and support, both within themselves and from other women. The private women's world of central Sudan is becoming more public but without losing the values and order of Muslim culture on which it is firmly based. It must be stressed from the outset that such changes and increased opportunities are relative to that culture and society: this remains a Muslim society with Islamic ideals, which continue to provide meaning and order for personal as well as public life.

In the following pages, I look at some of these changes and opportunities through the eyes and words of five Muslim women from the town of Sennar. In translated and edited interviews, which now spread over twenty years, supplemented by my commentary, they talk about their families and homes, their hopes and aspirations, their work and their social lives, offering insight into life in a contemporary Sudanese town from the perspectives of both ordinary and extraordinary women. In this revised, second edition, follow-up interviews with the women, their children, and their grandchildren chart some of the changes that have occurred in the Sudan over the last two decades. It is hoped that the accounts generate some understanding of individual people and the ways they have been dealing with the demands of rather tumultuous times.

My family and I moved to the Sudan at the end of 1979 and lived there for almost six years. From 1979 to 1981 Sennar was home, for my husband Simon and me, and our children, Alistair (Ali) and Katie, then aged six and four respectively. Christopher was to arrive in 1982, shortly after we moved from Sennar to the west of Sudan. We had come to Sennar from Pennsylvania where both Simon and I had completed graduate studies and had been teaching. Simon, a large animal veterinarian, initially took two years leave of absence from his position at University of Pennsylvania's veterinary school to learn something about global livestock problems. Eventually he was to spend ten years in development work and when he finally returned to a U.S. university, it was to Purdue, rather than Penn. He came to Sudan as part of a British government aid project to support livestock services in the country and was based at the regional veterinary laboratory in Sennar. Here we lived in the laboratory compound, in one of five government houses provided for staff and their families, and here I hoped to carry out ethnographic research into women's lives. I had already done fieldwork for my doctoral dissertation in anthropology at a Native American village on the northwest coast of Canada. I also knew the Sudan and Sennar, having taught at the Girls Secondary School at Wad Medani some years earlier, working with Voluntary Service Overseas, and during my stay there had made a memorable school trip to the river and gardens of Sennar. As we had planned our move to Sudan, I intended to look at the effects education was having on women's lives. Once we arrived in Sennar, however, this became increasingly irrelevant. We were living in an area of town where few women had received formal education. On the other hand they were active participants and leaders in their local communities, socially, economically, and even religiously, and I found myself excited by a range of other research possibilities.

Our first task was to master enough Arabic to communicate with our new neighbors. While a few of Simon's colleagues spoke excellent English, none of the women and children we met in the first few months at Sennar knew any. Alistair and Katie almost immediately learned enough Arabic to play with neighboring children, and for the next two years were to enjoy the freedom of daily sunshine, the safety of the laboratory grounds for a playground, and a very flexible home-schooling schedule. Our language skills were acquired more painfully, but gradually, with a great deal of support from our new friends, we were able to follow conversations and become more involved in the life around us.

After two years in Sennar we moved (in late 1981) to Nyala, in Western Sudan, and in 1982 to Khartoum where we lived until mid-1985. During this time I continued to visit Sennar regularly, staying for up to a month at a time with some of my former neighbors and remaining active in community affairs. Since leaving Sudan I have been able to return three times, in 1988, 2000, and most recently in 2001. On this last occasion I spent almost four months in Sennar, living with one of the women whose story is told in this book, and close to two others. Part of my recent research agenda was to learn what has happened to each of the women, to update their stories, and through their lives to understand some of the main changes that have occurred in Sudan over the past twenty years.

A description of women's lives through edited case studies was originally planned as part of a much bigger project aimed at documenting how Sudan has developed and changed. At first I intended to include studies of women from a wide range of backgrounds: rural as well as urban, young and old, housewives and professional women, rich and poor, Muslim and non-Muslim, and from a diversity of tribal backgrounds. In this way, it was hoped that social change among Sudanese women would be put into broad perspective. I met up with some of my former students who include teachers, veterinarians, lawyers, journalists, and bank officials as well as wives of important professional and public figures. As the wife myself of a doctor in Sennar, I was able to enjoy the company of the more prosperous families in town. As a housewife living in one of the poorest areas of Sennar, I was also involved in local networks of friendship and mutual help that gave me insight into very different levels of society. By early 1981 I had a large circle of friends and acquaintances, and had identified those I felt were articulate enough and willing to tell their story. My Arabic was competent enough to begin intensive interviewing and I had drawn up a questionnaire by means of which I intended to collect systematic information for analytical and comparative purposes. I set to work, visiting my chosen informants and hoping to amass boxes of cassette tapes of information.

Of course it did not work like that. Ethnographic field research probably never proceeds smoothly, and in retrospect I should have recognized that my project was both overly ambitious and impractical. The life that I was trying to document just did not allow for such a single-minded and academic approach. Even though the women were quite happy to help me, it was only rarely that the opportunity presented itself for systematic questioning. All the women I mixed with led full and busy lives and in their leisure time they liked to relax and chat with their friends. They were rarely alone with nothing better to do than answer my questions. Their lives were full of sudden contingencies: a sick friend to visit; funerary rites to attend; guests for lunch; help with a neighbor's cooking, cosmetic preparations, or ceremony; an urgent call to their home village; a headache. For women who worked outside the home, these demands were that much greater. Even if we did get a chance to talk alone for a few minutes we were invariably interrupted or joined by other women wanting to help. Group sessions were fun and told me a great deal about general matters but did not reveal much about individual lives.

Working in a contemporary urban setting of a developing country like the Sudan also presents its own difficulties. Shall I ever forget the time I recorded a pivotal interview with one of my informants, only to realize well into the conversation that the new Chinese batteries I had just bought in the market were quite dead? Attempts to redeem that situation by plugging the cable of my tape recorder into the house's main power supply met with equal failure: the electricity was off, as it frequently was in those days. Furthermore in the 1980s, simply providing for the family's daily needs demanded a great deal of my time. Essentials such as bread or sugar were not always available and it took a lot of effort to procure even basic necessities. Water, despite the proximity of the Blue Nile, ran infrequently and often had to be stored. Life in the town continues to be demanding, even within the constraints of a working life or the domestic round. This is especially so for women, who find opportunities for employment and diversion in many areas, some of which are described below. Women are busy, not just in their homes and jobs, but participating in and often directing the social and cultural life evolving round them and through them. It takes a certain mental and physical energy simply to keep up with different networks and activities, particularly in the grueling heat that Sennar enjoys for much of the year.

My research therefore had to be carried out with some flexibility. Formal interviewing could never be scheduled successfully but was carried out on a pragmatic basis, and for the most part consisted of open-ended questions, rather than the planned questionnaire. Initially this did not matter too much but it did lead to some frustration in attempting follow-up interviews and in completing case studies. Consequently, the research turned into a much lengthier process than originally (and unrealistically) anticipated. Plans to work with professional women still have not been realized, though this becomes an increasingly interesting topic as more and more women enter higher education and the formal workplace. Research with housewives, village women, and schoolgirls, not complete enough for extended case-study presentation, continues to provide background data for my various analyses. From interviews with local Sennar working women, however, who had received little or no formal training, I built up a fascinating and significant collection of case studies. These were transcribed, translated, and edited, keeping as closely as possible to the women's own words. I then selected the five case studies included in this volume. As the manuscript first took shape, I planned to include twice this number but it became both unwieldy and repetitive. However the following accounts covered the range of issues and activities in Sennar society I felt were needed for a general introduction to the culture or way of life of Muslim Sudanese women. Furthermore, they are interesting accounts in their own right. Not every informant was either as articulate or as forthcoming as the women in this volume.

Taken together, the stories of the five women cover the salient topics in the culture of Sudanese women in the early 1980s. They offer insight into Sudanese culture as a whole, but from a female perspective, one that twenty years ago was rarely stated publicly, though today women's voices are heard in greater numbers. On the whole, they are about a female world. In the chapters below, there are glimpses and comments on men and the wider world, but these are from the women's point of view. These are not deliberate omissions. Rather they are corroboration of the reality of the "dual social world" of Muslim society, marked less by physical barriers, at least in the poorer parts of towns like Sennar where living spaces are small, than by ideational separation. Men's lives, interests, and concerns are largely with other men; women's preoccupations continue to be predominantly with other women and their children. These points will be clarified by description in the main text and returned to in the concluding chapter.

To give focus to our conversations, I suggested the topic of work to all the women I interviewed *formally,* which basically means when we used a tape recorder. This was a subject we could discuss without embarrassment and was interpreted by us all as basically what women *did.* Mere income generation is just one aspect of those activities. They evidently regard their work as beginning when they get up to make the morning tea and fit their endeavors outside the domestic round in with other demands of their lives. There is no real segregation between "home" and "work." As they grow older this continues to hold true, although by 2001, only two of the women continued to work with any regularity.

All five women who speak out below were good friends of mine by the time we came to record these conversations about their lives, and they and their families were happy to help me with *my* work. On the other hand, they felt that certain topics could not be included for quotation even though in everyday conversation, with close friends, talk can be quite uninhibited. Originally some of the women did not wish their own names to be used, though as we worked on this second edition, all of them wanted to be identified, proudly showing off their copies of the first edition and ready, if not eager, to pose for photographs. The subjects themselves largely controlled the information given, ignoring questions they did not wish to discuss (usually probes into their marriages or families), which they felt were too personal or, in the case of the leader of *tombura zār,* about esoteric detail which she was unable to divulge.

Much of what they say follows stereotyped lines and conventions. Their fatalism and acceptance is very real. In general they do not grumble or complain about their lives, but accept what comes as from God. Efforts have been made to reproduce their expressions and attitudes and to edit their accounts as little as possible. Many, but not all, of their pious references are kept. In addition the sense of motivation in the texts is their own. Their practical, down-to-earth attitudes are very much in line with what I learned of Sudanese women when met on their own terms.

The income-generating activities of all the women in this book are part of the economic sector often referred to as "informal" and "traditional." These terms, found in opposition to "formal" and "modern," are still commonly used but need comment as they are misleading and a source of irritation to those so categorized. Both formal and informal, traditional and modern sectors are affected by the same ongoing processes of globalization, change, and modification. Though each of the occupations described in this volume is rooted in Sudanese culture, all have changed in response to broader forces impacting on local Sudanese communities. By 1985, they were being performed for cash, and the dynamism behind them was evident as Sudanese cultures developed within their own terms, not merely in response to outside forces for change. In 2001 I continued to be struck by the vigor of local institutions as well as by the unpredictability of local development. The fact that women are achieving a certain financial and personal independence from the constraints of their families and society as a whole continues to reflect trends in Sudanese Muslim society that are affecting the status and roles of all members of society. This is despite the political shift towards Islamization in the last twenty years, which has had profound impacts on contemporary Sudan.

The following chapters are essentially about ordinary Sudanese women in provincial Muslim society, a society where wholesale changes are occurring. They are an attempt to describe the pattern of that culture and understand a little about the women's world and how they move in it and perceive its continuities and its changes. Even though my aim was to keep the focus on the voices of Sudanese women themselves, this book is also inevitably about my own perceptions and experiences of Sudanese society. There is no completely successful way of describing another culture, as recent critical discussions in anthropology have shown. When I first decided to use life histories as a way of letting the women speak for themselves, there were few models to draw on. Since publication of the first edition of these narratives, a great deal has been written on the problems of ethnographic subjectivity and whether it is ever possible to empower one's subject through ethnography. These concerns were very real to me as I first struggled to give voice to the five women of Sennar and at the same time to translate those voices in ways that made sense across cultural as well as linguistic divides without destroying their authenticity.

My approach here is particularly subjective in that I selected five women and five specific careers through which to look at Sudanese society in general. This was done deliberately, and with care. I knew the women and the area for almost six years when I wrote the first edition and I continue to feel that those included here really do speak for many other women around them. These are ordinary women, content with their lot in most ways, even though in material terms they may have little. They accept their lives and situations with Islamic fatality and grace and make the most of what they have within those terms. Yet they are also determined, capable, and strong-willed, as their accounts quite clearly show. Likewise, many Sudanese women today are obviously able to plan and organize the changes affecting their society without drastic interference either from the men in their lives or from outside agencies and governments who do not always understand their motivations or their goals.

There are of course many other Sudanese women whose stories deserve to be told. A common criticism of the book I hear in the Sudan is that it ignores the visible accomplishments of the numerous women who over the past fifty years have achieved political, academic, or economic success despite the odds they initially faced. Several of my former students at Wad Medani Girls Secondary School went on to become the first female professional in their field—judge, veterinarian, journalist—and many others have made important contributions to their society and country. Hopefully their accomplishments will also be recognized in print. However my long experience in Sudan has been mainly with women like the five we meet in the following pages, and their lives and those of their families offer insight into a society and part of the world still not well-known in the West.

The second edition of this book contains the core of the original text, the narratives of the five women, largely unchanged from the first edition. My introduction and conclusion have been revised, as has my introduction to each of the narrative chapters. In addition, I have added a final section to each chapter describing what has happened to the women in the last twenty years. Where possible, I have included extracts from interviews I had in 2001.

Since the first edition of this book went to press, other significant accounts of Muslim Sudanese women's lives have also been published. Those interested in learning more about the people of the Sudan, particularly the women, are urged to consult them (Bernal 1993, Boddy 1989, Gruenbaum 2001, Hale 1998, Ismail and Makki 1990).

CULTURE
AND SOCIETY
IN CONTEMPORARY
SENNAR

The Town of Sennar

Modern Sennar is an expanding market town situated on the west bank of the Blue Nile, approximately 250 miles south of Khartoum. In 1980 and 1981, when the bulk of my research was carried out, it was the headquarters of Sennar District, with administrative and judicial offices centered in the town. After regional reorganization in the mid-1990s, it became the largest town in the newly formed Sennar State, although the town of Sinja is the state capital. Sennar remains a busy market and is an important intersection in Sudan's developing network of roads. In 1980, shortly after we arrived in Sennar, a paved road was completed, connecting the town with Wad Medani, and thence to Khartoum in the north and to Kasala and Port Sudan in the east. This gave a further impetus to a town that was already fast-growing and thriving. Sennar's historical significance, however, lay in its proximity to the Jazira Scheme, the oldest and largest agricultural scheme in the Sudan, whose primary product, cotton, remains a mainstay of the Sudanese economy.

Al-Gul'a, Sennar

The name Sennar is an old and famous one. Old Sennar was the capital of the Funj kingdom, which dominated a large part of contemporary Sudan from the sixteenth to the eighteenth centuries. A colorful English account of it was left by Bruce (1790), who visited the town in 1772. Even at that period, however, the empire was in decline. By the time of its conquest by Egyptian forces under Muhammad 'Ali in 1821, it had virtually collapsed and was a shadow of its former strength. From 1821 to 1885 the old capital served as a garrison for occupying Ottoman troops and administration. They put up strong resistance to the nationalist uprising under Muhammad Ahmad, known to history as the Mahdi (Promised One) and it took three assaults on the city before it finally fell, in August 1885. Survivors were taken as prisoners to Omdurman, and for the next few years, under the Mahdīya, the old town was virtually abandoned.

In 1898, after more than a decade of economic, ecological, and social disasters, nationalist forces loyal to the successor to the Mahdi, the Khalifa 'Abdallāhi, were defeated by an invading Anglo-Egyptian army at Kareri, north of Omdurman. A joint Anglo-Egyptian "condominium" government was established, which was to rule the country for the next fifty-five years. Old Sennar, as it became known, was virtually in ruins. The new government initially restored provincial headquarters there but in 1900 moved them north to Wad Medani. In 1903, district headquarters were also transferred from Sennar to a village known as Kabbosh, a mile or so south on the Blue Nile. Here new buildings were erected and a biweekly market was established. Slowly people began to move to Kabbosh, and by 1905 it had a population of 350 (Gleichen 1905:119). In 1909, the railway line was completed as far as Old Sennar, where a station was constructed just north of Kabbosh.

In the early years of the twentieth century, the condominium also implemented an experimental social policy in the vicinity of Old Sennar, which led to the establishment of a new town.[1] One of the biggest problems confronting the government was the large number of unemployed soldiers in the country, and to deal with this it introduced a program known as "colonization." Selected ex-soldiers and volunteers were given land in new "colonies," together with the means of moving there with their families, plus grain and tax concessions to help them get settled in their new homes. Three of the earliest colonies were founded near Old Sennar and were known as Kabbosh, Helmi (or Helmi Abbas), and Makwar. Kabbosh on the west bank and Helmi Abbas on the east bank of the Blue Nile are today large villages close to the modern town of Sennar. They are still largely populated by the descendants of ex-soldiers and have not experienced any drastic change in appearance or organization.

On the other hand, Makwar, situated on the Blue Nile about ten kilometers downstream from Old Sennar, was to become the modern town of Sennar. This area was soon targeted for extensive agricultural development, particularly large-scale cotton production; as early as 1904 government proposals were being discussed to irrigate the large fertile triangle or "island" of land between the Blue and White Niles, the Jazira. In 1913 initial funding for this was realized when the British government guaranteed a loan of £3 million, and Makwar was chosen as the location for construction of the dam to feed the irrigation canals. The First World War led to the project being postponed but work finally began in 1919 and the dam was officially opened in 1925. The whole construction project was finally completed by the end of 1930. During this period large numbers of laborers were attracted to the area, particularly Taʿaisha and West African (Fellata) immigrants. The ex-soldiers' colony was transformed from a sleepy little village into a busy commercial center. By 1922, there was a motion to deny the colonists of Makwar the special privileges still granted in Helmi and Kabbosh on the grounds that "Makwar had ceased to be a colonist village." Though the name of Makwar lingered on and indeed is still heard in the older parts of Sennar and Kabbosh, on January 1, 1931, the name of the town was officially changed from Makwar to Sennar, in order to preserve the reputation of the old capital.

By 1930, with the completion of the dam and the successful organization of the Jazira Agricultural Scheme, the town of New Sennar began to prosper. During the 1930s and 1940s people from the northern riverain area, from the Dongolawi, Sha'igīya, and Ja'alīyin tribes, were drawn here by the prospects for trade and commerce, and many of them now form the core of local business interests. The first schools were built in Sennar in the 1930s, a boy's elementary school followed (in 1939) by one for girls, where initial enrolment of fifteen students increased to one hundred by the end of the first month. Nevertheless it was a long time before elementary education for girls was to become common in the town and still longer in the Sudan as a whole. Although all the women in this volume regarded formal education as a priority for their daughters as well as their sons, and indeed saw some of them graduate from university, this is still not the case in much of the country at the turn of the twenty-first century.

In April 1950, the first town council in Sennar was inaugurated and laid the pattern to be followed in local government through the years after independence in 1956. According to the minutes of an early council meeting, there were then just over eight thousand people in Sennar, a figure strangely unaltered by the time of the first national census of 1955/6. This had doubled, however, by the housing survey of 1964/5 (quoted in El-Arifi 1980:398). By 1985, the town had expanded even more dramatically as migrants moved to Sennar in search of work in the agricultural schemes, the markets, and the new industrial complexes. Since that time the town has continued to grow and prosper, to incorporate new migrants from throughout the country as well as war refugees from the south and west.

Some of the early decisions of the new council are revealing about the state of Sennar at mid-century. There was no electricity or running water in town, even in the first-class district, and lack of street lighting was a problem, particularly along the main road where there were many water holes *(khor)*. There was already a hospital but there was no dispensary and funds were short. In October, Councillor al-Tahir moved that no services be made for foreigners who died in the hospital but pointed out that it was essential to appoint a *fakī* (holy man) and a woman immediately in order to carry out the washing of corpses, at a salary of £E18.00 a year for both.

During that year, the council eagerly awaited the arrival of a town planner to help them improve the state of the town. By the end of 1950, the

planner arrived. In the next few years, the town was reorganized; all existing districts were downgraded and plans were set in motion to build an
impressive first-class district, regarded as the "Face of the Town." This
was the area people first pass through when they come into Sennar from
the north; first-class government housing was built here alongside the
homes of the more affluent citizens. The new district was designed to be as
attractive as possible, with expensive houses, tree-lined streets, and facilities such as electricity and running water. The council also decided that an
area on the northwestern side of the town should be set aside for industrial
development. This has never been extensive but over the years peanut oil,
cigarettes, sugar, cotton, and textiles have been manufactured there. It is
from agriculture, however, that the town's steady growth is derived. The

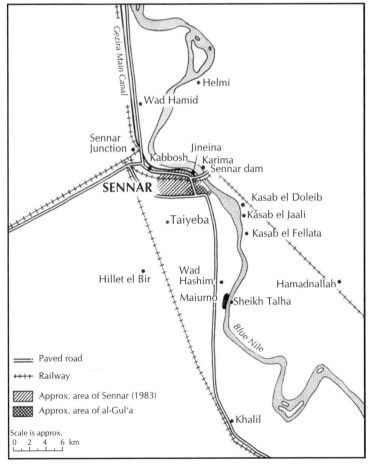

Contemporary Sennar and its surroundings

Sennar Sugar Scheme, the agricultural reform cotton schemes around Sennar, and particularly the Jazira Scheme, remain some of the country's major assets, despite problems with management and organization.

By 1973 Sennar was the seventeenth largest town in the Sudan (El-Arifi 1980:398). It was growing rapidly as new districts were planned and squatter settlements (known as fourth-class districts or, officially, native lodging areas) were regularized and provided with basic facilities. In 1980 there were fourteen districts and by 2001 four more had been added. These are still organized into different classes of district, a legacy from the condominium period, which are indicative of age and distance from the center of town as much as of affluence. Two first-class districts now flank the route by which one enters Sennar from the north and contain some elaborate and enormous homes. The district of the *muezifiyin*, "government officials," is the older and parts still have a distinctly colonial appearance with spacious lawns and shaded gardens. The district of the *mukhteribiyin*, "expatriates," is more recent and contains very grand homes being built by people working overseas. Shops, petty traders, and market areas are noticeably absent from these districts, although it is not far, across the railway line, to the main market of town. The second-class districts, Mazatt and Taktūk, are the oldest parts of Sennar, the heart of the town, close to the market and the main mosques. They also contain some fine houses but their smaller, walled courtyards distinguish them from the more cosmopolitan environment of the first-class districts. Third-class districts derive largely from the 1950s and 1960s and are distinguished by both their distance from the center of town and the type of property: the standard of housing is generally lower and courtyards are smaller. Many of the occupants were born in Sennar and surrounding areas and have lived in their homes for most of their lives. The three fourth-class districts I described in 1980 have now been upgraded to third-class, commensurate with the fact that they have running water, electricity, and most recently of all, telephone lines. These districts lie around the southern border of the town and were settled largely in the late 1960s and 1970s. For the most part, the original mud-baked houses and grass huts have been replaced with solid brick rooms and not infrequently by substantial homes.

Finally, following the completion of a paved bypass around the outskirts of the town in 1985, new residential districts have been developed there, giving former tenants in Sennar the opportunity to acquire their own house sites. At the same time, the town council built a central bus station just beyond the new road, adjacent to an extensive new market, and attempted to replace the old marketplace in the heart of the city. Unfortunately the new site was regarded as inconvenient by most of the merchants,

In the main market, Sennar (2001)

who chose to remain in the very congested old market area, as well as by the customers, who found the increased fares to the new market unacceptable. The "new" market therefore remains unused although the facilities it offers are far better than those in the "main" market.

In 2001 Sennar remains an administrative, judicial, and commercial center. District council offices, a law court, and a jail are located here; the large and varied markets service a wide hinterland; and it is an important junction for rail and road transport throughout the country. Sennar is also home to several faculties of Sennar University, the state medical center, and the main market.

Our home in the compound of Sennar regional veterinary laboratory was on the southern edge of town, in one of the former fourth-class districts, al-Gul'a (meaning fortress or hilltop) and it was here too that three of the women in this volume lived. Here most of my research was conducted and much of my commentary is based on what I learned from the women of this district. In the last forty years, this type of urban growth, arising largely from squatter settlement and developing fairly rapidly into solid, respectable neighborhoods, has provided women with accelerated change and often with increased opportunities, as well as with distinct social and housing issues. When we returned in 2000 and 2001, we found that most of our friends there are now the owners of large pieces of capital real estate, and although in other ways their income and livelihood have not changed dramatically, home ownership has clearly brought security and been the basis of their family's improved fortunes.

During the course of my early research in al-Gul'a, I carried out a household survey administered to women of 125 households in an attempt to determine women's attitudes to urban development and to life in the town generally. These supported what I was learning in informal conversations with women: they felt very positive about life in the town. Although they apparently came to the district or town to accompany a man (husband, brother, or father), the reasons most women gave for moving were the tangible benefits they perceived for themselves and their families, such as their own home with the prospect of modern facilities, improved schooling and job opportunities, and better and more varied health care facilities. They certainly did not see themselves as passive partners in the urban process. On the whole they have been energetic contributors to urban development though not necessarily in ways that are evident to outsiders or counted in official records. This text is an attempt to document some of these contributions.

Society and Kinship in Sennar

Sennar society remains largely Islamic and patrilineal, multi-ethnic, stratified, and dynamic. These are the main generalizations one can make, as there is great variety from one district to another, even between one family and another. In both rich and poor neighborhoods, one finds conservative extended households alongside a single nuclear family. In addition, since publication of the first edition, large numbers of Christians, refugees from hostilities in the South and the Nuba Mountains, have settled in the town, supporting four distinct church congregations even as they live side by side with their Muslim neighbors in predominantly poor areas.

Women in urban areas like al-Gul'a interact within two often overlapping groups: their neighborhood and their assorted relatives around the town. Two interlocking principles of social organization can therefore be distinguished, residence and kinship, with the former increasingly important. Residence and kinship used to be largely synonymous in Sudanese society. Even in the early days of urban development there was a marked tendency for ethnic or tribal groups to form compact districts, as Zachara the midwife explains in chapter 4. This is no longer the case as people become more mobile and both family composition and residential districts reflect greater variety.

In the Arabic language there are no generally applicable terms to refer to specific social units. All such terms need to be interpreted within a specific context. In Sennar, a variety of terms were noted but those discussed below are the most important and the most relevant for understanding the women's accounts of their families.

Residence

Ownership of property, of a house of their own, however modest, is very important to women in Sennar and this can be seen in the chapters that follow. It is not just the sense of security this brings, though that is evidently important. Women also acquire a very real sense of identity and independence, whether they are married or divorced. In some of the chapters that follow, it is not clear whether the women or their husbands own the property. Women certainly talked and acted as though they did. In the case of the three divorced women, the property was their own.

Household (al-beit)

The term *beit* literally means house but is used in a loose descriptive sense. "The house of the people of Fatima" is a way of describing a place or a social group. It can be applied to a single residence or to anyone living in a household, male or female. It is not uncommon in poor areas like al-Gul'a for several unrelated households to share a house or compound but to maintain separate households within it. Halima the hairdresser shared a compound with another family when she first came to Sennar, renting two rooms from them. "The house of Halima" then referred to her two rooms. The term is not used in Sennar to refer specifically to a nuclear family.

From the household survey I conducted in al-Gul'a in 1981, I found that the predominant household was overwhelmingly that of the nuclear family, though frequently one or more relatives were staying in the house for varying periods: a country cousin attending school locally or working in Sennar and maintaining his own home elsewhere; a sister come to help with a new baby; or guests simply on a visit of indeterminate length. Furthermore, many households in al-Gul'a are related, a link that is increasingly common as young people marry outside their immediate family, often across ethnic lines, and settle in their own homes nearby rather than with their parents.

The ideal of the extended family household also remains common in al-Gul'a. These include multigenerational families, spouses and families of siblings, polygynous families, and combinations thereof. In addition, there are multiple households (two or three unrelated families sharing a house), bachelors' houses, and occasionally individual men living alone, though the latter residences tend to be poor grass huts that are occupied only temporarily or seasonally. There is also an area of women's houses, commonly regarded as brothels, and a few instances of women living with their children.

Neighborhood (farīg)

Officially the town of Sennar is divided into districts *(hai)*, and certain of these district names are used as terms of reference. On the whole these are the names of the third-class (and former fourth-class) districts, where the sense of community is stronger, an observation made by several women who had the experience of living in several districts. Women in second-class districts were often unaware of the official name of their district, while women in first-class districts tended to have looser ties with their neighbors than I found in fourth-class districts.

Residents throughout the town attach far more importance to the neighborhood than to the district. Several terms are used for this: village *(hilla)* is heard frequently, but most common is *farīg.* Neighborhoods vary in size and cohesion. For women, however, they usually comprise only three or four blocks and can be easily walked from one end to the other. There are obviously overlapping neighborhoods, but women identify particularly with one group or another, according to the dictates of friendship.

A woman's social life is based in her farīg and includes ties with several other farīgs to which she belongs through a close relative. In 1985, Zachara the midwife, for example, lived in the same block as Halima (chapter 2) and the daughter of Fatima (chapter 3) with whom Fatima formerly lived. She visited them regularly and helped on any ceremonial occasion. Her mother and her sister formerly lived in other districts of Sennar, though within walking distance, and she shared in both their farīgs as well. Her sister-in-law, another midwife who trained with her, lived across the Nile in the village of Karima; Zachara was also involved with her farīg, connected to it by ties of both friendship and kinship. If she was in trouble or needed help with a social event, Zachara would expect to "call on" all of these groups and more to help her. Likewise, Fatima the market woman moved to the far end of the district but she continued to visit her old neighborhood for several years, helping her neighbors there if they had a special occasion. The ties, however, weakened over time, particularly when her daughter moved to another neighborhood. Fatima's primary farīg is now the grass-hut neighborhood to which she has moved and the other networks to which she is related through her children, including one in Omdurman where she has been spending time with another of her daughters.

These networks are individual and female-orientated. They are maintained by women visiting assiduously and they are activated by the sort of social occasions that demand a great deal of assistance from other women: births, circumcisions, engagements, marriages, funerals, or thanksgivings (*karāmat*) of varying sorts. Women's input is in terms of both personal services and financial help and is often totally independent of the men in their families. From the women's perspective, it is their own contributions that are decisive for the continuing success of such events and networks. This becomes apparent from Halima's discussion of her obligations or "duties" in chapter 2.

Kin Groups

Descent in Sennar, as in most of the Sudan, is primarily patrilineal. Not all the women I spoke with were quite as articulate about their antecedents as Zachara the midwife, in chapter 4, whose account of her family provides a good illustration of the principles discussed here. However they knew their male ancestors thoroughly, particularly through their father's line, while their grandmothers' backgrounds were soon forgotten. Kinship terminology is simple, distinguishing sex, generation, and relatives of the ascending generation, and is extended to cover all social relationships. Terms for friends and colleagues are still used only rarely.

The basic kinship terms are colloquial versions of standard Arabic references. Those in most common use are for mother (*umm*), father (*abu*), grandmother (*habōba*), grandfather (*jidd*), daughter (*bitt*), son (*wad*), sister (*ukhut*), brother (*akhu*), mother's brother (*khāl*) mother's sister (*khāla*), father's brother (*'amm*), and father's sister (*'amma*). All other categories are derivations of these. Virtually all people of one's parents' generation are either khāl, khāla, 'amm, or 'amma as far out, genealogically speaking, as one cares to go. Friends are also absorbed into the classification, depending on whether they are an associate of one's father or mother. Anyone in one's own generation can be called sister or brother as a token of friendship. Most of my neighbors called me *ukhti*, "my sister," sometimes adding *bitt ummi*, "daughter of my mother" (rather than of their father's co-wives, or their aunts) to emphasize our close ties, while their children called me *Khalti* (my Aunt) *Suzanne*. My husband, on the other hand, was invariably *'ammi Simon* as both a term of respect and a reflection of his links with their fathers, brothers, and husbands.

Traditionally the preferred marriage for a girl was with her *wad 'amm*, her "father's brother's son." Such endogamy is less important in

the town, where family alliance and solidarity is no longer a political consideration and girls usually participate in choosing their husbands. This is
done largely with the help of mothers and siblings. A girl proposes her
friend to her brother who then may arrange a chance meeting through his
sister. Women friends may try to arrange a marriage between their children but this is never accomplished without the participants' consent.
Marriages in Sennar today are rarely completely arranged. The bride is at
least able to refuse a match if not to instigate it.

In Sudanese society, marriage is very much a liberating process for
women. In the past the mechanics of an arranged marriage could be difficult and outwardly seemed to allow them little freedom of choice or action,
but invariably it led to greater independence. An unmarried woman, even
when she is no longer young, lacks both the freedom and responsibility of
the young matron, who grows accustomed to making decisions for herself.
There were unmarried women in al-Gul'a during our stay there, and the
reasons for their state varied but were usually prejudicial to them. Two
women I knew well were in their thirties. The mother of one had died
when she was small and she had spent the rest of her life caring for her
stepmother and stepsisters. Another, a second and favorite daughter, had
stayed home to care for her mother while her sisters had all married.
Socially they were both rather sad women who were always being turned
to for help by relatives, friends, and neighbors but who were not regarded
as having any real life of their own. When I met the second woman in
2001, she had recently been married to her brother-in-law, after the early
death of her younger sister, and she was raising his seven children, her own
nieces and nephews. Although she claims to have not wanted the marriage
at first, she is now clearly enjoying having her own home and caring family, and praying that soon she will also be able to have her own child.

Though the preferred pattern of marriage with a first cousin is disappearing in the town, a woman often refers to her father-in-law as her father's
brother, 'ammi. Yet a distinction is drawn between a woman's own family
and that of her husband, and between her mother's and her father's families.
There is a parallel group of terms for affinal kin but they are not used in
address and rarely heard in conversation. A brother-in-law is usually
referred to as the "brother of the father of my children." Behavior in affinal
relationships is characterized by mutual respect, sometimes bordering on
avoidance and even dislike. The relationship between a mother-in-law and
her son's wife particularly is fraught with tension, possibly even more so
today as mothers have less control in the choice of their son's bride.

The tradition of respect for one's father's family persists, evident
in many men's relations with their children. They remain the teacher, the

model, often unable to share a warm relationship with their sons, particularly as they grow older. A man's family is also expected to teach example and honor to the children of their descent group. By contrast, a woman's family is usually far closer to and gentler with her children.

Women remain close to their own families throughout their life. After marriage, the young couple is as likely to live with the bride's family as the groom's, though eventually most families now expect to have their own household. A woman also likes to return to her mother's home for childbirth and the subsequent lying-in period, and throughout her marriage, she continues to share mutual obligations with her family that do not concern her husband. It is for this reason, so that she can help her own family meet their social and economic obligations, that a woman needs some measure of financial independence, says Halima in chapter 2. In return, her family continues to support her, morally and financially, whenever possible. A woman's close male relatives, her *wilyān* (from *wāli*, guardian), are a particularly important group: her brothers, her father and his brothers (when she is young), and her sons and nephews, particularly paternal nephews (as she grows older). Similarly, throughout his life a man feels responsible for his *harīm*, his close female relatives: his sisters, his close cousins, and, as he grows older, his mother and her sisters.

Kinship terminology links social groups of varying sizes and significance. The terms *usra* and *āhal* are synonymous in Sennar for the bilateral, nuclear family, groups that, like residential groups, are based on a specific individual. Occasionally the terms are extended to cover the group that shares one's household. In addition, the ideal of the extended family, the *'aiyla*, is still very real: a patrilineally organized group, usually two or at most three generations deep. In many cases, such as that of Fatima the market woman in chapter 3, the 'aiyla remains in the village and Fatima and her āhal visit regularly to keep up their obligations there. In the past people generally preferred to marry within their 'aiyla but this is increasingly rare.

For women of some ethnic groups, but not all, a form of lineage is also important, overlapping with the concept of tribe. The picturesque term "mouth of the house," *khashm al-beit*, literally refers to a famous ancestor (or even contemporary relative) who has gathered an extended family group around him; but more figuratively it refers to the group of descendants who form a particular lineage or sublineage. The expression has been translated in various ways: lineage, subclan, sublineage, and is still sometimes heard in Sennar. In chapter 4, Zachara the midwife tries to explain what she understands by the expression but she has no doubt that it will have little relevance for her children.

On the other hand a sense of "tribal" or ethnic affiliation, *gabīla*, is still significant, particularly for people of the dominant riverain political groups. This is a common means of identification and refers primarily to shared history and cultural practices. However this is also waning as cultural differences are submerged in urban life and Sudanese nationalism is reinforced in various ways: through residential diversity, schooling, the media, and vastly simplified travel.

Women and Religious Life

The land now known as Sudan first experienced intensive Arabicization and the spread of Islam in the fifteenth century. Wandering Sufi teachers, from Arabia and North Africa, brought the message of the Prophet Muhammad, and once it was formally adopted by the Funj Sultanate in the early sixteenth century, Islam became established along the Nile area. As elsewhere, its success was due largely to the ease with which it assimilated existing beliefs and traditions into its rather loose contextual framework, a characteristic of Islam since the time of Muhammad. Indeed, Islam has been described (Trimingham 1949:105) as "not so much a creed as a social system, a living organism embracing all races and every side of life, which has molded and adapted itself everywhere to regional conditions."

In attempting to describe the practice of Islam, this presents a difficulty. While basic dogma is clear-cut and universally accepted, in practice, great variety is allowed. In contemporary Sudan many beliefs and practices continue to be associated with Islam that are outside that formal dogma. Many are part of Sufi practice, others are probably pre-Islamic, but over time all have grown and developed within the wider Islamic framework. Earlier sociological models of religion attempted to analyze this by distinguishing between great and little traditions or orthodox and popular Islam or even between orthodox urban and mystical rural. Such approaches are useful descriptively but oversimplify the complexity of each tradition and exaggerate the distinction between them. Although the religious establishment is uncompromising about what is orthodox theology and acceptable behavior, and the present government particularly has promoted its own form of orthodoxy, in practice there remains great variety of interpretation. Furthermore, women's belief systems have developed significant and harmonious blends of formal and popular traits that may be quite distinct from men's beliefs and conventional orthodoxy. To dismiss such practices as unorthodox or irrelevant is to ignore varied and vital aspects of contemporary Islam in the Sudan. Only by considering the practices and beliefs in daily Islam of all believers can the real appeal of Sudanese Islam be appreciated.

Today many Sudanese women receive some formal education, are exposed to the mass media, particularly radio and television, in which religious programs are popular, and may have the opportunity to visit Mecca. On their return from Mecca, they reinforce ideas of orthodoxy among their relatives and neighbors, organize Quranic study groups for women in the mosque, and are helping to raise the status of women as Muslims within their communities. At the same time, each generation finds satisfactory explanations in traditional, often non-Islamic, beliefs that continue to be reshaped and reinterpreted by changing circumstances. It is still true that women are excluded from some of the religious training and activities of men and may be exposed to a different religious upbringing that influences their own beliefs and worldview. This is not to say that women practice a religion distinct from the larger society. Their beliefs and practices are as much part of the orthodox whole as those of men; and indeed there is obviously as much variety in women's beliefs as between the beliefs of men and women. Yet often men and women seek different ends in religion. In central Sudan, for many women their religious practice is less a quest for oneness with God, which even someone like Bitt al-Jamīl (chapter 5), who was recognized as having extraordinary powers, would never presume to realize. It

Outside a mosque in Sennar

is more an attempt to establish peace and order within their own lives and social world by seeking harmony in the spiritual universe. This they try to accomplish through prayer and by following the formal commandments of God, and by conciliating and placating the spiritual powers they believe occupy the universe around them and whose displeasure can create all manner of problems.

The town of Sennar boasts many fine mosques, and it is a source of civic pride that so many of the leading citizens have chosen to found a mosque. In al-Gul'a, where buildings are modest, this is an aspiration that several businessmen have realized, and during the twenty-two years we have been visiting the district, a striking number of new mosques have been built, both by successful local men and by pious sons working overseas. It is the mosque that is the symbol of orthodox Islam, expressed in the five pillars of faith. From the mosque comes the call to prayer five times a day, with its associated ritual of washing, kneeling to face in the direction of the Kaaba at Mecca, and bowing the required set of prostrations. Women pray regularly, and for most the call to prayer gives an order to their day. In the past, they always prayed alone, sometimes in turn but quite separately from each other, unlike men, who by preference perform their prayers congregationally, led by an *imām*, a pious man who stands in front of the line of worshippers and sets the timing of each movement. In the newer mosques, it is not uncommon to find a women's room added, where women can also follow the imām's lead and listen to the Friday sermons.

The other pillars of formal Islam—profession of faith, fasting, almsgiving, and pilgrimage to Mecca—are observed equally conscientiously by most Sudanese women. In the profession of their faith, women can be effusive. Their conversations tend to be laden with references to the will of God and assertions of their dependence on and submission to God's favor. Fasting is formalized during the Islamic month of Ramadān, and this is a period to which everybody looks forward. Though it can be incredibly exacting at the hottest times of year, women participate enthusiastically. Indeed their participation is often all the more difficult as they continue fasting, forgoing food and water, while preparing the appetizing foods and drinks with which everyone breaks their fast at sundown. They may insist on fasting even when they are pregnant or nursing infants, although under Islamic law they are excused from doing so, and though they may suspend their fast during their menstruation, time missed is made up later in the year. Almsgiving is done routinely; food and drinks are shared, small offerings given even by the poorest homes whenever asked. Pilgrimage to Mecca is an ideal to which all aspire but which until recently few were able to accomplish. In the last few years, as increasing numbers of Sudanese men go to work in the Arab States, the pilgrimages of Haj and Umrah have become much more realistic ambitions for their relatives to accomplish with their support. For the majority, however, travel to Mecca remains an impossible dream; in the meantime they may visit a local sheikh's grave, where they are at least able to touch the soil on which a holy man walked.

The major Islamic calendar festivals provide a routine to the year. These are now recognized as national holidays in Sudan. ʿĪd al-Fitr (the small festival) follows the month of Ramadān. Preparations for this feast go on for much of the month of fasting: extensive housecleaning, preparing sweet cakes, cosmetics, new bedsheets, and new clothes for everyone. On the first day of the ʿīd at least, each household tries to sacrifice a sheep. In poorer homes, chickens or pigeons are substituted. The ʿīd itself lasts for four days, a time of real thanksgiving. Families join together and neighbors visit back and forth to show off new clothes, give presents to children, and share sweets and other luxury foods.

The big festival, ʿīd al-Kabir, is also known as the festival of slaughter, ʿīd al-Adha. Commemorating God's sparing of Ismaʿilʾs life from sacrifice by Abraham, it is a time for feasting in Sennar. Again, wherever possible, every household sacrifices a sheep for that which God substituted for Ismaʿil. The meat is shared and cooked over the next few days. In extended families, senior members sacrifice a sheep on different days of the ʿid, inviting the rest of the family and friends to share their feasts as well as making gifts of meat to those in need.

The five pillars of Islam are easily identifiable in Sennar at all levels, but the basis of practical religion for men and women varies. For many men, the observance of their religion and the profession of their faith are closely associated with the mosque. For others, it is in the practice of remembrance *(zikr)* performed with members of their Sufi brotherhood *(tarīga)*, that they feel closest to God. Sufism continues to be important in Sudan on several levels: religious, social, and economic. Brotherhoods such as the Sammanīya attract large numbers of followers throughout the country, particularly young people, providing them with religious education, important social networks, and a tolerant outlook on life that remains much admired in the country. Sufi music is widely popular, in public spaces as well as religious occasions. Meanwhile Sufi leaders exert a powerful influence through television performances and public appearances even though they outwardly eschew the political arena.

Since the arrival of Islam, the Sufi holy man has been a focal point of many Sudanese communities, which often grew up around the shrine of one of its holy founders. The central Nile area has a long tradition of such foundations, and a familiar sight is the egg-shaped *gubba*, the elaborate tomb of a saint built over his grave where his holiness *(baraka)* is believed to be stron-

Sufi tomb *(gubba)*
near Sennar

gest. Despite being banned during the period of the Mahdīya, and subject to criticism from the more "orthodox" parties in power in Sudan today, the Sufi Brotherhoods continue to exert an important influence in the country. Some ways are elaborately organized; others remain simple and ascetic. In Sennar an important thanksgiving (karāma) for all the brotherhoods celebrates the birth of the Prophet, al-Mulid al-Nabi or simply the Mulid, during the third month of the Islamic calendar. A large open area in the center of town is turned into a fairground and all the Sufi groups fence off squares, which they decorate with banners and where they hold various performances: prayers, singing, legendary accounts based on the life of the Prophet, and culminating in performances of the zikr. Special red sugar-molded candies are on sale and, particularly in the early evening, everybody—men, women, and children—enjoys strolling round to watch the town go by.

A living holy man is generally called a fakī (pl. *fugāra*) (see chapter 5 for a more detailed description). In the Sudan today the term is used widely and often inaccurately for any man who is particularly pious and active in his Brotherhood, who teaches in a Quranic school *(khalwa)*, who is believed to possess special powers, or who claims to be able to cure disease and spiritual problems. Many inherit their powers through family lines, and the same sort of religious leadership has been offered by certain families for generations. The source of their leadership is not necessarily in the goodness of their lives or in their knowledge of the Holy Book. It is because they are believed to possess special powers, baraka, which enable them to work miracles and cure ills.

Baraka, which is literally "benediction," refers to holiness in the sense of something given by God. Bitt al-Jamīl in chapter 5 describes her "gift" in this way though she never actually uses the term baraka, preferring to describe it as an "opening," *fath* (from God). The possession of baraka can be an arbitrary thing, unrelated to the goodness or piety of the recipient. Baraka may also be passed on to descendants of the holy man and transmitted to people who visit his tomb. Thus, outings to the tombs of local saints are popular for religious as well as social reasons. The favorite tomb near Sennar is on the east bank of the Blue Nile—that of Sheikh Farah wad Taktūk, a holy man who lived in the early eighteenth century. The eponymous village of Sheikh Talha is also a popular shrine, for West Africans particularly (though not exclusively) and his descendants are believed to have inherited his baraka.

Sufi Brotherhoods play an important unifying role in Sudanese society as participants from all types of backgrounds are brought together into associations of mutual help. However, while women and children may be members of a Brotherhood, it remains basically a male organization. Women may join the audience for the performance of zikr and, at certain points in the chanting, may ululate and even dance around the performers, or compose songs of praise to the head of the order and his family. They do not perform or attempt to approach God themselves.

The elaboration of many contemporary beliefs and practices occurs outside orthodox Islam, particularly among women, though their interpretations and accounts are not necessarily uniform. The spirit world is very real to most women and alongside their daily prayers is a range of other routine practices aimed at conciliating and propitiating different types of spiritual entities that can upset the order of their world. Most common is the belief in *jinn*, the existence of which is reinforced by the Quran where a whole Sura (chapter) is entitled "Jinn." They are the most ubiquitous and yet also the most vague category of spirits, capable of good as well as evil, and of assuming a wide variety of forms. A Sennar secondary school student described a jinn as simply "a soul or a shadow person . . . who is alive." Jinn are found everywhere, living in societies like those of humans and can harm the unwary. They tend to "possess" natural features, like rocks or mountains, and particularly occupy unclean sites such as toilets or rubbish dumps, places where the chance of disease is also great, and which thus become doubly undesirable. The best protection is avoidance of anywhere they are likely to be, but they can also be guarded against by charms or amulets, or by burning incense in places likely to attract them. On the whole, jinn tend to cause mischief or problems but rarely possess people. If they do it leads to madness. Not all jinn are harmful; some are peaceful and calm *(hadi)*. It is the envious and mischievous *(hasīd)* who cause problems.

Jinn are a species and in general lack individuality but some have specific names and characteristics. For example, Umm al-Subyan (the mother of male children) is regarded as the cause of miscarriage, sterility and problems in children while Umm Ba'ula is a fearsome woman spirit who steals children and whose name is invoked to punish children. Other types of spirits include *khalīja*, a category of very ugly spirits with threatening manner, and *huri*, mermaids or water spirits. *'Afarīt*, ghosts, are less elaborated than jinn but are definitely distinct. They are believed to appear in dreams and to hang around graveyards. *Sheitan*s, "devils," are capable of instigating real evil. They are believed to be led by Satan (Iblis) and are summoned in black magic, *kujūr*, when someone engages in trying to cause an injury to another. They may be controlled or manipulated by evil fakīs.

Most widespread of all are ideas about the Evil Eye, Hot Eye or simply the Eye, al-Ain. Strictly speaking this is not a spirit but rather a very widespread belief in magical power, which is activated by envy or conversely by good fortune. There are various precautionary measures. Prefacing any admiring comment with the formula or exclamation "*Ma sha 'Allah*" ("What God wills") or "*Salat al-Nabi*" ("May the blessing of God be on the Prophet") is a common safeguard among women in Sennar.

Finally in Sennar there continues to be elaborate beliefs about wind, *rīh*. Two sorts of wind are distinguished. *Al-rīh al-aswad*, the black wind, is tantamount to black magic. Women are afraid of it; they claim to know nothing about its practice and attribute it to disreputable foreigners, such as the Hausa from West Africa. The red wind, *al-rīh al-ahmar*, on the other hand is predominantly a beneficent force, with which women feel particularly involved. It is also known as *zār*, a set of beliefs and rituals widespread throughout much of the Middle East and northern Africa. It refers to both a belief in this particular type of spirits, which are possessing spirits, and the associated ritual that is also a form of healing.

Many women continue to feel their universe is "peopled" by all of these spiritual entities to greater or lesser extent. The last category, however—zār, the red wind—is most real to them. Although zār beliefs are common to men and women, the ritual and its associated knowledge is firmly in the hands of women, at least in this part of the Sudan. In addition, the fakī deals with complaints caused by all the spiritual categories except those of zār. These he refers to a practicing leader of the red wind who is invariably a woman.

Zār has been compared with zikr and it has been suggested that zār is a social and religious association of women that parallels male activities such as the zikr. This certainly helps in understanding aspects of the ritual and women's beliefs in general. Zār and zikr fulfill similar needs—ritual, emotional, and social—and largely cater to mutually exclusive members. They have had, however, very independent histories and development. Regardless of their very different status in contemporary society whereby zikr is largely condoned and zār condemned by orthodox authorities, zār remains a lot more than simply a woman's answer to men's activities.

In Sennar today, there are two distinct forms of zār, known as *burei* and *tombūra*. Burei is the most popular and the best known in the Sudan and has been widely described.[2] In recent years, however, tombūra zār has attracted increasing numbers of participants. In chapter 6, the leader of the Sennar tombūra group talks a little about her work. Tombūra and burei are similar in many ways, and indeed share many characteristics with a third form of zār, now dormant in Sennar, known as *nugāra* after the large drums used in its ritual. Just as zikr and zār are very parallel, so it is possible to compare the different Sufi Brotherhoods with the different "ways" or "paths" of zār. They differ in methods, organization, and ritual but not in "doctrine" or basic belief.

Women and Work in Sennar

As already noted, the following accounts of five women of Sennar are organized around the topic of work in which the women's own interpretation of work is used. Initially I introduced the topic to generate more general discussion but never attempted to limit that discussion or define it precisely. Rather through it I tried to develop a fuller understanding of the social and economic environment in which the contributors lived and worked. In the long term it has provided a useful yardstick for looking at how Sudanese culture has changed over the past half-century.

The women of this book were chosen for a variety of reasons. They were selected as much for what they represented as for their articulate conversation. Their activities and family backgrounds provide contrasting but important and often overlapping vantages from which to view the larger society of Sennar. It would be misleading to suggest that they are typical Sudanese women or that they have a lot in common. Their distinctive personalities emerge very clearly from the pages. Halima was down to earth, modest, and sincere, while Fatima was practical and indeed materialistic in her approach to life. Zachara the midwife was warm and talkative, even garrulous, and fond of philosophizing about life and society. Both Bitt al-Jamīl and Naeima, on the other hand, exuded a certain businesslike attitude that was evident from their conversations and initially, at least, was in surprising contrast with the nature of their work.

In their own way, however, each of the women was a success, and to achieve this they needed a certain degree of drive and determination. They all met with some opposition to what they were doing but they went ahead nonetheless. In the past, Sudanese families often disapproved of their women being employed outside the home, even when the material needs were great. There is still a great deal of ambivalence, in educated as well as more traditional families, to women assuming any sort of public role, and this has been aggravated in recent years by political developments within the Islamist state. In some cases women get around this attitude by working primarily from home. In others they openly reject their families' positions with views that belie any impression of passivity and weakness. Regardless of her material status, each of the women in the following pages exercised a certain choice in the course of her life and expressed some satisfaction with that choice. For all of them, marriage could have provided an alternative to working outside the home. They chose either to combine their work with marriage or to forgo marriage in favor of their job. The latter was not a choice forced on them, as it might be elsewhere. In a society where marriages may still be arranged, a Sudanese woman can usually be found a spouse, regardless of whether she is divorced, widowed, or handicapped in some way. Whether the arrangement suits her need not be the primary consideration.

On the other hand, the lives of the five women of Sennar were also typical of many urban women in the Sudan a generation ago. The routine of their day was similar to that of most of their neighbors, and remains so, beginning early with the morning prayers and usually ending quietly, surrounded by family, in the security of their own courtyard and home. Their days were patterned by the preparation of meals, the care of children, and their relationships with female relatives and friends, which continue to be expressed in regular and structured visiting. Their accounts are also spiced with the excitement of their lives, the daily dramas of life crises, sickness, and disorders that were familiar situations for all their neighbors.

In addition, their accounts are representative of many urban women who sought to earn some money of their own. When we first moved to Sennar, few women seemed to be involved in generating income outside their homes. Women themselves told us this and it was a widely held belief reflected, for example, in the national census returns of 1955/6 and 1973 (though admittedly this data has been subject to a great deal of criticism). In fact by 1980 large numbers of women did engage in some sort of money-making pursuit, increasingly so as the economic situation in the Sudan deteriorated. This apparent discrepancy was basically one of perception.

Both men and women perceive a woman's primary responsibility to be domestic. Even those who work full-time still have to cope with all the chores at home unless they have young daughters or relatives to whom they can delegate some. As a corollary, both men and women perceive women's activities outside the home as of little importance. It is often difficult to get women talking about their "jobs" unless one actually sees them at work, and in almost all cases they tend to be dismissive of their efforts. This is in marked contrast to their husbands' or brothers' attitudes to their own occupations and indeed to women's perceptions of what men do. A man's primary responsibilities lie in supporting his family and dependants and conversely, even where he spends a great deal of time looking after his children, it is his public role that is socially significant. For a woman to talk openly about her success at work is a criticism of the males in the family who have failed to support her.

It is also easy for an outsider to notice what women do not do rather than what they do. In 1980, Sudanese women were noticeably absent from most public places and their activities were usually carried out as discreetly as possible. For the most part they did not compete with men, and a significant feature of the jobs performed by the women in this volume is that they are largely independent of men. Certainly both midwife and hairdresser perform services exclusively for women. The others deal with both men and women but provide services that are easier for women to make use of when provided by a woman. Of the five women, only Bitt al-Jamīl, the holiest individual and the only one able to call herself al-Hajja (because she has been to Mecca) in 1985, performed a service that is usually provided by a man. This she did in highly individual fashion, not attempting to emulate the role of a holy man but adopting a gender-neutral public presentation of self. Each of the other careers reflects the segregation of men and women found in the Sudan. This reinforces the point that the lives of Sudanese women have been developing and changing within that framework of highly defined social rules rather than simply as a result of abandoning them. Such a point may be obvious but it is often overlooked as the "progress" of Sudanese women is assessed against a wholly alien set of standards.

Furthermore, all the women and the occupations they pursue are typical of women throughout the Sudan who are involved in similar activities either for profit or simply as part of their daily routine. For every Halima, there were countless housewives and young girls able to braid hair but who did not try to make a living from it. To braid a whole head neatly requires a distinct skill; in the past, every community had at least one such artist to complement the women's own efforts. Similarly, for every Fatima there are literally thousands of women in Sudan who engage in petty trading, especially in food items. One only has to walk the streets of a Sudanese town in early morning or evening to see this. Such women often leave home soon after dawn for the main market and bring back to their neighborhood baskets full of vegetables that they may spend all day trying to resell for a small profit. Their customers are almost exclusively other women who barter to keep down the price, and competition with neighbors similarly employed is great.

For every Zachara there were thousands of midwives in the Sudan, both those who trained at a modern school of midwifery and, less commonly nowadays, those midwives who learned from a relative the traditional techniques of delivery. Their work is more intimately associated with women's lives than any other career, and the discussion Zachara offers is pertinent for understanding all Sudanese women.

In terms of both career and success, Bitt al-Jamīl was virtually unique. Her work, however, illustrates the lives of thousands of women in the Sudan whose social, physical, psychological, and religious problems she was able to confront. Such difficulties are highlighted from the perspective of the women who feel called to help them; a limited group but apparently growing in number. In addition to the rare holy women, it includes the more numerous leaders of the zār spirit possession groups. In 1985, there were at least two other leaders of tombūra zār in the vicinity of Sennar and five leaders of burei zār. In 2001, I found one other leader of tombūra and five in burei, though the number of women who attended these events was probably greater than in the 1980s. Such women "healers" or leaders are now found all over Sudan, in rural as well as urban areas, and the account of Naeima's career in chapter 6 gives insight not only into their work but also, like that of Bitt al-Jamīl, into the needs and difficulties of the many ordinary people who come to her for help and reassurance.

The contributors to this volume also share certain characteristics that in themselves reveal something about the changing roles of women in contemporary Sudanese society. They can be summarized briefly as follows:

1. They were all middle-aged. In 1980, Naeima was the youngest at about 40 years of age and Halima the oldest in her mid-fifties: in 2001, Naeima was still working, in her early sixties, but Halima had long since retired. All of them had been working for many years and, in the majority of cases, had entered their present occupation when they were in their early thirties. Fatima was also working then but was later to change her occupation (see chapter 3).

2. They had all been married at least once. Two were still married to the same husband; the other three had all been divorced and lived without a husband. Halima was divorced twice and did not remarry. She was the only one to have been a co-wife.

3. All but one (Naeima) bore children. Bitt al-Jamīl had two, Halima three, Zachara five, and Fatima eight surviving children, most of whom in 1985 were an ongoing responsibility and support. Naeima did not give birth but regards herself as the mother of her deceased sisters' children and remains involved with the upbringing of her brother's children, who at one point shared the family compound with her.

Basically it was a combination of these three factors that enabled a Sudanese woman to work outside the home with the least inconvenience. Marriage made her an adult and gave her at least a measure of responsibility for herself. It weakened her ties to her father; furthermore, women never regarded their husband's authority over them as equal to that of their own male relatives, which at marriage was somewhat curtailed. Once they reached middle age and the end of childbearing years they no longer had to observe the demands of modesty so carefully, and indeed they have achieved the age and respect where they can dictate to many of the men as well as the women of their family. Finally, the fact that they had children, especially daughters, of their own who were able to take over some of the domestic routine, freed them from many onerous chores at home. It is still basically young teenage girls who perform most of the domestic work in the Sudan. Even those who are attending school are expected to come home and do their share of the cooking, washing, and child-minding while their brothers rest after their arduous day studying.

Of the five women, only Bitt al-Jamīl was in a position to employ a full-time servant to help with the chores. It is worth noting, however, that each of the others employed part-time help: a washerwoman who came more or less on a regular weekly basis and washed all the heavier items. Like several of the women here, she was paid partly in cash and partly in kind. In 2001 I was delighted to find the washerwoman Hajja Fatima still working in al-Gulʿa, and indeed we lived in the same house for a couple of months though I saw little of her because of her busy laundry schedule. She too, of course, provides a service directly for women, shares the characteristics discussed here for working women, and is very much a part of this same female economy.

4. They each had minimal formal education. In this they were typical of their generation. Even elementary education for girls did not become common in Sennar until the mid-1970s. Their atten-

dance at Quranic school varied but in no case did it provide them with competent literacy. Only Naeima, who had two years at the government elementary school, could read reasonably well.

5. They were all self-employed. Arguably the midwife was responsible to the town council and the medical authorities but this was only if problems arise. The running of her working life was left entirely to her.

6. They were all influenced by and aware of the fast-changing urban environment in which they lived. Though they all lived in the town of Sennar, even those born in the town distanced themselves a little from it by placing their origins elsewhere. Yet none of them had any wish to move and certainly not to the place they came from. They appreciated that it was town life that gave them the chance to succeed outside the home. The fact that they lived much or all of their lives in an expanding urban environment exposed them to many opportunities that were denied to their rural sisters. Of the five women, the first three lived in al-Gul'a. Naeima lived in a third-class district to the north of them, an older and better-established neighborhood with slightly grander homes. Bitt al-Jamīl lived in a fine old house in the second-class district of town, close to the river and to the market, a real indication of her success.

7. They were devout practicing Muslims in the local Sudanese tradition. They observed the five pillars of Islam and organized their lives accordingly. When we conducted the interviews, only Bitt al-Jamīl had been to Mecca. Halima and Zachara were to go a few years later when their sons were working in Saudi Arabia.

8. Equally in the local Sudanese tradition, they held elaborate and vivid beliefs about the spirit world. In particular they were all involved with zār. Zār provided Naeima with a means of making a living. In the other cases it gave a significant perspective to the women's outlook on themselves and the world around them.

Other case studies I collected from working women and do not include here for various reasons were from a government cleaner (farasha), washerwoman, literacy teacher, secretary, factory worker, zār coffee lady, singer, and play-group leader. It is interesting that the first occupation, that of a government cleaner, remains the most popular job for uneducated women. It carries a certain status as well as some security and a regular salary. It is also generally accepted that it involves very little work.

Although the following are primarily socio-cultural accounts of women's work, the economic data are equally significant. The expression "shadow economy" was one I coined in 1985 when first drawing attention to the situation of working women in urban Sudan, and it is a useful way of conceptualizing what amounts to a distinct economic subsystem. Particularly as a result of the recent economic and financial crises, women in urban Sudan continue to work in ever larger numbers and with increasing ingenuity, in often female domains where they have long been productive but where their efforts went unnoticed. Furthermore, women have their own methods of saving and investment that are largely independent of male control: they invest part of their earnings and services in almost exclusively female economic systems. It is possible to view this cycle of women working–earning–investing as distinct from, though not independent of, the main economy. The phrase "shadow economy" also conveys a picture of women working in relatively invisible places, calculated to give as little public exposure as possible. Furthermore, this shadow economy refers to activities that are often either ignored or not known of, even by other women. A woman's primary role and obligations in urban Sudan, no less than elsewhere in the country, are perceived as domestic and her extra-domestic activities are consistently undervalued both by her and by others. By 2001, many more women were working in the formal sector; through education, women employees are now visible in most professions, offices, and public places as well as continuing to work in jobs such as those described below. Yet they continue to regard their work within the home, kin work as well as housework, as being most important.

When asked in the 1980s why they work outside the home, urban women offered two reasons. Primarily they need to feed and support their family. They also stressed, however, the importance of providing for their own needs without being dependent on someone else. These needs included attractive clothing, toiletries, and a certain degree of spatial freedom for themselves and their children. However, they also talked of contributing to systems of saving and investment, which, though almost exclusively female, they regarded as vital to the maintenance of the existing social order and which they saw as increasingly important as other forms of support weakened or failed.

The rotating credit association, known locally as the box *(sandug)* is a widespread institution, documented for the Sudan and elsewhere.[3] For at least sixty years this has been the main way for women in the Sudan to accumulate funds for major expenses: for schooling, house repairs or extensions, special social occasions such as births, circumcisions, engagements, and weddings. A certain number of women contribute set sums at specified intervals to a savings group known as sandug, and at each interval one of the contributors takes the whole amount. There are various permutations to this basic idea; household items as well as money are saved, memberships in a sandug are shared and subdivided, but the principle remains the same. The leaders of the sandug, in Sennar invariably female, assemble a group of participants, women they trust and associate with regularly over long periods, for an activity that is a means of enforced saving as well as of insurance. The introduction of Islamic banking to the Sudan in the last two decades has in fact helped to strengthen this system of saving, which is now found in businesses and offices as an alternative form of investment and security. It is primarily an economic activity although the contributors are usually either friends of the organizer or recommended by one of the other members who thereby assumes responsibility for them. The only social function associated with the sandug is the regular visit to or by the leader to assemble the money. The organization of the sandug is usually voluntary but some organizers do take a percentage of the savings for their work, especially when large sums of money are involved.

Successful organizers, known as "ladies of the sandug," are highly regarded individuals. In addition to their integrity and organizing skills, they often possess a certain level of education (for bookkeeping) and of income (in order to cover any losses, a contingency not unknown). They may become involved in the first place because either they or their husband want to save on a regular basis, and they continue to run the sandug for personal savings as well as a local service. In the 1980s I knew a woman who had been organizing a sandug in al-Gul'a since she first moved there from her village eleven years earlier. During that period, her family prospered and through careful savings was able to set up their own transportation business (of public cars) as well as extend their property considerably. She was particularly admired because she offered financial advice to the contributors, drawn largely from her own successful experience. She also organized her sandug in a very personal way, deciding herself, on the strength of need, who should have the savings at what time. By 2001, she no longer ran a sandug, but her family's visible success continues to be attributed largely to her business acumen.

The system of duties, *wajib*, (pl. *wajba*), is even more widespread than that of the box and is found in town and country. However, it assumes more significance in poor urban areas, where extended family support is lacking, than in rural areas or in more affluent parts of town. Wajba refer to small money gifts that are given to the hostess by guests at any celebration (karāma): naming party, circumcision party, wedding, or homecoming. On such occasions, a written record is kept of the sums given. These should be returned with interest at some later date when the donor herself has a karāma. At such a time, every woman has a wide network of people she can call on. Wajba are in fact part of an intricate system of reciprocal gift-giving/delayed investment in which women engage and which helps to support the pattern of social life. To fail to reciprocate a wajib obligation can put into jeopardy all of one's own wajba dues. Word quickly gets around of any neglect or omission. A wajib relationship implies obligations or duties on both sides, and although these are not as great as kin ties, they are a significant form of investment and insurance. Those who cannot afford to repay wajib obligations in cash may do so in services, and indeed many women offer both forms of assistance if they are particularly close to the family concerned.

Investment in the material sphere is highly elaborated. Investment in the spiritual sphere, however, is also important. Besides giving alms to the poor in the spirit of Islam and usually in the form of food, many women make a more concrete investment in their spiritual lives through the institution of zār (see chapter 6). With the increasing popularization of the red wind, many changes have occurred in its organization. One of the most interesting is its involvement in the money economy. Financial contributions by participants are very important and are variously used in the service of the spirits. Equipment and supplies have to be bought, participants such as the drummers, the woman who serves the incense, the person who makes the coffee, all have to be paid a small sum. In return, however, the spirits offer financial assistance and incentives to those who are in need, even if the need is simply encouragement or moral support. Furthermore, certain popular zār spirits can bring some income to the women they possess, usually women who are regarded as having very strong powers in zār but who have not made the full commitment to train as a leader *(al-umīya)*.

Finally, the economic situation of the women in this book needs to be put into some sort of context. The period when the research for this book was first undertaken (1979–85) was a time when the cost of living was rising very quickly in the Sudan and former necessities were fast becoming luxuries. Economic depression has been exacerbated in the last twenty years by war, political instability, and repression. Unemployment remains high, even for those with advanced education, and the political and economic climates have added to individual difficulties. Many people, primarily men, have for several decades been going abroad to find jobs and personal security, at first mainly in the Arab States, but also more recently in Western Europe and North America. This issue recurs several times in the texts. Halima's nephew, Zachara's son, and Naeima's nephew were all working elsewhere in the Middle East at jobs of various levels: driver, shopkeeper, carpenter, teacher. Even more so today (2001), it is the remittances of such expatriate relatives that give a family any real security. Many single men feel they have to work abroad for a few years if they are ever to get married, while married men rarely take their wives and children with them because of their need to save to buy a home or simply to send money home for their family. Such periods of working abroad were at first not regarded as permanent moves from the Sudan, and as soon as the financial objectives were achieved the workers planned to return home. However, largely for political reasons, many people have now stayed away for years, taking their families overseas with them, no doubt recognizing that their stay abroad may be prolonged.

For those left at home or unable to find such opportunities overseas, the economic struggle in contemporary Sudan has been great. Each of the women below grumbled about current prices and inflation and found it increasingly difficult to manage. None of them, however, thought of herself as particularly poor. They all owned their own homes while around them they could see others who were far poorer. In 2001, there were no obviously homeless people in Sennar (as in 1985), but there were many individuals and families who barely had enough to eat.

In 1981, the official rate of exchange was approximately one Sudanese pound (£S1), or 100 piastres, to one U.S. dollar. A loaf of bread cost 25 piastres (approximately a quarter), a ride in a public car was 10 piastres, and sugar was anything up to £S2 a pound. A government laborer earned approximately £S42 per month and a government cleaner £S28 per month. A shop-floor worker at the local spinning and weaving factory earned £S30 a month. These were not large incomes, but were not enormously disparate from other government salaries whereby a new secondary school teacher, with a university degree, earned £S60 monthly, and a new veterinary graduate, £S70. By 2001, a new form of currency, the dinar (equivalent to £S10) had been introduced. Reflecting the tremendous inflation that had occurred, one U.S. dollar was worth 256 dinars (£S2,560). A ride in a public car in Sennar now costs £S200 and the government cleaner's monthly wage is £S600,000. It should be noted that locally money is still reckoned in pounds, even though the dinar is the international currency.

When we had the interviews, Halima the hairdresser's monthly income varied. She worked for approximately twenty clients a month and received the average equivalent of $1.50 a hair-do. This she supplemented with small sums earned from food processing.

Market women could make as much as $10 profit a day. This was potentially a large monthly income but subject to distinct contingencies. There were days when Fatima made nothing or even suffered a loss. It

Buying bread in the market (2001)

was not possible to keep up the pace of work that she describes indefinitely. She also had to make a considerable capital investment in terms of equipment and recurrent supplies.

The allowance for a government midwife in 1985 was equivalent to $20 per month and with inflation has not improved by 2001. After each birth she usually received gifts of cash (anything up to £S5) and food, particularly meat. Consequently in some months, when she had plenty of work, the midwife had a manageable income; at other times, she had to get by on £S20.

The holy woman was obviously successful, financially and in other ways. In a typical morning such as that described below, she earned about £S10 simply from consulting fees. In addition she had income from the medicines she prescribed and, perhaps more significant, she earned occasional windfalls of £S50 or more from grateful patients. Furthermore, she had fewer outlays than, for example, the leaders in zār. She was the first to admit that God had indeed been gracious to her.

The leaders in zār have a more private income. They have obligations to the zār that are impossible to assess. Incense and refreshments have to be purchased for each consulting session, and after we made the interviews in 1985, Naeima completed a special room for zār that obviously took a great deal of zār income. How much of the fee paid by each patient actually goes to the leader is unclear. On ceremonial occasions, gifts are made to the leaders themselves as well as to the spirits. Many leaders of zār, however, find it hard to manage. This was especially so during the earlier period of research when several resorted to selling refreshments outside their homes: tea and coffee, cakes and snacks, great pots of soup made from goats' legs, and so on. In this, they appeared to be particularly successful. Indeed, how could their tea fail to be more invigo-rating than that of other, more ordinary women?

Endnotes

[1] Information on the condominium history of Sudan is largely derived from the Sudan Public Record Collection, particularly files CIVSEC 5/6/33, CIVSEC 57/3/C and PUB/ 3/2/7.

[2] Boddy 1989; Constantinides 1972; El-Nagar 1975, 1987; Kenyon 1991, 1995, 2001.

[3] Ardener 1964; Geertz 1962; Kenyon in press; Rehfisch 1980.

AL-MUSHĀTA
Traditional Hairdresser

Halima the hairdresser and her family are among our oldest and closest friends in Sennar. It was her daughter Miriam, the secretary of the veterinary laboratory where Simon worked, who was the first to visit me when we moved to the town in 1979 and helped us settle in to our new home. It was her younger daughter Asia, then a high school student, who taught me to read and write simple Arabic and who organized her friends to help me carry out household surveys for my research. Halima herself had never before met a light-skinned foreign woman, and it took some time before we could communicate with ease. However a few months later, Miriam and her new baby went back to live with her mother when her husband left to work overseas, and my children and I became frequent visitors to their home. I then enjoyed many hours chatting with Halima, sometimes while she was braiding a customer's hair, often with many of the neighbors joining us. After we moved away from Sennar, this became my home too—and indeed when I came back to town in 2001, I spent several very happy months living in Halima's new guest room.

Hajja Halima (2001)

Halima is a slim, stooping, grey-haired lady who was probably born between 1920 and 1925. With a quiet, self-effacing manner in public, she is, as she wryly notes, often regarded as *miskīna*, a common Sudanese description (generally complimentary for a female) that encompasses qualities of shyness, passivity, and modesty, as well as the more immediate translation of sad or pathetic. Such qualities hide Halima's inner strength of character, which becomes evident from the narrative and of which her family is very much aware. In the 1980s, at home she was affectionately referred to as the President or "Nimeiri" after the ruling president at the time, although since she has been to Mecca, everybody, including her children, calls her Hajja. In her neighborhood, she has always been accorded a great deal of respect and her views and opinions are generally deferred to even as she grows elderly and frail. She is a religious woman who holds a conservative view on many matters, yet her religion is more in deed than in word. Her conversation is less punctuated by pious exclamations than many of her neighbors', but she is punctilious in observing her prayers and encourages her family to do likewise. On Fridays she attends the small local mosque, where she used to sit in the outer passageway with other women. Since making the pilgrimage to Mecca, however, she and her son have financed the building of a separate women's room there. She also attends neighborhood meetings at the mosque, but although once she returns home her opinions are readily and forcefully given, she would never express them publicly. She is quick to help those in need, with small gifts of money as well as a sympathetic ear, and despite her increasing years continues to support her large extended family and neighborhood friends.

Halima is also much respected locally for her experience of traditional Sudanese ways, especially medicines and rituals. Among her many visitors are those who come to ask about cosmetic recipes, home remedies for simple illnesses, or advice on ceremonial events. Certain roots, weeds, and seeds Halima knows how to boil, shred, dry, and administer for colds, cuts, or bodily ailments. Anything complicated, however, she refers to the clinic or the hospital, preferring to treat only her family with home cures. A great believer in the strength of custom she is constantly encouraging her daughters to follow familiar paths. Yet she also holds modern ideas about how life should be lived and has aggressively encouraged her children to seek education and professional careers. They all readily accept changing situations, traits no doubt learned from their Nigerian forebears, who adapted to life in both Arabia and the Sudan.

Halima is of Fulani, West African origin. In central Sudan all people originating from west of the Sudan are referred to, in rather derogatory fashion, as Fellata (fem: Fellatīya; pl. Fellatīyin), the term Fulani reserve for themselves. For centuries there have been movements to Sudan of peoples from West Africa, predominantly Fulani and later Hausa, either making the pilgrimage to Mecca or escaping political strife in their own lands. They established various settlements along the routes to Mecca, and some stayed in the area, married local women, and became integrated into the local society. The village of Sheikh Talha was founded in about 1830, on the east bank of the Blue Nile, ten miles south of modern Sennar, by a group of migrant Fulani, and was later organized round the veneration of the tomb of the founder, a saintly man whose descendants inherit his baraka to this day. This village became a focal group for later Fulani groups coming to the Blue Nile and remains an important Fellata town and shrine. In 1906 the village of Maiurno was established on the west bank of the Blue Nile by Fulani refugees from Sokoto, after their defeat by British colonial forces. Though en route for Mecca, the refugees (led by Mai Wurno, fifth son of the late Khalifa of Sokoto) were encouraged by condominium officials to settle just south of Sennar, and thus to provide labor for the emerging agricultural schemes. Although many Fellata, like Halima, have moved to nearby towns, Maiurno remains the Fellata capital in Sudan, a place where Fulani is the main language and where the physical appearance of the town is quite different from the rest of the country. Close ties remain between Fellata people in Sennar and their relatives in Maiurno.

Halima herself was born in Maiurno, and still has a family home where she stays periodically, in the center of the large compound occupied by her father's relatives and members of his old household. She is related to many of the influential people in the town and continues to visit regularly, to keep up her duties and obligations. She had a sheltered upbringing in Maiurno but was fortunate in that she received some edu-/ cation and her father allowed her and her sisters to acquire some skills. Her failed marriages forced her to become financially independent. She could cook, she could sew, and she could dress hair and by these means she was able to support herself and her three young children. Gradually her work as a hairdresser precluded the other activities, and for the last twenty years or more of her working life she established a regular clientele around the town of Sennar.

The career of the hairdresser provides a useful introduction to women's lives and work in the Sudan. Like many other occupations it is a service performed by women and for women. It carries little training, little status, and little remuneration. Yet for thousands of women in the Sudan, unrecorded by national statistics or awarded any official recognition, it has provided a livelihood or at least a way of supplementing their income to a manageable level. It is also an example of a traditional art form that has been passed on for generations and in Sudan at least is so commonplace that it passes largely unnoticed. Finally it is a tangible way to approach the subject of change as fashions, including hairstyles, are constantly being transformed, in Sudan no less than in the West.

Dress and appearance are very important to the identity of Sudanese woman, both nationally and individually, and are a visible reflection of her perceptions of herself and the world around her. Her appearance is carefully cultivated and highly distinctive. Until recently, few mature women were seen publicly without their *tōb*, the decorative length of fine cloth, usually nine meters, which is wrapped in standardized manner around the body, with a fold to cover the head but leaving the face uncovered (El-Tayeb 1987). Wearing the tōb, an awkward and cumbersome garment for those not accustomed to it, has modified the movements of Sudanese women, who walk and act in it with particular style and grace. This national dress shows no sign of disappearing although a few generations ago serious attempts were made to "emancipate" educated Sudanese women and to encourage Western dress in public. More recently, government-enforced reaction to Western influences was expressed in the promotion of what is regarded as modern "Islamic" dress: long skirts, long sleeved shirts, and headscarves pinned under the chin *(hijāb)*. This is now required attire for women in government employment and is commonly seen in public alongside the tōb and other Middle Eastern fashions such as the black *abiyah* overcoat. The latter is often a gift from relatives working outside the country, signifying important connections as well as foreign fashion, though abiyah are now also available in local markets. On formal or ceremonial occasions, however, the tōb remains the favored dress for young and old alike and continues to be regarded as the "national" dress of Sudan.

Equally distinctive are the perfumes and cosmetics used by Sudanese women: the strongly perfumed paste *(dilka)* used for skin massage by both men and women; a highly perfumed oil used to anoint the body at night *(karka)*; a perfumed deodorant applied generously to the body and head *(khumra)*; perfumed incense wood *(bakhūr)* variously used as a room freshener, spirit-warning, medication, and smoke-bath; the reddish brown dye obtained from the *henna* leaf *(Lawsonia alba)*, used to stain hands and feet in often elaborate patterns, and applied with scented oil. These toiletries all belong to a system of body care and massage that form an important part of marital relations. They are now available for sale in specialty stores in the market, though they continue to be made at home according to traditional designs and recipes, varying only in the amount of expensive ingredients individuals can afford to include. Increasing access to foreign perfumes and spices may have modified what was formerly used, but the demand for such "traditional" toiletries is still great and they remain a vital part of Sudanese culture. The frequent and varied use of incense in particular is evident in each of the following chapters and is part of the pursuit of beauty, cleanliness, order, and serenity which underlies much of everyday life.

For Sudanese women, beauty is important less as an abstract quality or in their material surroundings but rather in terms of their own physical appearance and well-being. While they generally do not spend much time caring for their household furnishings or creating craft items to decorate their homes, they do devote a great deal of time and energy to keeping their personal selves attractive within very well-defined terms. Neatness and cleanliness are paramount. Married women remove all bodily hair except for that on their head, which in the style of *mushāt* is carefully groomed and disciplined in a very rigid fashion. Depilation of bodily hair is done by means of a sticky boiled concoction of lime and sugar, and the skin is then oiled and smoothed. Smoke-baths, using special woods for perfume and skin color, are taken regularly to soften the skin as well as for other therapeutic reasons. In the area of the kitchen, married women have their own personal smoke-bath pit, discreetly covered with a mat when not in use.

Only married women are supposed to follow these preparations. Other cosmetics are enjoyed regardless of marital status. *Kohl* or *delāl*, a black powder made from a gum arabic, brightens the eyes; nail varnish, sometimes with henna, decorates tips of fingers and toes; *sibgha* darkens both the hair and henna decoration; and a range of commercial perfumes, at various prices, is available at every corner shop.

In the past the female body was also decorated more permanently, though these "traditional" forms of body scarification are now disappearing. Many middle-aged women bear facial scars *(shelūkh)* and dyed lips *(shelūfa)*, which forty years ago were common in the Sennar region. Some women told me how as young girls they longed for cheek scars, for beauty and for maturity, and begged their relatives to mark them despite the trauma of the actual operation. Lower lip dyeing has also virtually disappeared in the riverain area, although it used to be routinely performed on girls when they became engaged. This was a service provided for a groom by his mother-in-law to-be, whom he rewarded with special gifts. The bride was said to welcome it because it protected her modesty after their wedding night. Her family would not see the marks of the groom's kisses on her lips.

Equally distinctive was a Sudanese woman's hairstyle. Other African women braid their hair but do not employ either the same styles or the same symbols as in Sudan. Hair fashions, no less than other aspects of women's lives, are changing as many women opt for simpler styles or begin to copy the styles they see on television and in magazines from other parts of the world. Some of Halima's more gloomy predictions in the following section of this chapter are becoming a reality as few brides today choose the elaborate hair braiding she describes, and working women cover their head with hijāb in public and braid their hair, simply, themselves. Those who continue to wear the so-called traditional style of mushāt can repair it themselves, rebraiding sections of their head or helping friends with theirs. To redo the whole head neatly, however, takes the skill and experience of the *mushāta*, who therefore continues to find work throughout the Sudan even though the demand is declining.

In the 1970s and 1980s, many women made a living from performing this simple and vital service for other women. Despite this being an old and valuable art it received little recognition. The role of the hairdresser carries little status, even among women, and remuneration remains low, certainly a lot less than middle-class women are prepared to pay to the henna painter, the other professional beautician in contemporary Sudanese society. This may be because the art of henna painting is new. Older women recall how in their youth they simply used henna dye to stain their feet and hands black but did not paint the intricate designs that are popular nowadays and most fully elaborated for a new bride. The henna painter provides an occasional, ritual service, a luxury for most women. The mushāta, on the other hand, provided a routine but essential service until very recently.

Though regarded as the traditional Sudanese hairstyle, the type of braiding Halima describes does not appear to be that old and probably only goes back a couple of generations in the Sudan. According to El-Tayeb (1987:60):

> Most unmarried women in the Riverain Sudan went about with their heads uncovered until comparatively recent times. . . . The hair was worn in a braided style called *rasha* (spreading) . . . a fashion still prevalent among certain Hassanīya Arab women. Hair was parted in the middle and then braided in rows of parallel plaits down the sides of the head in layers. The top layer of braids finished just above the ear and then the hair was spread out and stiffened with mutton fat. In the early part of this century this style began to go completely out of fashion with the settled Riverain women.

It was probably the rasha hairstyle that was described and illustrated by Cailliaud (1826:288) when he visited the old Funj capital of Sennar in June 1821. He depicted a young girl of Sennar in a grass skirt with cowrie shell decoration, barechested and barefooted. Her hair was braided "*en une infinie de petites tresses*" but set off by a straight fringe and fell in an even length. The same hairstyle made a big impression on Stevens (1910:71) who visited the Sudan in the winter of 1909. Below, Halima herself recalls having the rasha hairstyle for her first wedding day, in about 1945. Obviously the new style of mushāt became popular only gradually. There were two basic differences between the styles. One was the size of the braiding. Rasha employed a larger braid, and therefore fewer layers were needed to complete the braiding of the whole head. Even more distinctive, however, was the coating of grease that covered the rasha braids and gave the style both a rigid cast and a penetrating odor. The later styles of mushāt were rubbed with, sweet-smelling oils to keep the braids sleek and supple and to clean them, and no woman used rancid oils or fats on her hair.

Halima's income from hair braiding was never great but it enabled her to raise her family and to acquire her own home in the mid-1970s, when she became eligible for a large corner house-site in a newly settled district on the south side of Sennar. Over the years she has gradually built a comfortable home there for herself and her family. At the time we made the original interviews in 1980–1985, she had a simple grass hut and two mud-baked rooms connected by a rough lean-to *(rakūba)* of old sacking. It was in the shade of the rakūba that Halima braided the hair of clients who came to the house, since for much of the day the rooms were too hot to occupy. The hut Halima regarded as particularly her own. Here she slept on a simple wood and rope bed though in the other rooms she had modern metal-framed beds. The hut served as kitchen, storeroom, smoke-bath, and general center of the home. The front room, close to the road and the gate, was the men's house, used by her son and family guests. The second room, set further back, was the women's room and housed china closets and wardrobes of clothing, bedsheets, and cosmetics. Here women guests could rest, though Halima's close friends usually sat with her in the hut or under the rakūba. Finally on the corner of the site was a detached room that she rented out as a shop to the merchant Ibrahim. Near the front gate were a simple toilet and separate shower room and in the center of the compound, under the shade of a large lime bush, was the tap and water hole. A screen of acacia bushes separated the men's front courtyard from the women's area to the rear. A fenced chicken run, a mud-baked pigeon coop, and a large goat pen completed the outbuildings.

Halima's home was typical of most of the houses in her area, an older part of the district settled in the late 1960s. It was supplied with running water and electricity in the mid-1970s and by 1985 every home in this area had its own toilet. In 1980, the road in front of Halima's house, one of the main public transport routes from the center of Sennar to the southern districts, was paved and made passable all year round. By then Halima owned a desirable home, and by 2001, this had become a substantial property. The former men's room has been replaced by a large wood and cement building, funded by her son who is working in Saudi Arabia and consisting of a spacious guestroom plus a room reserved for his family. The corner shop is presently closed for business and is used as a storeroom that Halima anticipates her son will convert into a business when he finally returns to live in Sennar. Further back Halima herself also has two new rooms and an enclosed veranda. Gone are the grass-hut and the lean-to, along with the various pens and coops for livestock for which Halima is no longer able to care, though for many years, they provided food for the family as well as a small but important secondary source of income.

Halima enjoyed her job, although once her children became adults and independent, her own financial needs were less pressing. However, her work gave her money in her pocket and enabled her to feel some control of her family's affairs. In addition she felt a sense of creativity, a distinct pride in her skill in accomplishing an important if utilitarian art form. Though she would have found it difficult to express this in words, her smile of satisfaction on completing a head of mushāt, or on being complimented on her work, spoke for itself. Most importantly, perhaps, through her work Halima regularly met old friends from differing walks of life and, especially with her wealthier clients, vicariously enjoyed foreign experiences and tastes of luxury and extravagance. It gave her the opportunity to be involved with other people's lives, to learn about happenings in other parts of town and country, and to participate in a wider social arena than she found in her immediate neighborhood. Besides being professional hairdressers, the Halimas of Sudanese society were very real social and cultural brokers, bridging the gaps between differing social groups and circulating information in a very personal way.

Halima al-Mushāta (1981)

My name is Halima and I work as a mushāta here in Sennar. I first started to dress hair when I was small. I remember some old women, one named Zachara and another called Asha, used to come to our house and give my sisters mushāt at home. From the time I was about 8 or 10 years of age I watched them carefully and by the time I was 15, I had learned it properly. In the past all Sudanese women had mushāt. A bride had a special mushāt, a new mother had mushāt at the end of her forty days lying-in period, every woman had mushāt for the 'īd. There was a lot to do. In the old days there was work every day. Then there was only mushāt. Times have changed. Today young women of all the tribes do not want any sort of braids. They just want to comb their hair; all young unmarried girls do this. Even brides no longer have mushāt; they just comb their hair and have gold [jewelry]. Everywhere is the same nowadays. Only young married women still like mushāt.

I like the work. It is easy. I go and braid hair, come back and see my children, and the next day I go again and do more mushāt. However, I have applied several times to become a cleaner. I got myself a nationality certificate and work permit and applied for government jobs as a cleaner but so far it is not to be. If I found a job like that, I would probably give up mushāt. It would be better both for pay and for security. But I could not stay at home doing nothing. My heart is hot. If I am at home, I sweep, I empty the water hole, I clean the bathroom; all these things I have to do. I do not like to see things lying on the ground all year round. I cannot just stay on my bed doing nothing. That is why I go out to work.

Family and Early Life

My father was born in Kano, in Nigeria. He left there a long time ago, before the time of the English, to make the pilgrimage to Mecca. My mother was also from Kano but she was taken to Saudi Arabia when she was only 5. We still have many relatives in Nigeria but I do not know them because we were all born here in Sudan. My father saw my mother in Mecca and married her there.

My parents stayed in Mecca and Medina a long time and then they came to Omdurman. This was in the days of the English; Omdurman was not like it is now. They stayed there for several years. My mother had her first child in Omdurman. Then the family moved to Maiurno where I was born.

My father became an important trader in Maiurno. He was a great man, a friend of the Sultan Muhammad Bello, and made lots of money. He had four wives and they all bore him many children, praise be to God. My own mother gave birth to seven children, four boys and three girls. Altogether fifteen girls and eighteen boys were born to my father but only one boy survived, my brother. He became a man and married. His wife was pregnant and then, in the seventh month, my brother died. His widow gave birth two months later and then she too died. Their son Ahmad is still alive and is now working in Saudi Arabia. He is my only brother. My parents and my brothers are all dead. My mother died only five years ago. For several years before that she stayed with us here in Sennar and she was over 80 when she died. I am now the oldest of us all. I have five sisters still alive and they are all in Maiurno. I often go and visit them, sometimes just to greet them or if they have a celebration, a birth or a wedding, we go to help.

And if we have something here, like my daughter's wedding or a karāma, they come to help us.

We did not go to school but we read in Quranic school in our home. When we were small our father brought a man and his children and gave him a home and money. He told him to teach his children and said, "When you finish I will send you on the pilgrimage." We read for seven years and then the fakī said he wanted to go to Mecca. Our father traveled with him to Saudi Arabia. Then he brought another teacher, a Bornu. He taught us for ten years and then he too went to Saudi Arabia with my father. After that my father used to read a little with us until we were married. I cannot read handwritten letters but if I see it written in a book, I can read it. I know the alphabet well.

My mother did not work outside the home. She just did the housework. My father did not mind if we worked in the house. He did not say anything if people came to us at home but he would not let us go out. Neighbors came, other people came and they would pay us too. We did their hair for them and made tea and coffee and enjoyed chatting together. Afterwards we walked the girls to their homes. We also used to do sewing. People who came for mushāt often wanted bedsheets. Everything was cheap then. We used to make sheets and tablecloths, crochet men's skull caps and handkerchiefs, all sorts of things like that we did but at home. In Maiurno many women still work at sewing and weaving in their homes.

While we were growing up and newly married, our father was very successful. But then he died. It was after that I started doing mushāt regularly. I had been married and divorced twice. Neither man was my relative. In the old days, you married your brothers, your father's brothers' sons, but now you can marry anyone, from outside your khashm al-beit or even your tribe. The father of my two older children was a friend of my father, a trader, and he already had two wives. I went to live with them in Haj 'Abdallah but we quarreled a lot. I was not happy. After my son was born and while I was still nursing him I became ill. They took me to a famous holy man in Shikaba. He did *kheira*[1] for me and found I had the red wind. A holy man would not call it zār. He just opened the Book and said it was the red wind. The father of my son came and asked, "What is wrong with her?" and the holy man told him I had the red wind. He said he should leave me with them for fifteen days and then come and make a karāma.

Our father paid what was needed, and after I had stayed there for a month he brought a sheep and made the karāma. It was good. They did not drink blood or alcohol or do anything bad. People just came on a Friday and made the karāma and brought the *fātiha*[2] and I became well. Before I left, the fakī also told them to make new gold jewelry for me and to bring me a gold signet ring. I still have it. He said that I must not be unhappy when I return home, that I should do henna and incense and perfume myself and that I would be happy. I have never had that illness again, that illness of the red wind. I sometimes go and watch zār but I am never possessed myself.

In the end, I left that man. After my daughter was born, I returned to my father when she was only a few months old. He arranged for me to marry my second husband but I left him before our child was born. I only stayed with him for about six months. He was a driver. He had also been married before and had four daughters, but he had divorced his first wife. Then I refused him too. Even now he comes and sends letters to me but I do not want him. I did not want to marry again. Many other men came and I said, "No. Go away. I don't want you. I'll bring up my children alone and they will be good for me. If I have small children and marry again my children will be unhappy when they see someone come in place of their father. Now I am with them and they are happy and they will grow up strong and will stay with me. But with another man, they will run away." A man comes to marry you and sees your children and says, "Your children are bad. They should not do so and so." If he is sitting outside with the men he will chat about you. "Her children are bad, her children shout, her children did this." I just wanted to stay alone with my children and work and have no one to tell me off or to tell them off and make us all unhappy. I decided I did not want to marry another man who would come and shout at my children and beat them. I said, "No. I shall stay and do mushāt and make *kisra* [unleavened bread] until my children grow up and finish their schooling. Each one will learn to support himself and they will also support me when I become old and cannot work and have to stay at home."

In those days I did not have any money from my father or my children's fathers. We lived on what I earned. Living was cheap then. One cent would buy a meal. You paid a cent for breakfast and gave the man another cent for dessert. Stew was cheap, soap was cheap, and two pennies worth of charcoal would last for two days. I did not have a hard time. Our total expenses were just £S4 to £S6 a month. Now everything has become so expensive.

When I started to work, my children were still very small. My son was only 7 and my daughters were 4 and not yet 2. But thanks be to God, we managed well. I found a room to stay in the house of al-Haj, the tailor. They are also Fellata people, though not the same as us, being from the east. They had a spare room plus a small room like a kitchen. I asked them if we could stay with them, if they would rent those rooms to me for £S2. So you see I never lived alone, I was with these people. If I went out, the children came home from school and stayed with the landlord and his family. They looked after them very well, like their own children. I would come back and find everything was fine. When the children were very young, women used to come to me in the house. Only later, when they went to school, did I go out to work. Life was good.

Work as a Mushāta

Many women, from different tribes and districts, work as mushāta. I work all over Sennar, not just in al-Gul'a. I go to women in the districts of the merchants, Mazatt and Bunyan, and to the senior secondary school where the wives of the headmaster and one of the teachers send for me. When they want a mushāt at school, they send a car for me at ten o'clock, I go and do their hair, and then they bring me home again in the evening. Elsewhere I can take a public car and go myself. I go to about thirty women regularly. In the district of Mazatt, there are maybe fifteen women, and in al-Bunyan, there are five. Here in this area I have about ten steady customers.

Mushāt is better than combing. Mushāt is pretty and it makes the hair tidy. Without it, you have to do your hair in the morning and the evening, but if you have mushāt you can leave your hair for a month or forty days.

There are three main mushāt: the regular mushāt, which is called *mahlab*; one called *kufāt*, in which the braids are bigger than ordinary mushāt; and one called *simsim,* in which the braids are very small, like the needle. Simsim is the style for a bride. It is sometimes called *dugāg*.

For all three types of mushāt, you part and braid the hair in front separately from the hair in the back. The front part, the bangs, is

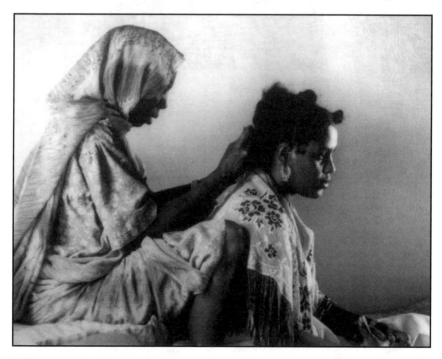

Halima at work (1981)

Regular mushāt
(1981)

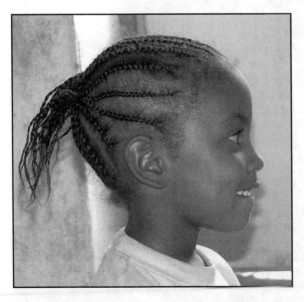

Sudan gafal hair style
(granddaughter of
Fatima the market
woman)

called *masīra* and it is found in all mushāt. Sometimes young girls braid their hair without masīra. They pull their hair back from the face and braid it towards the crown. This is called *Sudan gafal*. Only young girls do this. A woman either combs her hair or does mushāt at the back and then makes the masīra in front.

Most women today who have mushāt have the mahlab with medium-sized braids. Sometimes a woman might want kufāt because you can do it more quickly and it does not hurt your head. Also it lets the hair grow.

When I come to do mushāt, I part the woman's hair with a special pin [*mukhrat*] into four sections. Then, starting at the back I part the hair one by one and braid them and finish them in turn. For this I use a bodkin [*ishfa*]. In the old days we used to buy an ishfa for a penny, then it became 5 cents, and now it is 25 cents. You can buy them in the market. I have my own ishfa but I do not take it with me to do mushāt. Women usually bring their own comb, needle, and oil or wetting solution. When you part the hair and comb it, then you put oil or dilka on it so that it does not hurt when you braid in the mushāt.

In the old days, a wedding was particularly hard work for the mushāta. The bride used to have a special hairstyle that was very decorative and very difficult to do. It would take up to seven days to make the mushāt simsim for her, bit by bit. Her family came and called me, a week before the wedding: "Come and do mushāt for the bride." On the first day, all the family came. Some put £S1, others £S2 or £S3 in the place where the henna was ready for the bride. This money is all for the mushāt. Then they called all the youngsters and they made a little karāma. They sat the bride down and brought incense and perfumes like Rev D'Or and they made breakfast. They ate this and sprayed the perfumes and then beat the drums while I started the mushāt. It took four, five, or even six days if she had a lot of hair. We used to braid her hair and thread silk hair into the braids. After the bride got up, when her hair was ready, they collected the money from the place of the henna and gave it to the mushāta. All the young girls used to come and stand around, watching me do the bride's hair. . . . Some would give 10, some 50 cents, another would give £S1, altogether they would give maybe £S10, just from their collection. Then I would get another £S10 or so for the mushāt of the bride and more again for doing the other girls' hair. After the wedding, if they were good people, they gave the mushāta a dress or a tōb or a bowl full of the perfumed wedding oil. Once I was given five washing soaps and five toilet soaps. They used to give us oils and henna and invite us to decorate ourselves too. They shared everything with us.

But this is done no longer. About ten years ago, people stopped doing all this. Brides began to go to the *coiffeur* [commercial hair stylist] to have their hair straightened and styled and to bring false hair attached to a cap of gold that they wear for the Sudanese dancing. Hardly anyone marrying nowadays asks for mushāt. They all want to have their hair combed and styled. Even my own daughter did not have mushāt for her wedding though she has it done now.

When I was young, people used to do their hair into something called rasha. They did this when they did not want to keep repairing their hairstyle or for a bride because it would stay tidy. When I was married they did this for me. First of all they braided my hair into a very beautiful mushāt with bangs. After that, they brought clarified butter and wet the hair all over. Then they took wax and oil and put them on the fire to melt. When this was hot they put it over the hair, bit by bit. When it cooled, they sprinkled dried henna over the top of the head. In those days, women of all tribes liked the rasha. I remember how they made me sit down and did my hair for me like this at my wedding and then brought gold and henna and new clothes. At that time, the bride did not dance. We were just dressed up and taken to our new house. But now nobody likes the rasha. Sudanese, Fellata, all the tribes say that rasha is dirty and it has completely disappeared. Really, it was dirty. If the weather was hot, the fat and wax became hot too and ran all over the place. If you took a bath or a smoke-bath, it would melt. Smoke-baths can be very hot and the rasha would be in a dreadful mess. Nobody at all does rasha anymore. It was really very ugly.

After that, women started to do their hair with silk threads braided into their hair when they wanted to celebrate something as well as for a bride. Then people started using a finer thread, which was very beautiful in the mushāt and people preferred it because it was not so heavy. Finally, people stopped wanting any type of artificial hair. Nobody wanted it, not even brides.

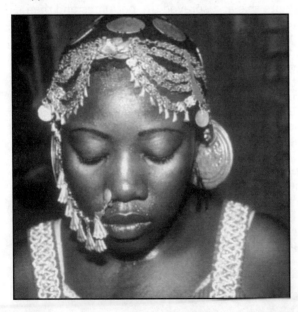

Bride (1981)

Bride dancing (2001). Note the henna painting and the incense.

In the old days, I used to braid false hair into the mushāt but I was worried about this and recently I asked our imām about it. I told him that I had heard it was wrong to mix artificial hair in the mushāt and wanted to know if I was committing a sin. He said yes, this is wrong. You can do the plain mushāt but to mix false hair with it is sinful. So now I will not braid false hair of any sort into the mushāt.

There are those who say that mushāt itself is sinful. The Muslim Sisters say that it is forbidden [harām] in Islam and comb their hair their own way. But mushāt is acceptable [halāl]. Even Fatima herself, daughter of the Prophet, did mushāt. Nowadays education makes women say that mushāt is not right. They see it as something difficult, uncomfortable. Yet in its day, mushāt was very beautiful. Today, a bride is just brought out with a combed hairstyle and dressed in new clothes and gold. She sits in a covered platform for people to see her, or she dances. It is not like in the past.

Here in the Sudan we believe that the bride is beautiful. Even if she is an ugly girl, at the time of her wedding, when she is dressed well and decorated with henna and perfumes, she is beautiful. Everybody wants to go and see her because they know that she will be lovely. A bride should not be too fat or too thin and then she will move well when she is dancing. Do you remember how, in the old days, the bride used to dance with her neck? The neck dance is truly Sudanese and was very beautiful. Nowadays women just jump about. That is very ugly. They do not know how to dance any longer.

I only know how to do mushāt. I could never make henna for someone. It is the young girls who know how to do this well. For a wedding, people also need a hanāna, a young woman who comes and draws with henna on the bride's hands and feet. A good hanāna earns £S20, even £S50, for a bride's decoration. She draws patterns over the hands and feet with henna dye; then they rub oils into the henna to make it very black and beautiful. Henna is sometimes used on the hair, usually by old women with white hair who want to dye it red, but I do not do this.

I used to do mushāt for brides and for young girls at weddings and then for an ʿīd I did mushāt for the bride again and for all the young people. Then there was work every day as everyone had mushāt. Today there is the coiffeur and the comb, and young people no longer want braids. Maybe only one bride in a hundred has mushāt.

General Comments

When my son became a man and my daughters were growing up, we were able to buy our own house. We came here to al-Gulʿa and bought some land and built our own place. My children are all here with me now. My son studied at the lower secondary school and then finished. He refused to enter the higher secondary school, saying, "My mother is tired. I don't want her to wear herself out further. I want to work to help her bring up my sisters." Now he is working for the water company and he supports himself. My first daughter completed senior secondary school and works as a secretary while my younger daughter will complete senior secondary school this year. Then she wants to study and get a certificate to become a teacher. She should teach for one or two years to establish herself. There is no hurry for her to get married. After she has finished studying and becomes a teacher, then she can marry if she wants to; but she must not leave her job. Once she becomes a teacher, a man who wants her can take her like that. If he cannot accept her as she is, he can leave. My elder daughter has always worked, even after her marriage and after the birth of her daughter. I am happy for her, because she does not depend on a man and say, "My husband does this and that for me." The man is like the morning shade. Maybe if she leaves her work and stays at home, one day he will not support her. His family might tell him to marry so-and-so's daughter and he will leave her. She would no longer have work to go to. But if she works she can support herself, like a man.

Nowadays, my daughter goes to her job in the morning and I stay home with my granddaughter, Nadda. Since she was born, we stay together till her mother comes home at two o'clock. There is no way I can go out earlier. If it were not for Nadda I would go out to do mushāt after breakfast. The morning is better. If I go in the morning, I complete the head in one day. Now I go out at two, stay out three hours, and come back at five. In that time, I can do half a mushāt. It takes me two days now to do a whole head. I told my customers, "My daughter has had a baby. If you agree, I will come at two. If you do not, you will have to look for someone else." Some said they agreed as they could do their cleaning and make kisra and tidy their houses in the morning. By the time I go to them, they have had a bath and are ready for me to do their hair.

My day is busy. I rise at 4:30 for the first prayers and do not sleep again. After saying my prayers I get straight to work. I light the coals, make the tea, sweep the place down, and, if I have to, I make the kisra. Now my daughter is living with me, she makes kisra. That is a job for young people, though in the old days I used to do it all myself. Then I take the goats to the herder at the river. I only have three goats at the moment as two have died recently. My daughter has chickens and we also have pigeons.

On my way back from the river, I stop in the street and buy vegetables and bread and the things we need for the day. When my daughter goes to work, I am ready to stay home with Nadda. I eat lunch at home with her and then at two o'clock, I can go out to work. I start the mushāt and at three they have their lunch. After lunch we drink tea and chat and then I can get back to work around four o'clock. I do more mushāt and come home at five. Even then I do not just lie around and rest. I go to see what the girls have done. We pick things up from the floor and tidy every-thing up. I go out every day. On Friday, I stay home if we have guests but if no one comes, I go out to work after I come back from the mosque. I usually go to the mosque on Friday or if there is something special. In Ramadān, I go every day unless I am ill.

I do not make bargains for my work. I take what I am given; it depends on the customer. One gives me £S1, another £S2, another £S1.50. I ask for neither a little nor a lot. Sometimes I am given soap or pigeons or sugar or coffee beans; people give me all sorts of things. But if someone gives me too little or is unpleasant to me, I will not go to her again. No, I just keep quiet. For that reason, people say that I am modest [miskīna].

I have more than enough customers at the moment. The 'īd is approaching and then I will have to do mushāt for all my regular customers. I have no time for someone new. After the 'īd, when all my customers have had their hair done, I could go to someone else, but I will only go to a woman if I know her or if someone I already work for tells me about her.

Besides mushāt, I sometimes can make some money from sell-ing foods like okra. I buy the vegetables fresh in the market, dry them, and then pound them to a powder and sell them in paper cones from Ibrahim's shop. Since we have had a refrigerator in the shop, I also make iced Popsicles for the children. I make a sweet drink from the hibiscus, fill small plastic bags with this, and freeze them. We also sell those from Ibrahim's shop. Sometimes, too, I buy sweeping brushes cheaply in the country and then resell them at a small profit. These things all help.

My children do not like me to go out to work. My daughter wants me to stay at home and just make popsicles. My son is not happy either. I say that I want something in my hand. He says that he will give me my expenses. I say that I also want to do something, I like to have something of my own. He is still not happy. But not all men are like this, just like not all women want to work. Not all Fellata think alike and not all Sudanese say the same things. We are all different.

Today there are many women out working in the Sudan. You find them selling tea or coffee in the streets or as cleaners such as those at the district commissioner's office, and, thanks be to God, they can all earn some money even without a school certificate. These women are 30, 40, 50, even 70 years of age. Anyone can be a cleaner; they work by day, sweeping, cleaning, bringing tea, tak-ing messages. They certainly are not lazy. They work hard and become good at their jobs. Then they have some money of their own and if, for example, a woman wants to marry her daughter or has a circumcision in the family she can contribute to the expenses.

Even a married woman needs her own money. She might give some of her wages to her husband but she also has her own needs. If her sister wants to get married, for example, she has to give her pots and plates and glasses. Her husband is already bringing them food, bedsheets, bread, sugar, and so on. Can he also give her money for her to give to her family? No, of course not. His income is small. If he does give her anything, it will be slight. But if a woman works and has her own money, not just her husband's, there is no problem. She can do it herself. And if her family is hungry and her husband is not there, she can quickly help them by herself. Only if a woman has a lot of gold can she manage without working.

A woman has many wajba. If another woman gives birth or has a naming ceremony or a circumcision, you give wajīb to her. When the women are making henna for the bride, they make a collection. In the old days, the mother of the groom gave £S3, which is now nearer to £S5, saying, "This is for so and so [the bride]." Then all the other women also give something for the collection. On the day of a circumcision, too, the family makes our traditions. We say these are also wajba. For all these you have to give what you can. If you are a close relative, you have to give a lot, maybe £S10. If you are working, you can do it. If you do not work, there is no way you can contribute.

We give wajba for a birth, a naming ceremony, at a wedding, and after a circumcision. We Fellata used not to circumcise girls. In the old days, the Fellata peoples circumcised only boys. Before the English came we all had our own customs. Nowadays we circumcise girls too. Sunna circumcision is fine; if you look in the Holy Book, you will read there about Sunna. But the other form, *fironi*, is bad; it is harām. When our mothers came from Nigeria and were staying out in the west, 'arab midwives came to them and made that circumcision for them. Now all our daughters have it.

If someone comes home from abroad, you also give wajīb. The family makes a karāma and you give them sugar. If you cannot bring sugar you give money. Recently my nephew Ahmad returned from Saudi Arabia. He came and greeted me: hello, Halima, how are you, and so on, asking after my health and my family. I said to him, "Take this for the karāma," and gave him £S5. Next time it will be £S7. These wajba are always increasing. For such occasions you have to give money. If you do not give, people will ask why and say bad things about you. Everybody will be angry with you.

Hajja Halima (2001)

Shortly before I returned to Sennar in August 2001, Halima's daughter Miriam telephoned me in Indianapolis from the local phone shop. Their new guest room was completed, she said, and they wanted me to stay with them during my coming visit. I worried that Halima, now approaching her eighties, would be too frail and tired to have a foreign guest for several months, but my fears were quite unfounded. Halima continues to live in her old home, accompanied at night by some of her granddaughters and neighbors but for the most part looking after herself and her home in remarkable fashion. She (and I) took meals at Miriam's house, a few minutes walk away, but most of her days were spent at home, cleaning, washing her clothes, and quietly reading her Quran in the shade of her new kitchen. I never felt she saw me as either a foreigner or a problem, except once when I was ill with stomach problems and wanted only to stay in my room and sleep. She sat outside, wringing her hands and praying, and calling for her daughters to do something to help me.

In her modest way, Halima looks with pride on the growth of her family. She now has sixteen grandchildren and one great granddaughter, born in May 2002 to Nadda and her husband Omar. They were married in June 2001 after Nadda graduated from senior secondary school. Both Halima and Miriam had wanted Nadda to get further training and her Uncle Abdel Magid, "Abdu," was prepared to support her at university for four years. However she was adamant that she wanted to marry Omar, a nephew of Halima. He had come from Wad Medani to work in Sennar three years earlier and had been staying with his aunt during the week. Nadda, a beautiful and spirited young woman, often saw him at her grandmother's house, and a love match had clearly developed. Omar is an engineer at Sennar's electricity corporation and is a part-time student of economics at Sennar University. He is also a very active Sufi, having trained with the late Sammanīya Shaikh Ibrahim Abd al-Rahman Shatut of Wad Medani, and is now working closely with his successor and grandson. Until their marriage, Nadda had been far more interested in popular music from the Middle East or the West than in religious music, but she is now beginning to share her husband's devotion to his Brotherhood.

Both Halima's daughters and their children live nearby. Miriam, the proud owner of her own home for the last five years, is only a block's walk away, and Halima spends a lot of time with her and her daughters Mozalifa, Murwa, and Muna, who are all still in school. Miriam's son, Mustafa, completed middle school and is working in the market as a trainee-mechanic, but his dream is to join his uncle Abdu in Saudi Arabia, where wages are so much better than in Sudan. His father, Daoud, also worked in the Middle East as a young man, but despite all the family's efforts, has not been able to return and now drives a public car (owned by Abdu) in Sennar.

Asia, Halima's second daughter, is also the mother of five children. Despite her mother's ambitions, Asia married after completing high school. Her husband, a local man unrelated to them, has been working in Switzerland for over twenty years, and Asia spent the first few years of their marriage with him in Zurich, then in Geneva. She loved the life there but after returning home to have her third child, found her residency permits for Switzerland no longer valid. She now lives with her children in their spacious family home adjacent to her husband's family, a few blocks from her mother. For several years, her husband has not returned from Switzerland to Sudan, and to her sorrow, she has learned that he has taken another wife. All her children, two girls and three boys, are in school and the oldest is hoping to enter medical school in the near future. Asia herself has also begun training for a medical career. After completing a short course at the Sennar Malaria clinic, she works at the local university as a technician to the medical assistant, diagnosing malaria cases. Halima has reservations about Asia working outside the home while her children are still young, especially since her husband continues to support her generously. She tells Asia she is behaving like a man and is openly critical of her activities, but Asia, like her mother, is fiercely independent and continues to work.

Halima's son Abd al-Majid left Sennar for Saudi Arabia in the mid-eighties. His cousin Ahmad helped him find a job in al-Ta'if, southwest of Mecca, where he has been working ever since, managing a supermarket. In 1992, he was married to Halima's sister's daughter Hassina, from Maiurno, and they now have six small children who all live in al-Ta'if. There is no doubt that Abdu's increasing prosperity has helped the rest of his family in Sennar. He keeps in close touch with his mother, installing a telephone in her house even though Halima is extremely reluctant to answer it, and indeed her increasing deafness makes it difficult for her to hear it. It is Abdu who has improved his mother's property, and recently she and his sisters legally put her estate in his name, ready for his long awaited return to live in Sennar.

Abdu, a Muslim Brother, has become ever more devout since going to Saudi Arabia and is always ready with advice for his sisters and their children and is generous in his support for his extended family. His stay in Saudi Arabia enabled Hajja Halima to fulfill her life-long ambition, of making the pilgrimage to Mecca. A year after he moved there, he sent his mother a ticket and took her on pilgrimage to Mecca and Madina. Her second visit was about four years ago. After his marriage, Abdu and his wife wanted Halima to live with them permanently in al-Ta'if. Again Abdu sent her a ticket and she stayed for six months, during which she went to Mecca twice. I asked her how was Mecca?

> Beautiful, there is no problem. You can find anything there. . . .
> I went for Umrah and stayed there till Haj, the second time I went
> for Haj. Ma sha 'Allah, there were so many people on Safa and

Marwa's day: no one stood, everyone was running, then sitting at the place for prayer. No one knew anyone else. . . . There were people from all different places, many people from Khartoum, also from the West and from the East, many, many people. We turned around the Kaba and came back. Then we went to Madina . . . Mecca, *ya salam*, it is very beautiful place. . . .

We talked about life in Saudi Arabia, especially in al-Ta'if where Abdu works very long hours:

Abdu has rented a beautiful house—three rooms and kitchen, bathroom and hall. One room is for him and his wife and baby, another for me and the children. . . . The mosque is near his shop and he goes there at sunrise for the first prayer, while we pray at home. Afterwards he goes straight to work and we stay at home as it is far [from his work]. At breakfast time he comes back home and returns to work until five o'clock when he goes for prayers. He doesn't come back till early in the morning after they close the shop. His sons don't want to sleep. If we gave them supper they said, "We don't want to eat till our father comes home." Only after he returns would they take their supper, and we sleep a little. Then it is the call for prayer again.

This was in the month of Ramadān. Ramadān there is very beautiful. We fasted Ramadān, and after Ramadān 'id, then we fasted five or six days more.

Abdu has stayed there for more than fifteen years. Hassina is very happy and wants to stay but Abdu is not comfortable. When he comes back home he asks his sons "Did you read? What did they give you in your school? What did you do?" He wants to know things like that, but he comes back only at night for a short rest before he returns to the shop.

Halima liked the people in Saudi Arabia, though she seemed to have little contact with them as she and Abdu's wife rarely left the house.

Only on Friday did we go outside the house when we went to the mosque for morning prayers and to read Quran. We took our own book but everywhere you can find the Quran. Many women were there, all sitting together, behind the men in the first rows, all reading from holy Quran, all wearing long *jallabīya*, then trousers and a white tōb. Till today I keep my tōb and trousers from the Haj, clean in the cupboard.

However Halima was not really happy in Saudi Arabia. She clearly missed her family in Sudan, and the rich social life she enjoys in Sennar. Also she did not like the climate—it was too cold for her in the mountainous region of al-Ta'if. She became ill and pined for home. Indeed when she returned she was really ill, not just from cold and arthritis, but suffering confusion and general weakness. Gradually she has regained most of her strength and memory and nowadays is more or less back to normal.

Halima may not have met many Saudis in al-Ta'if, but one of her most memorable experiences concerns Saudis in Sennar. She recounted the story several times, how some Saudi businessmen who worship in the same al-Ta'if mosque as Abdu told him their dearest wish was to build a mosque in Sudan, which they knew to be a poor and backward country. Abdu took this as a sign: his deceased father's village had only a poor, rough structure for worship and his life-long ambition had been to see it replaced with a fine mosque for all to enjoy. When Abdu next came home on leave, the men gave him money for a new building and after some time, a beautiful mosque was completed. Then two of the Saudi sponsors decided to come and see it. Abdu was back in al-Ta'if, so Miriam's husband, Daoud, met their plane in Khartoum in Abdu's public car and brought the guests straight to Sennar, to the local hotel. However, they were disappointed they were not to stay with the people, so Daoud brought them to Halima's new guestroom. Miriam and her neighbors spent the next few days cooking kebabs and steaks for them, treating them as honored guests. On their second day in Sudan they went to pray in the new mosque. Afterwards the whole village feasted on the two sheep sacrificed to honor the guests. Halima is still breathless as she recalls their visit, all the wonderful things they had to say about Sennar, the Sudanese, and about Islam in the Sudan.

Halima and Muna relaxing at home (2001)

As for her work as a hairdresser, that now seems a distant memory. Halima has not worked as a mushāta since she first went to Mecca. She stopped partly because of her age, but mainly because Abdu persuaded her to give it up and to let him support her. She agreed that not many women have mushāt nowadays and particularly brides no longer want it. There are a few mushāta still working in Sennar, but there is not much work. If they want a braided hairstyle, women generally prefer a simple style that their relatives or friends can do for them; but most women no longer bother with it. Since Shari'a law was introduced, in public they wear tight-fitting headscarves (hijāb) to cover their heads. There is no longer any need to fix up their hair as they did when they wore only the tōb which tended to slip off their heads and reveal their hairstyle.

Endnotes

[1] *Kheira* is a method of diagnosis used by the fakī. Before sleeping, he prays, reads some special verses from the Quran, and repeats the patient's name. In his sleep he will then find the answers he is seeking.

[2] *Fātiha*, literally "opening," describes the first verse of the Quran, which is used as the Islamic salutation of sympathy.

3

SITT AL-KUSHUK
Market Woman

I first met Fatima in 1980 when she was living in al-Gul'a with her daughter Abla, next door to Miriam, daughter of the hairdresser. Abla was then a young matron with three small children, and I saw her frequently at informal gatherings of neighborhood women. Since Fatima was out working all day I rarely saw her, apart from an occasional evening party. I had known her by sight for more than a year before I really talked to her or was even aware that she worked in the market. She sometimes used to ride to the house of zār with me and some of the other neighborhood women but she did not talk much or attend many other neighborhood activities. She was not often mentioned in conversation and only when it was general knowledge that I was interested in writing a book about women's work did I become aware of where Fatima spent her days. Neither she nor the other women held her activities in very high esteem even though Fatima was obviously successful. Yet she was to prove a most articulate informant and provided interesting insight into women's lives in general.

Fatima is a soft-spoken, self-effacing woman, outwardly far less assertive than her words at the time of our original conversations sug-

Fatima (2001)

gested. Then she had a slim figure and pleasant round face that broke into frequent smiles. Her graying hair suggested that she was older than she looked, which could not have been more than 50 years of age. She had been married for about thirty years to a close relative and they were to remain together till her husband's death (in 1991). They had eight surviving children, ranging in ages from 30 to 10 years, and all but the two youngest daughters had left home. She was very proud of her family and took every opportunity to talk of them and of her increasing number of grandchildren. Despite her quiet demeanor, Fatima was very much in charge at home; her husband was a mild, unassuming sort of man who said little when we met.

Fatima is a village woman. Naemulla, where she lived until well after her marriage, is a small rural settlement in the Jazira region between the Blue and White Niles. She continued to visit her family there regularly until her husband's ill health prevented him from working or traveling far in the mid-1980s, and since that time her links there have weakened. Her own children, raised largely in Sennar, feel few ties to it. Indeed their jobs and marriages have taken them all over the Sudan and the family today is scattered and unlikely to return to their family village.

Like many women of her age and background, Fatima worked outside the home, off and on, since she was young, mainly because of need but also because of precedents within her extended family. Despite the fact that she had no formal education, various employment options were open to her, of which food processing and trading have long been among the most common. Food preparation is a central concern for Sudanese women and is associated with tasks they start learning when they are very small and that dominate the order of their day. It is also, in a basic domestic sense, associated with female identity. While men may work as cooks in the large restaurants in town, they do so only in the public sphere, to work with strangers. In the home food is very much organized and controlled by women and is perceived as their responsibility by society as a whole. In more affluent families, men may do the daily food shopping in the market, but in poorer homes, women also have to go to the market in the early morning to buy the day's food. In almost all cases decisions about what foods to buy are made by women, who also do the preparation and cooking.

Duties and training associated with food begin early. Small girls begin to run errands to the corner shop, to serve drinks to guests and older women, and to lay the tray for meals. By the time they are young adolescents, girls are able to prepare simple meals and are expected to assume a large share of the domestic work. By the time they marry, they are well able to run their new home themselves.

Food activities also order women's days. Mealtimes are flexible only in so far as the family takes them when they are hungry or ready to eat. A woman's responsibilities are more rigid. Meals have to be prepared in good time so that they are available as necessary. The housewife's first job of the day, after her morning prayers, used to be to light the coals and make the early morning tea. Because of the increasing scarcity of trees and wood, charcoal has become expensive in Sudan, and the luxury coals are saved for special jobs such as roasting coffee beans. Most homes in Sennar now use gas for cooking, which makes routine jobs easier and quicker.

Once tea has been served, a housewife is very busy, unless there are several women in the house to help. Breakfast is cooked early, even though the meal might be taken late. The making of unleavened bread (kisra) is hard work, best done before the sun is high as it entails bending close over the hot plate and burning wood to cook the fermented batter quickly. Even when gas is used for this task, it remains a hot and sticky job, one generally delegated to a junior woman in the family. Egyptian beans, the other favorite staple for breakfast, used to be left to soak all night and put on to boil as soon as the tea was made. Nowadays most women send a child to a nearby shop to buy a cupful of beans from the large pot simmering much of the day, thus saving on time as well as fuel.

Making kisra (2001)

Breakfast however remains a major meal of the day. Formerly it was eaten between 9:00 and 10:00 A.M., and many places of work gave employees a break at this time to go home to eat. A few years ago, the government put the clocks forward an hour in the Sudan, ostensibly to allow people more free time in the cool hours of late afternoon. A result of this is that today (2001) two times operate in the country: what is known as "real time" (old time) and "new time" (government time). So officially, breakfast is now between 10:00 and 11:00 A.M. However, most activities are carried on according to "real time," and meals continue to be taken when the sun is at the same height in the sky.

After breakfast has been cleared away women enjoy a respite of a couple of hours, a time for visiting or cosmetic preparation or simply taking a rest. Preparations for lunch begin by midday ("real time"). This, the main meal of the day, takes up the most preparation and now, by "new time," is not eaten till late afternoon, usually between 4:00 and 5:00 P.M. Stew, salad, and bread or kisra form the basic meal, although if guests are anticipated, as many separate dishes as possible are prepared. When guests arrive unexpectedly, as is usually the case, neighbors pass a portion of their daily stew over the fence so that the lunch tray is as full and varied as possible. This type of reciprocity in food activities is particularly common in poor urban areas where households are small and often only one woman is preparing food in each house.

In places like al-Gulʻa, the evening (9:00–10:00 P.M.) meal may be leftovers from breakfast and lunch or simply hot sweet tea with milk, unless guests are present. If they are, then a similar tray to that of breakfast is served.

For many women, food processing and sale remains an important means of earning a little income. This is not new. I. Pallme (Pallme and Petherick 1980:85) was an Austrian traveler in the Sudan in 1837–1838, and he made the following comments on the women's market in El Obeid. (He does not mention what they were selling.)

> The portion of the market occupied by the women affords a most singular sight, for they sit crowded together without order or regard for personal comfort, and the small vacant space is densely filled with buyers, who will not budge an inch to make room for each other. . . .

A few years later, J. Petherick, a Welsh mining engineer who lived, traveled, and traded in Kordofan from 1847 to 1853, also left a description (Pallme and Petherick 1980:92–3) of women's activities in the market at El Obeid, including the type of goods for sale:

> Beyond this [the gallows!] is the *zoog* or marketplace, thronged each day from 3:00 o'clock P.M. to sunset. One double range of small mud-built booths, and two other parallel rows of temporary sheds, composed of a few posts covered with matting, form the only shops of the vendors of valuable goods, barely affording them shade; whilst the purchasers, and hosts of natives disposing of less valuable commodities, are exposed to the full power of the sun. Hundreds of women—free and slave—of all shades . . . form interesting groups; and, seated on low stools, are vendors of fruit, vegetables, sour milk, *merissa*, water, balls of grease—the native pomatum, used by males and females.

> Equally striking are the Baggara women, numbers of whom, from a neighboring encampment, attend the daily markets on their stately oxen, laden with bundles of wood or large receptacles containing the produce of their dairies. . . .

The tradition of women working as petty traders, especially associated with food items, is more marked in western Sudan and has also been brought from Nigeria and other parts of West Africa by Fellata immigrants. Within the last forty years, however, increasing numbers of women from all ethnic backgrounds have begun trading in some way, to try to earn a little income. Fatima herself is from one of the main riverain tribes, the Jaʻalīyin. For these women, resale of vegetables, bought early in the morning from the main market and then displayed for sale along the

Street vendors (1981)

side of the streets in their neighborhood, is a common way of making a small income. Slightly more effort but also greater profit is involved with food processing and resale; herbs, spices, peppers, or okra are dried and pounded; peanuts are roasted or made into peanut butter; pumpkin seeds are dried and pounded; sugar cane is cut down into small pieces; kisra, savory cakes *(ta'mīa)*, and sweet cakes *(ligimat and khabīs)* are cooked, generally for regular customers. Such activities are usually part-time, in the sense both that they do not take up a full day and that they might be pursued for a while and then dropped, either in favor of something else or because of other demands. Part-time activities are by far the most common means for a woman to earn some money in the Sudan.

Fatima's work represented one of the more ambitious and also more lucrative attempts to make a living, using basic female skills of cooking, marketing, and food presentation. In Sennar, many women are involved on a small scale, selling just tea, or a stew for supper, but few make quite such a commitment, in terms of either time or money, to their work as Fatima. The economic crises of the past few decades have also caused more and more men to compete with women and it is now not uncommon to find men sitting near the side of the road, next to a pot of simmering stew or pile of vegetables. Nevertheless, petty trading, especially in food items, remains the easiest way for poor women in the Sudan to make some money and it is still largely associated with them. Large numbers of women are a common sight sitting by the side of the main town streets with their stove, kettles, and glasses, serving tea or coffee to passers-by. For such women there are no overheads or investments, though profits are small.

By the 1980s, however, it seemed that market women were beginning to come of age in the Sudan and to enter into more ambitious and competitive forms of trading. In a separate space at the back of the main market of Sennar, specific premises had been made available to women traders by the city council. Most women who rented these huts *(kushuk)* used them for simple teashops, serving tea, coffee, and sometimes light snacks. They had to pay rent to the council or (by 1985) to the original "owners" of the huts, but were assured of a regular trade and did not have to work very hard for it. There were also a few women like Fatima who in addition to paying rent invested in a large range of equipment and put in long hours every day. By working very hard their returns were then much greater than those of mere "tea ladies." It is significant that Fatima is the only person in this volume who was able to charge a specific remuneration for her services. All the other women, to a great degree, took what payment they were given, being involved largely in providing what was perceived as a "traditional" service. Fatima was very much a part of the market economy although her actual activities were no less "traditional" than those of her colleagues described here.

Besides market women there are also women traders, *delalīya*, who retail food and goods either from their own homes or door to door. Sometimes they specialize in certain items; one delalīya we knew bought brushes and baskets cheaply from a village outside Sennar and with her own full basket went from house to house to resell them. Another woman, the neighbor of Halima and Fatima, traveled monthly to the People's Market *(al-suk al-Sharbi)* in Khartoum to buy sheets and clothing, which she attempted to resell in her neighborhood. Generally she worked from her home although whenever she went out visiting she took a few samples with her.

Sennar's main market is a busy thriving center. The variety of goods sold, as well as the customers and salespeople one encounters there, reflect the wide hinterland that it serves. It is not uncommon to pass cattle and camel traders from the west, part of the commercial chain that stretches from Darfur to the Nile and moves livestock regularly along to the main markets of Omdurman, disposing of some at each of the major markets en route. Even more routinely, one encounters nomads from villages to the east of the Blue Nile, West Africans from villages to the south of Sennar, and farmers from settled communities in the Jazira area who come to the market to sell their produce or to stock up on provisions.

The prosperity of today's market contrasts starkly with a description of Sennar from 1909 (though at that time the market was probably located near the site of the railway station, a few kilometers north of the modern town):

> ... the marketplace boasted about thirty poor shops opening on to a central space with a few simple goods for sale: burmas, or earthenware jars; hippopotamus hide whips, called *kubajs*; grain and some vegetables. There was also a shop run by a Greek that contained some Manchester cotton-piece goods and shoddy ware from Birmingham. As the people had so little money, anything more elaborate was unnecessary. I could not help thinking that if a Greek could come to Sennar to better himself, Greece must indeed be a miserably poor country. (Jackson 1954:38–9)

Today, Sennar's main market extends over an area of approximately a square mile. Located in the heart of the town, close to the river, it is where all roads in Sennar converge. Like other main markets in the Sudan, its very formal order is obscured by a superficial appearance of untidiness, noise, and clutter. At the center is a large square where the main meat market and stalls of fresh produce are located. Surrounding these are a variety of refreshment booths and the more substantial shops and retail stores that specialize in different sorts of manufactured goods: groceries, hardware, fabrics, and pharmacies. Some are still owned and run by Sudanese of Mediterranean extraction, whose families have lived in the area for several generations. Beyond these businesses, tradespeople are concentrated largely in kind; goldsmiths are in one area, cloth merchants in another; most tailors work along adjacent streets and blacksmiths are found by the river; vendors of mats and grasswork are grouped near several stalls of clay pots and long lines of traditional wood and rope beds and stools. At the north end of the market, leading to the railway line and to the sheep and goat market on the other side, is a row of stalls run by men selling fabrics and manufactured goods, many from East Asia. The women's huts used to be at the opposite end, on the south side of the market. Meanwhile fresh produce is hawked all over the market by enterprising youths, but there are several other areas for retailing fruit and vegetables where clusters of squatting women are also found, selling peanuts and peanut butter; bottles, empty and full of oils; pounded herbs and spices; small piles of fruit and vegetables.

In the early 1990s, as in several other major Sudanese towns, the town council attempted to develop a local people's market by moving the main market to the outskirts of the town, close to the new town bypass and bus station where there was room for expansion and ready transportation. Spacious market stalls were erected and instructions given to the petty traders that they were to relocate to the new site. The stalls remain today, unused and neglected. A few traders moved out for a short time, but found that it was too far for customers to come, and they had very little business. They returned to the old marketplace, having lost their original facilities and forced to start again, sometimes on the pavement by the side of the road. Over the years many have succeeded in finding new stalls to rent and gradually have been able to rebuild their businesses. The old market itself appears more congested and busier than ever, but recently the town council, acknowledging its earlier failures to relocate it, has taken steps to develop the existing premises. A grand entrance to the market has been erected, close to the main road, and this is now flanked by a new hotel, which provides, in air-conditioned comfort, a restaurant as well as accommodation facilities for Sennar's more important guests.

Besides the main market, each district in Sennar has its own smaller market. These vary in size but generally deal only in fresh produce in the early part of the day. At the southern side of town is the market known as Suk Libya and, because of its distance from the main market, this is probably the second largest market in town. This is where Fatima's husband worked in 1985, selling produce he bought earlier in the day from the main market.

In addition to markets, Sennar has a wide range of shops. The larger stores are almost all close to the main market area but throughout town there are numerous small corner shops that cater to immediate needs. In 1980, I was told by the sheikh of al-Gul'a that in this district alone, there were sixty-eight small businesses, which included general stores, tailors, laundries, mills, and restaurants. At that time, the cattle and camel market was also in al-Gul'a, on the southern end of town, but this has now moved close to the main market, and government housing has been built on the old site. Meanwhile I estimate that the number of shops in al-Gul'a has at least doubled in the last twenty years.

In the following pages, Fatima describes how she managed a small kitchen-service in one of the women's stalls on the edge of the main market in Sennar. Restaurant is too grand a term for the type of operation she had, and she herself reserved that word for the larger institutions run by men in the middle of the town. The men's restaurants usually have one or two indoor rooms with tables and chairs scattered about. Most of their customers, however, prefer to eat outside, either in the shade of the walls and roof, or, especially at night, out on the pavements and areas behind their kitchens. Such establishments are large and well placed, being grouped together in a central part of the town and market area. Many customers are regulars who treat the restaurant in part as a club. The premises, when extended out on to the street, are often spacious. These restaurants have places to sit, taps for washing, and a varied menu, though they do not usually serve tea or coffee, which are available separately from women vendors or small teashops nearby.

There was little real competition, however, between the men's restaurants and what the women offered from their "kitchen-kiosks." Men's restaurants did a large part of their trade at night, serving supper, when the women's part of the market was closed. Furthermore, the men's restaurants are frequented entirely by males while the women's huts were used by both men and women. As a general rule, women do not like to eat or drink in public but sometimes, such as when they come from some distance to shop in the market, they find it unavoidable. For such women, stalls like Fatima's were discreet and quiet, being located in an uncrowded area on the edge of the market. Here they could take their meal without feeling that everybody was watching them, from a tray of food that was prepared by another woman.

The particular kiosk that Fatima rented was a small, corrugated-iron shed, one of a line of similar huts, close to the river. Two lines each of twenty-four identical sheds, separated by a small pathway, were used as either tea and coffee shops or small restaurants. They were all run by women. Each kiosk had a door in back and in front so that the lady of the kushuk could serve customers on two sides. On either side there were similar huts, some serving just tea and coffee, others selling kisra and cakes, and yet others that at any given time were closed owing to sickness, family misfortune, or simply lack of tenant. Inside her kiosk, from 6:00 A.M. each morning, six days a week, Fatima presided over her business, which she ran single-handedly, though in holidays and after school hours one or more of her younger children would lend a hand. The limited space inside the kiosk was fully extended. The only seats were a small stool on which Fatima sat to tend her stove, and, leaning against one wall, a rope bed that doubled as a surface for drying dishes when she was busy and a bed on which to recline when business was slack. She had no chairs for customers, who either squatted on the ground outside or, if they preferred, joined Fatima inside and perched on the end of the bed.

In addition to the bed and the stool, there was the usual range of utensils *('idda)* found in any Sudanese kitchen. Under the bed was a large round tin bowl *(tushit)* used to wash dishes and also to store food and dishes when not in use. Against the other wall were stacked round trays, large ones for holding food, and small trays for serving coffee or tea. Nearby were a couple of colorful food covers. In one corner, near the stool, were two stoves, the traditional square metal *kanūn*, in one of which the coals glowed from early morning till Fatima was ready to leave in the evening. Stacked near the stoves were cooking pans: large short-handled saucepans for stews, round shallow woks for frying meat, large and small kettles for making tea, and another pot that was half kettle, half saucepan, used for boiling coffee. Tea glasses, coffee cups, and bowls were all stored neatly; sieves, pestle and mortar, metal coffee pots, metal spoons large and small, wooden food grinders; all were ready for use. Most Sudanese women acquire a range of utensils such as this when they marry, and many of these items are arranged proudly in a prominent position in the home.

Trade was brisk for much of the day. People arriving at the market early stopped for a cup of tea, and this ran into the breakfast custom. By midday there might be a short lull when Fatima could rest a little, but lunch had to be ready at 2:00 P.M. and was served until about 5:00 P.M. When there were no more customers or when she ran out of food, Fatima packed her things, taking all the leftovers home for her family's supper, and locked up the kiosk for another day. Fortunately she was near the main stop for public transport around town, and she did not have to wait long for a public car to take her home. When she lived with her son and daughter, not far from us, the car would stop just a few yards from their house. Once she moved, however, she had to walk from the last bus stop in town.

Her new home was a grass-hut in a very new district on the edge of Sennar where most facilities had not yet reached. In the mid 1980s, they had no public transport or electricity, no water or sewerage. Life was difficult, but Fatima was optimistic in the pride of home ownership. Housing remains an ongoing problem for women moving to the towns. Often in their home village they have their own house or share in the family home, which may be modest but has no overheads and could be very spacious. In the town, the same women and their families may only be able to afford to share one or two rooms or huts with another family and have little privacy or security. Rents are high and the extra costs for water and food can be so great that there is scant opportunity to save for one's own house. Fatima considered herself fortunate that she and other members of her family had been able to afford their own homes.

Like Halima, Fatima worked a long day. She rose early to say her prayers, and by 6:00 A.M. was already in the market. At the time of the interviews, her two daughters still at home were able to take care of themselves and their home, helping with chores at home and in the kiosk, after the school day was over. Some days Fatima was so busy she barely had time to rest during the day, though usually she enjoyed a respite in the middle of the morning, either for a brief nap or to take her stool outside and sit in the shade of the wall chatting with the women who worked alongside her. There was a very sociable air about the kiosks, and Fatima also enjoyed talking with customers, many of whom came to her on a regular basis. Her new neighborhood was very quiet, since there was no electricity in the district and not much happened there in the evenings. People tended to go to sleep early and were ready for their early morning start.

Because of the informality of her business, Fatima closed shop if something urgent occurred in her family. Both the marriage of her son in Port Sudan and the sickness of her daughter in Wad Medani took her away from home for a couple of weeks. On those occasions, she simply locked up the kiosk and her customers went elsewhere till she returned.

Fatima Sitt al-Kushuk (1981)

I was born in the Jazira in a place called Naemulla. All my relatives, my brothers and sisters, are still there. We still have our own house with goats and everything. We were very happy there but about fourteen years ago we were moved to Sennar. Now that house is rented out and we only go every few months to collect the rent money, £S50 per month.

My tribe is the Ja'alīyin from the north of the Sudan. My father and mother were both from Naemulla, the same village. My father worked as a driver. I was married early to my cousin, my mother's paternal cousin. He is a Kahli from the Khawahla tribe and was also from Naemulla. In those days there were no schools, just the Quranic school where the boys studied, so I do not read or write. I just stayed home. I never worked in those days. I had my children, now four boys and four girls altogether. However I always had an ambition to be a midwife and to work in my country. My mother had never worked, but both my father's mother and my father's sister were midwives. All the women in his family worked. They were traditional midwives, because they had not studied at the midwifery school and they did not know how to use injections.

Thank God, we were a big family in our village of Naemulla. My mother and my sisters all lived in the same house as us. They kept my children while I used to go out to the villages to deliver babies. Then, when the children were still small, I applied for and was able to attend the school of midwifery. This was before my youngest children were born. Till that time I had just worked without any training, following my aunt and my grandmother.

The work of the midwife is easy, but after we had studied at the school of midwifery, we were able to work properly, with all the right equipment. I worked as a midwife for fourteen years. It is a good job and I was very content to be delivering the babies in our homes, in the homes of our sisters and cousins and all our villages. I used to go there and back by car. People usually take you to the delivery and bring you back home again. If a woman was delivered at home, praise be to God. But if she had not delivered in twenty-four hours of labor, we would take her straight to the hospital in Wad Medani. If she started to hemorrhage or the placenta did not come down or if there were any problems at all, we took her straight to the hospital. Women would come to us with all sorts of problems: headaches, fevers, something that women get during childbirth called *klubsh* [calcium deficiency; see chapter 4] . . . there are many women's illnesses. We would try to help them. But during childbirth we went straight to the hospital if there was a problem. If we could manage at home, fine, we delivered the baby, gave the woman injections and tablets, and she would be reassured and safe. If she was not able to deliver easily, then we took her to hospital. The doctors know more than us.

I was happy with the work but really there was very little money in it, just enough for food. There was a small salary from the government of £S12 a month. Then we usually got something from the baby's family: meat, half a sheep, or some money. But only two or three women have babies each month. I could make a little from circumcisions but not a lot. Before we attended the school we did not circumcise at all. Only once I had learned the government circumcision, where the incision is done well with anesthetic and stitches, did I perform it [see chapter 4 for details of this].

The father of my children did not object to this work; in fact he was very happy with it. When he was transferred to Sennar, however, he said "I cannot stay alone in Sennar while you remain here. The children are small." So I resigned from the job and came with him. I could not work as a midwife in Sennar as it is in a different province. This is Damazin province and I would need to have a work certificate from the office in Damazin. My children were still small, at school, and I just decided to stay home and work from there.

My husband used to work for the government, for the water corporation. He was transferred here to another department. Now we have our own land and house and we are happy in Sennar. Most of my children are here with us, though the older ones are married with children of their own. Asia is our first child and she is in Wad Medani with her husband and children. All my children, boys and girls, have studied at school. Fath al-Rahman studied at the senior secondary school and knows English. He is the manager of a company in Port Sudan, a big company with foreigners working there. He is soon to be married. 'Abu al Ghais, my next son, also studied as far as the lower secondary school but then he stopped. He is a driver and has a license to drive a taxi. Then there is 'Abu Obeid, 'Abu Sofyan, Abla, Huwaida, and Ruwaida. The two youngest are still in school.

When I first came to Sennar, I worked at night, making and selling tea. Just before sunset I used to go to 'Abdallah's shop near the tarmac road with my glasses and things. I prepared and sold pumpkin seeds, beans, and tea with or without milk. I sold them at the entrance to the shop and returned home at nine o'clock. This is the countryside; there is nothing to do here during the day. In the mornings you can only find work in the main markets of town, not out here in the sticks.

Four years ago I found this kiosk to rent in the main market. I pay the owner £S2 a day for it. Of course I would like to have a kiosk of my own but there are none left. It was a long time ago when these kiosks were started by the town council. They were given to the older women who applied to the council and who then worked in them themselves. In the old days girls did not go out to work and young girls never even went to the market. Only older women used to go there and sell unleavened bread [kisra]. But now those older women have grown very old and have stopped working in their kiosks. They have started renting them for £S2 a day to younger women to work in. They use them to sell kisra or tea or whatever they like but they have to pay this rent of £S2 a day to the owner of the kiosk.

My friends were already working in the kiosks and they said to me, "Fatima, instead of just staying at home, why don't you come and work in the market? Rent a kiosk, and you will find a profit." So I went to the market and found a kiosk, and now, thanks be to God, I do make a profit.

It is very tiring work. Every day I rise at 4:00 A.M. with the call to the first prayers. I get up straight away and after saying my prayers, I make the kisra for the day. I have to make a lot, using at least half a kilo of flour and the fermented liquid. I fill my tray with it and cover it well with a good clean cloth to go to the market. I find a public car and I am in my kiosk by 6:00 A.M. I just bring the kisra from home, everything else is there.

When I first arrive at the market, I go and buy the food for the day. Then I come and light the coals so that I can make tea and coffee. Then when people come early to the market they find it waiting. We are ready for the first customers to arrive.

When all those wanting tea have gone, we begin to prepare breakfast. As soon as I get to the market each day I go to the butcher and buy mutton and liver: £S5 worth of sheep and £S4 worth of cow. I also buy vegetables, tomatoes, cucumbers, and bread and start getting ready for breakfast. We make a meat stew from mutton that we serve with bread and we cook liver and we make an *umregeiga* [traditional stew made with okra] of meat that we serve with kisra. The traditional breakfast costs 75 cents while the mutton or liver, served with a plate of salad and a loaf of bread, costs 125 cents. We do not make beans. You can buy beans in the restaurants in the market that the men run but we do not bother. Tea or coffee is served separately. Coffee costs a quarter and a glass of tea is a dime.

Many people come to the market each day. Many come from outside Sennar, from the villages and from the east, to the market to buy their provisions and sell their produce. They often come and eat our food. Some come regularly because they like a good breakfast but they do not want to eat in the restaurants because the men's food is not so good. Women's food is clean and delicious. Both men and women come to eat in the kiosks. More than twenty-five come to me every day. When the women of the east come into town to shop, their men bring them and sit them here. They have breakfast and drink tea, followed by a pot of coffee, and their men do likewise. After that they go into the market to buy their supplies. Then they leave for home in the public cars.

After breakfast I can rest a little. At 1:00 P.M. I have to put on the stews for lunch. For lunch I serve two stews, maybe potato and *mulūkhīya* [traditional stew made with Jew's mallow], plus a salad and kisra. We have bread only for breakfast. Lunch of a bowl of stew, salad, and kisra is also 75 cents and tea and coffee are extra. After people have finished lunch we wash the dishes, clear up, and leave the market between five and six o'clock. We take the public car and thank God, it goes most of the way to my new home, even though it is far away. The father of my children is already there and the children have come from school.

It is forbidden to work in the kiosk at night. They do not have any electricity; it has been disconnected, so that nobody can work there after dark. From about 5:00 P.M. the police are there. They wait by the kiosks until they are all closed and they know that everybody has left. Then they stay until morning, looking after the furniture and equipment. Since the women pay a tax on these

Fatima at work (1981)

kiosks to the council, the police stay to guard them and make sure that nothing happens to them.

The furniture and equipment in the kiosk are all mine. I have food trays, plates, and pots. There are also twelve small coffee cups, twelve tea glasses, two sugar bowls for serving with coffee, and four spoons: two big spoons for tea and two others for the coffee. I also have two decorated stands to put under the coffee pots so that people are pleased with its appearance. I have four small trays for tea and coffee and six coffee pots, two large and four small. The big ones serve two people and cost 50 cents. The small ones fill two coffee cups and cost a quarter.

Each day I make about £S25 to £S30. From that I take the money for my supplies and what is left is my profit. Besides meat and vegetables, daily I need two packets of tea at 75 cents each plus four cups of sugar which costs £S2, and half a cup of coffee for £S1.35. Then I buy charcoal by the sack straight from the lorry for £S6.50.

Before we leave the market all we women meet and pay into our savings box. We share this and each day we all pay £S5 into it. If there are a lot of us, it can reach £S100 or even £S150. Zachara Fadl al-Moula is the lady of the box.

I am an old woman now. There is no reason why I should not work in this way. When the woman is young and ignorant, she does not like to go out, but I am no longer young. If I was, I could not even go to the market. My brothers would not like it. But now I am an old woman with children, I do not have a problem. I am able to work in the market. My children do not object, for since I am an old woman there is no talk about me. But if I were a young woman I would not go. Neither my children nor their father would accept it. We say we are old now. There are some even older women working in the market and there are also younger women there. Some young women have their first child on their laps and are working in the market selling tea. Some young women are divorced from their men and then they have to work. They are young, the same age as my daughters. But we are finished with all that. We will not have more children and we do not have any problems. Our husbands and our children are here and we just work to bring up our children well and to have some money in our pockets. When you have money you can be happy. You can dress well. A tōb is now at least £S55 or £S56 and nice *shib-shibs* [sandals] are over £S30. In the market I can make much more money than the midwife. Each day I come back from the market with £S10 or £S15 in my pocket.

The father of my children also works in the market. He has retired from the government and receives a pension. When he finished work there he went and got a commercial license. Now he goes and works with it in the small market called Suk Libya, selling vegetables that he buys early in the day from the main market. We do not go there together as I go to the women's place of the kiosks and he goes to the men's place. In Suk Libya too, not just anybody can work. Everybody has their own place. Each individual rents a certain area and can only work there. You find both men and women but they have separate areas.

We do not work on Friday. We take Friday for a holiday, stay at home, and do not open the kiosks. If people we know have a wedding or a circumcision, we go and visit them. If there is a woman with a baby we go and congratulate her and for a funeral we go and give fātiha [see chapter 2]. If there is a zār being held in town I just go to chat with the people. Most people in my district have zār. None of my family had it, neither my father's family nor my mother's. Zār is not always inherited. It is just an illness that people get, the red wind. I became ill during childbirth. It was the Evil Eye. I had zār since early on but after the birth of my fifth child, Abla, I became ill and had no milk for the baby. They took me to the hospital and treated me but it did no good. So my family said, "Maybe this is a zār illness." They brought the umīya and she did the incense treatment and found it was zār. There were a lot of people [in my head]: Bashir, 'Abd al-Gadr al-Jilani, Lulīya, the English Khawāja, Khawāja Girgis . . . a lot. Immediately I prepared for a Chair [ceremony]. Sheikha Zeinab came and held it in my house. We killed three goats. We did the karāma and the beans and the procession. All those who were sick went down. Everyone who had zār bought their clothes and their perfumes and money and were possessed. Then they gave money to the umīya and to the women who beat the drums. You could see their pockets were full of money. As soon as they went down they gave it away to the umīya and to the women beating the drums.

After that Chair I became fine. I have not been ill with zār again. It was Lulīya who held back the milk and made me ill. They brought her clothes and a scarf and a special velvet dress from Saudi Arabia. In those days there was no velvet here in the Sudan, you could only get it if you knew someone traveling abroad. We had some relatives who had gone on the pilgrimage to Mecca and they brought it back with them especially for Lulīya. They brought it for me and I wore it with the special clothes they made for me, and I slaughtered the karāma. That was it. I became better. Now I am fine but if someone has a zār ceremony I go to visit and in Rajabīya we all give £S1 to the umīya. All the women with zār contribute so that she can buy the things necessary for the karāma: sheep, sugar, beans, cigarettes, and so on. I do not have very strong zār. I just sit quietly with everyone and pay my money like everyone else. The zār is still with me but I do everything it wants. It likes sandalwood oil and the perfume called Bitt al-Sudan so I always keep them in my house. If you have all these things at home, perfumes, clothes, and so on, the zār spirits do not become angry, but if you fail to do as they wish, they are annoyed and make you ill.

Sometimes on Fridays we just stay home. I am very tired. How could I not be? I come back from the market with aching feet, exhausted from the cooking, the serving, and the traveling but what can I do? A person is forced to do something with children studying in schools and the cost of living so high. Is it easy to bring up children? Everything is so expensive. If I do not work in the market and make use of my arms, no one else will bring anything for us. A person who does not work does not have any money, and you need money if you are ill or if there is a death in the family or if someone needs to go to the hospital in a special car. If your child is sick you also have to pay for injections and medicines. If you do not have the money in your hand will anyone give it to you?

Life is not so bad. We have our own house-site for which we do not have to pay rent. When we first came to Sennar we had to rent a place here in al-Gul'a. The townspeople had built all these houses and were renting them out, apart from those they were living in. Some people spend twenty or twenty-five years renting a place; the landlord just makes money from them. We rented several different houses with our children. Before I bought this place, we used to live with our son Fath al-Rahman. He was not married then, he was just a boy. Abla lived there too with her children and their father in the other room. When my son married we left that house and went to live in our own block, Huwaida, Ruwaida, their father, and me. Our own place is better. We bought the block of land with the money we had earned and we had a hut and a lean-to built on it. We already have lots of furniture but at present we have no place to put it all. There is a lot to do. Now we want to build the foundations. Just to add these might cost £S3,000. My boys working in Port Sudan will have to help me so I can build properly. Right now we do not even have a toilet. We have to go out to the countryside or to the gardens or the other side of the tarmac road. Such things make life difficult for us. But if God gives me good health, I will build a fine house, complete in every way.

I am happy with the work of the kiosk. I do not want anything else. God willing we will stay here in al-Gul'a, we will live in our house here, we will not go back to live in Naemulla. Our children are here with us. We will just go back to Naemulla to greet people or to a wedding or a funeral. We are happy here. How could we not be happy? This is our own house and al-Gul'a is not a bad place. Some parts of it are not so good, with Nubans and their drinking and bad people like the Ethiopians and the Eritreans, such as in that area just near the abattoir and the veterinary compound. Back there, you can find bad people. But here in our district, people are good and kind. The people's sheikh of the district lives near us. It was from this sheikh that I bought my plot of land. We were renting a place and then the owner sold it. The council took all those people who did not have homes and were paying rent and told them to buy land and build their own places. I applied straight away and got ownership of a plot. It was expensive, £S1,050 altogether, but it is good land. Now Abla also has her own house-site, thank God, near the house of the sheikh. They have already built a wall round it and are ready to build a house. In the coming year, if God wills, you will find her in her own home with all her things, her refrigerator and her fan, around her. Yes, this is a good place, a peaceful place. We have no drinking or theft; these are fine people, the sons of Arabs. They pray and fast and do not commit sins and covet or steal other people's things. They are truly the sons of the people.

Fatima and the Women's Market (2001)

On my return to Sennar in 2000 and 2001, I had some trouble finding Fatima. Her daughter Abla has moved away from the neighborhood and not bothered to keep up her ties there, having failed to come and help her old neighbors on several important social occasions. The women I talked with had also not seen Fatima for a long time. They thought she had moved away, possibly to Omdurman where her daughter Huwaida was now living; but nobody was very certain of her whereabouts and had not seen her, in the market, on special occasions in the district, or at zār ceremonies.

In a broader sense, even more disturbing was the disappearance of the women's market. I went to find it, briefly, while in the main market in 2000, but decided I must have been looking in the wrong location as those I asked for directions waved vaguely in different directions. In 2001, I was more determined. Accompanied by my two research assistants, Hanan and Hiba, I made an expedition to the market specifically to locate it. Several of our neighbors had told us it was in the same place as before, but this was clearly not so, as all that remained there was a large garbage dump. In the marketplace, we were directed to different places by amiable vendors, but without success. There were no kushuk, and no women working in the sort of area that had previously catered primarily to women customers. One male vendor told us that women now work all over the market, but particularly near the meat market. There we did indeed find several women squatting on the ground, selling bottles of oil, paper cones of peanut butter, a few eggs or dried pumpkin seeds; but of the stalls or secluded teashops, there was no sign. Finally I pieced together what had happened. When the city council had relocated the market to the outskirts of town in the early 1990s, it had knocked down many of the existing stalls, including all the women's kiosks, as an incentive for traders to move to the new site. Although most merchants still declined to leave the old site, women traders were left without any facilities, and indeed, since that time few women are to be found during the day serving food in the market, except for tea and coffee, or light snacks. For the most part they squat outside the more popular shops or stalls, sometimes with a stool to sit on but no shelter or storage space. It is only in shade of evening, on the outskirts of town, that women may be found serving stews and bread. Market women today enjoy far fewer facilities and support than Fatima had in the mid-eighties. There are no longer women in Sennar market who can be described as Sitt al-kushuk. While it seems unlikely that this was the outcome of any official political policy, it is no coincidence that in the early days of the Islamist government, women were actively, even forcibly, discouraged from working outside the home, and their movements were considerably restricted.

Fatima herself I was finally able to track down, but the news of her was also not encouraging. Of the five women and their families, Fatima and her children have fared least well. Her daughter Abla, who, I was to learn, still lived not far away in al-Gul'a, had recently suffered a terrible tragedy when her oldest son drowned on a high school trip to the river. We clearly needed to visit and offer our condolences to her. She and her husband have eight surviving children, but the loss of her son has been a great blow. Furthermore, Abla's husband has taken a second, younger wife, another cause of pain. Finally, we learned that Abla's brother, Sofian, had recently been in a bad road accident and was hospitalized in Omdurman.

Market women today (2001) in the center of the main market

This had led to Fatima's precipitate departure from Sennar about the time I arrived in town, when she went to stay with Huwayda in Omdurman, to be near Sofian. Fatima herself, said Abla when we visited her, was not in good health. She was largely confined to the house because of problems with high blood pressure. Abla sighed as she spoke of her mother and said Fatima has just become very old. Halima the hairdresser was later to comment that Fatima is much younger than she but certainly Fatima does not enjoy the same good health and fortune.

Abla expected her mother to return to Sennar shortly, and I went several times to Fatima's old house. What looked like the same grass hut and lean-to seemed unchanged from when I had visited it in 1985, and the surrounding acacia fence was just a little more worn than I remembered. This property she now shares with her youngest daughter Ruwayda, recently divorced, and her three grandchildren.

Fatima had still not returned when the time came for me to leave Sennar, but a few days before I left Sudan I was able to visit her in Huwayda's house in Sowra 42, a new development north of Omdurman. Dismounting from the public truck, we asked a shopkeeper where the people of Sennar lived. He pointed immediately to a house one block away. There we found Huwayda chatting to neighbors outside her door, not surprised to see me as Abla had telephoned that I might be coming. She led me into the house, straight to a darkened room off the large compound, where a much older and sadder Fatima was resting. The years have not treated Fatima kindly.

In brief, her oldest daughter, Asia, died fifteen years ago, after many years of ill health. She left two small children, a son and daughter whom Fatima has raised in Sennar. Her granddaughter recently completed high school and her grandson is already working as a laborer, having left school early. Fatima's husband died in 1991, after a long and tiring illness. Her sons then insisted that she stay home, that she stop going to work in the market. This also coincided with the time when political pressure was being put on women to stay home. However Fatima was thus left without any source of income. She fell behind on the rent for the kiosk and town officials seized possession, also confiscating all the equipment she had left inside it. Shortly afterwards they knocked down all the stalls in their fruitless bid to relocate traders to the new market. This was the end of Fatima's market career. She has not worked since, lacking the resources to start again even if her health permitted.

Things would have not gone badly for her, however, had her sons been able to support her. They apparently do not offer much help at all, though they are all working nearby. The oldest drives a public minibus but has at least two wives and families to support. The second, who graduated

Ruwayda and her
infant son (2001)

from senior secondary school, works for the government, and the third, an
English graduate from the University of Khartoum, works for an international transport company. They are both married and preoccupied with
their own families. Sofian, the youngest brother, is also a driver and is the
only sibling not yet married. With only a primary school education, he
was able to find a job in Saudi Arabia and was to have moved there in
2001. Had this happened, Fatima's fortunes might, at long last, have been
reversed. However shortly before his departure he was in a serious car
accident, suffering (among other things) a broken arm that has proved
hard to heal, despite the support of his mother and sisters. If any of her
sons were able to assist her, Fatima kept noting, life would be a lot easier.
Since no one is working outside the country, there are no remittances to
help improve their fortunes.

Abla and her family are probably the most successful of Fatima's
family. Her oldest daughter attends the new University of Sennar, working
towards an economics degree. She is also married and hopes soon to join

her husband in Germany where he is working. Meanwhile she stays with her mother who looks after her small daughter while she is at school. Hawayda, Fatima's third daughter, whom I recalled as a young girl help-ing in the kushuk, completed two years of higher secondary school before her marriage. Her husband is also a driver and they have five children. Ruwayda, her younger sister, finished high school and then married a sol-dier. When she discovered he was taking a second wife, they divorced, and she returned home to her mother with her infant son. In all, Fatima has 26 grandchildren and one great-grandchild.

We spent a pleasant afternoon with Fatima and her family, looking out across the Kareri hills. Work was really a nonsubject—though repeat-edly the topic of Fatima not having her own income, not having any money, came up. Fatima's illness, her daughters said, is "the illness of money," caused by lack of funds. Zār spirits might also have something to do with her misfortune. Fatima told me she continues to attend zār cere-monies. She was actually attending her group's thanksgiving ceremonies in the month of Rajab, when she heard of Sofian's accident and departed so hastily from Sennar, leaving all her clothes and equipment in the leader Zeinab's house.

Ironically this was the woman who twenty years earlier had been so independent and whose career had shown the most promise for a finan-cially secure future. Her success in the market was aborted by family as well as political developments. Sadly she is now the saddest (miskīna) of the surviving women.

"We have left the work to the young girls," said Fatima sadly. "In the past most of the workers in the kiosks were old women. Now you find young girls in the market, wearing gloves and stockings, cosmetics on their faces and bodies, all smooth and beautiful.

"When we were working we had saving-boxes and each month one of us took it all. Then we were rich! Now I am ill with rheumatism and for ten days I have just lain on the bed at Hawayda's house. That is all."

AL-DAIYA
DISTRICT MIDWIFE

In the same town block in al-Gul'a as Halima, though at the opposite end, lives the midwife Zachara. They have been neighbors for almost forty years and together they have watched their families grow and prosper. I met Zachara soon after I got to know Halima, and as she learned of my interest in women's work, she invited me to accompany her on her rounds, as well as to visit her relatives and friends. Whenever I return to Sennar, Zachara is among the first to welcome me, entertaining me with the news of the neighborhood, poking gentle fun at her friends in stories that readily bring smiles.

Zachara the midwife is a familiar figure in al-Gul'a. Wrapped in her official white tōb and carrying her grey metal box of equipment, she is still to be found walking the streets to attend to her patients. She confided once that her ambition was to make enough money to buy herself a little car so that she would not have to walk so much; but first, she added, she should perhaps save for a refrigerator, which would be more useful for the rest of the family. By 1985, she had her refrigerator, but she has never managed to get a car, though with the help of her children she now lives quite comfortably. Although she worked long hours, her own income was

93

Zachara and Sue Kenyon with the first edition of this book (2000)

slight, and even when it was supplemented with gifts, she has always been dependent on help from her family for any luxuries.

Zachara is of the Ta'aisha people, of which the Abbasiyin ("People of Abbas") and Naasa (see below) are lineages. These were the relatives of the Khalifa 'Abdallahi who succeeded the Mahdī in 1885 and came originally from western Sudan. They were among the first people to settle in new Sennar after the overthrow of the Khalifate in 1898, when the leaderless Ta'aisha were forced to flee in all directions. Zachara touches on this period below when she describes the travels of men like her father who were drawn to Sennar by the opportunities for work: in the newly developing agricultural schemes and the construction of the dam. They were one of the earliest groups to settle in the new town and occupied what is today a prime site, near the river and spreading south from the center of the town.

By the time we taped the following account of her work in September and October 1981, I knew Zachara well. I visited her frequently in her home and accompanied her to her relatives on the east bank of the river. I had also worked closely with her on several occasions, attending births and circumcisions, and watching her on follow-up visits to newly delivered mothers. This had given me a great respect for the way she worked and for her very professional attitude to her job. I had also grown to like her enormously. We had first met early in 1980, in a neighbor's courtyard. I found Zachara lying on a bed, drinking coffee and entertaining the other women by reading fortunes from cowrie shells. She is good company, talking vivaciously in a loud throaty voice and chuckling frequently. On this occasion, her plump frame stooped low off the bed as she kept gathering up the seven small shells, throwing them once more and, in turn, providing us each with a new slant on our futures. I learned that I was very fortunate and very rich and, God willing, would soon have a new pair of shoes. This amused everyone as the shoes I wore, a long-cherished pair of clogs, were indeed down at heel. Fortunes told, Zachara proceeded to ply me with questions about myself and my home. She always shows a lively concern for other people's lives and ideas as well as pride in her own achievements and those of her family.

Zachara is a religious woman, as befits the daughter of a *mūezzin*. Her conversation, more than most, is punctuated by frequent references to God and her admonitions to women in labor are to show faith, to call on God, rather than simply groan and cry. She prays regularly and sometimes attends the mosque. Before she made the pilgrimage to Mecca, like most of the women in her neighborhood, she saw no contradiction between this and her belief in and support of zār. In the 1980s, I went with her to burei zār ceremonies where she thoroughly enjoyed herself. She had a rather irreverent attitude towards the ritual, waving mischievously to onlookers as she marched in the solemn procession to sacrifice an animal for a zār karāma. Yet she knew a great deal about zār procedures. Once, when the butcher's wife was holding a three-day ceremony for zār nearby, there were heavy rainstorms and the drummers were unable to get through to the house. It was Zachara who persuaded another woman present that together they could beat the drums and enable the ceremony to continue.

This readiness to take the lead is typical of Zachara and distinguishes her from many of her neighbors. She has a strong personality, is ready to make decisions, to act, in contrast to many women in the Sudan who are frequently more retiring in group situations. She is forthright, determined, and concerned, caring and also inordinately curious about other people and places. She is most attached to her family and her home. She is justly proud of her children and cared deeply for her parents who used to live nearby. When I first knew her, her home looked very imposing from the outside with its high wall, large gates, and tree-shaded courtyard, though inside, her three rooms were simple mud and brick structures, albeit decorated with great care. By 2001, these had been transformed into a large modern house with many modern appliances.

Largely because of the demands of her work, Zachara's day was far less structured than that of Halima and Fatima. Apart from the weekly examinations she held at the local health clinic, she had very little regular work but most of the time was "on call." Like other practicing obstetrical specialists, she suspected that babies deliberately come in the middle of the night and was therefore often to be found catching up on lost sleep at irregular hours. Usually she knew if she was likely to be needed for a delivery and could plan her time accordingly. On several occasions we made trips together, once to the grave of Sheikh Farah wad Taktūk for a thanksgiving karāma of no special reason; another time to visit her relatives in Karima whom I knew from elsewhere. Zachara obviously enjoyed a day out and took full advantage of the fact that I could drive her where she wanted to go. On other occasions, she was unable to join me because she knew a delivery was imminent and needed to stay within calling distance. Until recently she did not have access to a telephone, but her patients generally sent one of their other children or a relative to tell her when she was needed. If there was any possibility of a problem, she did not go far and always left word where she could be found, ready to attend to her patients. She was also careful to follow up a childbirth with regular visits for several days afterwards, though the frequency of visits depended partly on the experience of the new mother and partly on the nature of the birth itself.

As she points out, her work tends partly to be seasonal. Circumcision operations, which have to be planned ahead of time, were usually scheduled for the school holidays or for certain Islamic occasions, such as the Prophet's birthday, which are believed to be particularly auspicious. At such times, she expected to be very busy. She tried to schedule only one appointment a day, and to stay on and enjoy the celebration that followed. It was not uncommon for several girls to be circumcised at the same time, especially where sisters or cousins were close in age. In such cases, only one midwife would be called upon, generally the local district midwife unless someone in the family was qualified to do the operation. Certain midwives earned a reputation for clean, attractive circumcision scars and were in much demand.

Zachara continues to lead a full and active life. In the 1980s, it was difficult to find her at home because when she was not out visiting patients or delivering babies, she was invariably catching up on her social calls. Because of the unpredictability of her working life, she tended to set the pace of her social life herself, relaxing with friends when she had the time and shutting her gates firmly when she needed to rest or to catch up on her chores. She did most of the domestic work herself, although when her half-brother and his family lived with her, his wife did much of the cooking and her teenage daughters helped with washing clothes and sweeping the courtyard and rooms. She was proud of her cooking and whenever she was free, she enjoyed helping neighborhood women prepare a thanksgiving meal.

The midwife is a central character in any Sudanese village or neighborhood, familiar to children from birth and involved with female health problems throughout their lives. Each district in Sennar now has at least one official (government-appointed) midwife although there are also many other women who help deliver babies if necessary. These women have not undergone the formal training that Zachara has had but have learned only by experience, sometimes from their mothers or from an older relative (as in the case of Fatima in chapter 3, who worked with her grandmother). Such untrained midwives are usually referred to as either *daiyat al-bāladi*, country midwives, or *daiyat al-habl*, rope midwives, after the traditional method of giving birth. Many are quite proficient, especially in childbirth, but do not have access to any form of equipment or anesthetic and often have only rudimentary knowledge of hygiene and infant care.

The government midwife, on the other hand, has undergone a formal training, knows something of anatomy and physiology, and can administer medication and anesthetic (in this case, the drug pethidine). Though often uneducated or illiterate until recently, the government midwife is technically proficient at home deliveries and can provide basic prenatal and postnatal care for mother and child. Certainly vis-à-vis the traditional specialists, today the midwife is a distinctly modern paramedical practitioner. Yet until fifty years ago, she was just another traditional healer. Hers was a very old job, for which knowledge and training were handed down, often through family lines. In the past few decades, the work has been modernized, rather than superseded by educated modern practitioners. It has left the midwife in the position of being both part of her community and also outside it, associated as she now is with the practice of modern medical techniques.

There are several other traditional curers practicing in districts like al-Gul'a. Besides those involved in spiritual curing (see chapters 5 and 6), ordinary people may consult with the bonesetter *(basīr)* and the barber *(hallag)*. The bonesetter is a practiced masseuse who is also skillful with herbal remedies. By 2001 the bonesetter I had known earlier in al-Gul'a had died and most people in town now consult a family that has held knowledge of this profession for generations. Several members are skillful in treating aches and pains in various joints with vigorous massage and are able to help with back problems or problems of dislocation. Some bonesetters specialize in treating children. The barber performs boys' circumcisions and also treats certain complaints by applying hot metal to various parts of the body. For diarrhea or tooth complaints, he cauterizes the gums, while for hepatitis (the sickness he is believed to cure best) he lays burning wire in prescribed manner on the upper arms. It has been suggested that the application of heated pressure on particular parts of the body may have the same alleviating effects as acupuncture (Ahmed El-Safi, personal communication). Cupping *(hajjama)* also continues to be practiced in Sennar, though I was not able to see any practitioners at work. Many individuals also have special home remedies from herbs, seeds, roots, and bark (as in the case of Halima the mushāta in chapter 2).

The midwife brings to her job a knowledge of such traditional Sudanese practices and the same beliefs and values as her patients. Yet at the same time she has undergone a formal training in aspects of clinical medicine. Since her training is brief and she may not have had much formal education, she remains very much a part of the local community, to which she is often related. Yet the nature of her job also places her outside the community and in the sphere of hospital personnel. By professional medical staff, however, she is regarded as a very poor relation, even though, in much of contemporary Sudan, the midwife remains the only modern community health worker. In her district she works alongside other traditional curers in dealing with daily ailments as well as attempting to promote clinical medical methods in her work.

As a consequence of these conflicting demands and attitudes, there is a certain ambivalence towards midwives generally in Sudan. There, the reputations of many midwives, like nurses, are regarded as a little tarnished and this is a clear reflection of the unconventional lives they lead. They go out from their homes, often alone, at all hours of day and night; they enjoy a particularly close physical intimacy with their patients; they possess a certain knowledge that their friends and neighbors do not have; they are not subject to the same social constraints that other local women observe because of the priority given to the demands of their job.

The role of the Sudanese midwife is contradictory. On the one hand she is more closely bound to the intimacies of women's lives than anyone else; on the other hand, because of the very nature of her job, she is herself quite different from the women she helps. Often when midwives fail to reconcile these factors, they earn the dislike of the women they are trying to help. Certainly midwives seem more controversial in the Sudan than any other occupational group, and individually, they are frequently gossiped about and scrutinized. Criticisms of midwives seem to have less to do with their job performance or with demands for payment than with the nature of the job itself. It is as if their involvement with sexuality, and particularly female sexuality, is at once reassuring and threatening. While women do not hesitate to discuss with midwives their intimate problems, they will also gossip about those same midwives as if they are a distinct class of social problem, such as prostitutes. The midwives are obviously aware of these tensions. The pressures of both their working and nonworking lives often lead to a certain amount of personal and domestic disorder. Many midwives are divorced. Many also suffer from visible and tacit stress ailments, and they are particularly prominent in zār activities.

Only against this background of conflicts and anomalies can the career of the midwife in modern Sudan be fully appreciated. She has a central and vital role to play and is in some ways very much the intermediary, the broker, the bridge between new and old ways, in both medicine and other cultural assumptions. Yet in other ways she ends up by belonging in neither place. This is both her strength and her handicap. Nowhere was this more evident than in the controversy about female circumcision in the Sudan. Some Sudanese wanted the harsher, traditional form of the operation for their daughters, while others believed that a new, milder procedure was quite acceptable, and a few were prepared to renounce the custom altogether. The midwife, however, was blamed by all sides, either for perpetuating the custom in order to bring herself a steady income, or for not operating in the traditional manner. Yet she herself was part of the community she ministered to, had herself been circumcised, and did not really comprehend a society where women were not adequately circumcised.

Midwifery in the Sudan was first organized professionally in the 1920s, a time when educational opportunities generally opened up for women. Formal education for girls had begun in 1907 when Babikr Bedri opened the first school for girls in Rufā'a and also from that time there were a few girls attending boys' elementary schools in Khartoum, though such places were few in number. Previously the only opportunities for learning to read and write were through the Quranic schools, which were also predominantly male institutions. Then, in 1921, a teacher-training institute was established in Omdurman Girls Training College, which was to lead to a rapid increase in the number of girls' elementary schools. In the same year, the first formal education for midwives began with the establishment of Omdurman Midwives Training School, under its first principal, Mabel E. Wolff. She set about to organize a four-month practical course for rural midwives, introducing them to Western concepts of hygiene as well as a different method of delivering babies.

From the outset, female circumcision posed a dilemma for the school. It is apparently a very old custom and may indeed date back to pharaonic times. Certainly at the turn of the twentieth century it was very widespread in the northern Sudan and despite vigorous government efforts over half a century, showed little sign of disappearing when we lived in al-Gul'a in the early 1980s. Then we found that it was actually spreading as peoples from south and west, the Dinka, the Nuba, and the Fellata, began to copy their neighbors and to circumcise their daughters.

In northern and central Sudan, two types of female circumcision are recognized, referred to locally as Sunna and fironi (pharaonic). Sunna, meaning "Traditions" in the sense of following the "rightful path" of Islam, is sometimes referred to as "Government Sunna" in that it was actively supported in government legislation, which attempted to eradicate only the harsher, pharaonic form. Sunna circumcision consisted of removing the prepuce and glans of the clitoris and often the whole clitoris. The pharaonic form, on the other hand, was far more drastic and painful and completely changed the outward appearance of the women's genital area. It involved the removal of the clitoris, labia minora, and most of the anterior parts of the labia majora (referred to as excision) as well as the stitching together or infibulation of the reduced sides of the genital orifice. Together with the removal of all bodily hair, the total effect was a sort of neutering one. There was no outward sign of a woman's sexual parts other than a faint scar where the genital slit should be and a small opening at the vaginal entrance. Women who have undergone such operations are vulnerable to all sorts of side effects as well as to great discomfort when they commence sexual relations and when they go into childbirth (El Dareer 1982).

In the 1920s, pharaonic circumcision was almost universal in the northern Sudan and was performed under the most difficult conditions. Despite the horror with which the founders of the Omdurman Midwives Training School viewed it, they realized that one small group of midwives would be unable to persuade Sudanese women to give up genital excision. Therefore Miss Wolff and her successors chose to teach midwives a modified, "intermediate" form of circumcision, performed under more hygienic conditions. The wound in the "new" operation was less extensive than in the traditional, pharaonic form and healed more effectively (Sanderson 1981).

The attention of the condominium government was drawn to the problem, however, and in the following years many of the graduates from the midwifery school themselves, as well as other influential Sudanese, began to speak out against female circumcision. In 1938, the new principal of the midwifery school banned staff midwives from performing the operation of genital excision at all. Formal opposition culminated in 1946 when the legislative assembly passed a law making pharaonic circumcision an offense punishable by fine and imprisonment. Sunna circumcision remained legal. Surveys in the 1970s, however, showed that the pharaonic operation continued to be performed on more than three-quarters of the female population (El Dareer 1982:1). Legislation was largely a failure, although in educated and influential circles this remained a controversial issue for well over half a century.

After Independence (1956), education for girls developed rapidly. Junior and senior secondary schools multiplied and several regional schools of midwifery also opened. The school of midwifery in Sennar dates from about 1970. Until that time, student midwives from the Sennar area had to go to Omdurman or, more frequently, to Wad Medani to study, an inconvenient measure since many of them were, like Zachara, mature students with a family to care for. The opening of the Sennar school also reflected a general increase in the number of government midwives and a corresponding decline in the work of the traditional midwives, who found themselves being displaced, at least in the riverain area.

Since pharaonic circumcision is illegal, midwifery students are not taught how to perform the operation itself, but inevitably they are shown how to open and reclose a circumcision scar for a delivery. This effectively prepares them for the circumcision operation itself, and until recently, they found that the steadiest source of income was from operations of this kind. It is evident from Zachara's account that she herself did not see anything wrong with this work and she was obviously rather proud of her artistry in operating. She is, in fact, confused about the differences between Sunna and pharaonic circumcision. She was warned at school about the hazards of the pharaonic operation and did not want to perform that herself; yet the type of operation she did, which she often refers to as Sunna, was of the intermediate type, first introduced by Miss Wolff, which involves both excision and infibulation.

In 1985, I assumed from what was then going on in Sennar, that it would take several generations for female circumcision to disappear in Sudanese towns. There, while pharaonic circumcision was being superseded by the intermediate form, I found no sign that the operation was being discarded. At the time we were doing these interviews, attempts were being made on radio and in the mosques to persuade women that the custom is not necessary and is actually injurious to their health. For the most part, the women felt they knew better. Their decisions and attitudes had nothing to do with midwives or education, but rather reflected the importance of tradition and a reluctance to be the first to abandon what was seen as an integral part of their culture. By 2001, however, I found that things had changed very rapidly. Many parents have rejected circumcision completely for their daughters, and one mother estimated that in Sennar today, most girls born after 1992 are not circumcised. This is taken up in the final part of this chapter.

As important rites of passage, birth and circumcision traditionally have been surrounded by a great deal of ritual in Sudanese society, though this varies somewhat according to the ethnicity of the family, their economic status, and the position in the family of the newborn. Firstborn children are often accorded the greatest extravagance. Pregnancy itself is greeted enthusiastically but treated fairly pragmatically. A pregnant woman carries on her life as usual. In al-Gul'a there is a small health clinic where Zachara works, which provides prenatal checks and which women use with varying regularity. A woman likes to go to her mother's home for the birth and she moves there towards the end of her pregnancy so that she has help preparing for the birth as well as with the delivery and the postnatal period. Preparations include the manufacture of the necessary perfumes, oils, and incensed woods, of sugared biscuits, and of baby clothes, and the purchase of new nightclothes for the mother-to-be, including a special *firka al-garmasīs*, the brightly colored silk-like length of cloth on which she will rest during her lying-in period. Other more mundane items are also needed: plastic sheets for the delivery, a new tushit (tin bowl) for the birth, new glasses for serving drinks to the many visitors expected, possibly a sheep for the karāma after a safe delivery or the naming ceremony.

Pregnancy is not an illness, and childbirth is regarded as an exciting part of the natural process by Sudanese women. That is not to deny that they expect the actual delivery to be difficult and look forward to it with some trepidation. The early stages of labor are no problem; then the pain is described as "cool." Later stages of labor, however, and especially the episiotomies all circumcised women undergo, are definitely "hot" pains. These are local distinctions that are used to contrast mild and severe pain, although the cold–hot opposition is also applied in other contexts of Sudanese life. Here, however, it reinforces the fact that it is not the actual delivery so much as the cutting and stitching that women dread, which is why they choose their midwife carefully.

With the birth of her baby, the new mother traditionally enjoys a forty-day rest period. She is fed foods regarded as especially nutritious and easy to digest: pigeons, soups, and special custards made from dates or sorghum, milk, sugar, and eggs. She herself has nothing to do other than care for her baby. She has plenty of visitors and is rarely alone. The baby is never left, particularly during the first few weeks when it is most vulnerable. At seven days, the child is named and it is then that a sheep is usually killed for the celebration.

Much of the ritual and symbolism in circumcisions are similar to that in weddings and childbirth. The girl (like a new mother) is referred to as the bride *(al-'arus)*. She is prepared for the occasion with new clothes and jewelry, including nightdresses for her lying-in period. The women prepare the perfumes, oils, and incensed woods, and the sugared cakes for the visitors; purchases are made: plastic sheet and new tin bowl for the operation, special colored sheets to wrap the girl in after the operation, a sheep for the celebration to follow. In the past, the operation was usually performed when a girl was between 4 and 8 years old. If it was left for later than that (usually for financial reasons, for even the simplest type of occasion involves a payment to the midwife and some type of celebration), women felt that it was more difficult for the girl. The operation and recovery were more painful and, perhaps more important, the girl herself had by that age become a source of ridicule to her playmates, who were well aware of her physical condition. She was taunted for being unclean, and other children refused to play with her.

By 1985, most circumcision operations were carried out between April and July, the long school holiday and the hottest time of the year, so that they were done early in the morning, soon after sunrise. Sometimes a night of partying preceded the operation; the street outside the girl's house was closed off by large screens, chairs were assembled on either side of the road, a microphone was set up, and dancing might go on all night. Immediately after the operation, a sheep was slaughtered, cooked, and served the same day. The girl and her close female relatives were fed the choice dish, raw liver chopped with onions and sprinkled with lime and hot pepper. Guests were fed breakfast and lunch, and they gave money gifts to the girl while someone kept a record of the amount. Sometimes in the late afternoon, a trip was made to the river by close relatives and friends. For the next few days, the girl was given special foods, similar to those given to a bride or to a woman after childbirth. She was encouraged to lie still, but by 1985, the period of recovery was fairly brief.

Midwives are also involved in marriages and even more commonly in remarriages, as Zachara describes below. Because of the nature of pharaonic circumcision, the help of the midwife is sometimes needed in order for the marriage to be consummated. Conversely, before a second marriage, the bride-to-be may ask the midwife to neaten her circumcision and tighten the flesh around it. This service is also in demand after childbirth, and Zachara did it fairly routinely.

Perhaps because she has undergone a formal period of training, Zachara has far more to tell about her job than the others who learned their work informally and found it difficult to organize their information and thoughts about their occupations. Zachara needed less prompting in her interviews and provided twice as much information as the others in the volume. There is an obviously didactic tone to her account. She is used to teaching student midwives and she worked with me in the same way, assuming that I wanted to write a book about training for midwives. She emphasized repeatedly that the only way I could learn the skill was through practical experience.

Zachara al-Daiya (1981)

My name is Zachara Ahmad Seif al-Dien al-Bushari, midwife of al-Gul'a. I graduated nine years ago this year from the school of midwifery. I am in good health, thank God, and I am working well. I circumcise and I deliver babies and, praise God, nothing bad has happened to me in those nine years. I thank God I have had no problems with the doctors nor made any mistakes. In nine years, no woman has died during childbirth with me. If a woman died, my heart would stop beating. This is my good fortune, and if God is willing, I will always be so lucky because my heart means well and I perform my procedures properly. I get courage from God because however kind and loving I may be, when it comes to my work, these feelings go away. I do not listen to my emotions but work with courage and daring and am not afraid.

I always had an ambition to be a midwife. When the father of my children divorced me, I did not really consider any other work. Dr. Farid suggested that I work as a cleaner in the hospital. I told him that bearing in mind my children and my situation I had to work but I really did not want to be a cleaner. Every day you have to get up at 6:00 A.M. and go to work. Furthermore certain jobs like cleaning itself, cleaning the ward and toilets, and taking bedpans off the patients are humane tasks but a bit difficult. Also my heart is bad. I had no ambition to do it and there was not much money in it. Midwives, thanks be to God, make a lot of money. The government gives us an allowance of £S20 a month and people are also very good to us.

In fact the job of a midwife is also a very humane one. If you find people who do not have anything, you do not say: "You have to give me so much." If people give to you, you thank God. If they do not, you can see their state and keep quiet. Those who give to us cover those who do not give anything. We excuse people who do not give. We do not complain about them; that is wrong. We should be patient and God will send us a generous patient to cover the others. There are some poor people who give to us and some rich people who are miserly. But we provide a service and do not expect anything in return.

I am very happy with this work, thanks be to God. I cannot say I am not content because I am. My health is good. Every day I see happiness and thank my God. People like me. They come to me and I cannot say no; I work well for them. I try to please everyone who comes to me. If God puts the baby in my hands I deliver it. You cannot turn someone away and say: "I've just come back from a delivery and I am tired. I cannot come with you just now." That is not possible. However tired your body may be, you must go. You cannot turn anyone away unless you have a sickness certificate. This would be wrong, you would be making a grave mistake. If the woman has difficulties or is hurt, it is your problem. Even if you have just come home tired, you have to go. It is your duty.

No other woman in my family ever worked before me. At first they were angry and told me not to do it, though now they see that the work is for my own good and for that of my children. In the beginning, though, they opposed my working and said many things to scare me. They used to threaten me and say: "Don't dare become a midwife. You are young. Those people who come and take you to a childbirth will kill you . . ." But I never believed them. I had the ambition to work. I told them: "Let them come and kill me. If someone takes me to kill me, it would be a fine thing. Does a man want to take me to his wife or to slaughter me?" I do things my way. If my head says something, I must decide upon it. I do not do what other people say. I do what is good for me and that eases my conscience. I was not afraid, thanks be to God. I have not come across any of the things that they say about midwives. I work well and people greet me well and bring me home safely. Nothing has ever happened for me to complain about.

Family Background

I was born here in Sennar. I also gave birth here to nine children. I had six boys; four died and two are alive. Then there are three girls. Five children are not bad. It is a lot from God.

I live with my children here in Sennar in my own house in the district called al-Gul'a. My oldest son is at the University of Khartoum. My second son got his school certificate and now works abroad, in Jordan. He is a carpenter for a large company. Someya, the oldest child, passed her school-leaving examinations but was not accepted into the university. She has now applied to work in the bank here in Sennar. If she fails to get that job, she may become a teacher in the junior secondary schools. She has been to Damazin about a teaching job but they still have not sent word to her. Then my other two daughters are still in secondary school. They have not done badly, thank God.

My people are the Ta'aisha. We are the Abbasīyin, from Abbas's children. My husband was also Ta'aisha but from a different branch or khashm al-beit; they call them Naasa. We are all Ta'aisha but each person belongs to a particular branch, to that of their father.

Patrilineal

They belong to father's side

My children and I are all Ta'aisha but they are also Naasa. My mother was my father's cousin, his father's brother's daughter, and they were both children of Abbas. Each tribe and each branch of the house is distinct and we all live separately. Like you English, you say, "I live in England." Egyptian people live in Egypt. Isn't that so? Though it seems to me that the English are spread around rather a lot. Everybody here also had their own tribe and their own homeland. Even in Sennar, the tribes live separately. This area is still all Ta'aisha. Other peoples have not mixed with us. The Sudanese are behind us and we the Ta'aisha are at the front. The Humeidab are over that way, near the center of the town, by themselves, a different group; and the Fellata are at the back, also separate. Everyone belongs to their own tribe and each tribe has its own distinct living area. But times are changing. Nowadays if someone does not want to live in a certain place, he moves elsewhere and anyone can take his house, Fellata, Sudanese, any tribe. We are becoming mixed in our living habits.

My father was Ahmad Seif al-Dien al-Bushari. I was named after his sister Zachara. His mother was Birkhita—or was that his mother's sister? I am not sure if it was his mother or his aunt. He was not from Sennar. He was in Omdurman at the time of the killing there. My father was an old man when he married my mother, then a young girl. At the time of the Mahdīya, my father was a young boy. I think he was 7 years old when the Mahdīya was hit. His family died in Omdurman. Zachara, after whom they called me, was older than him. They lost her during the fighting. They looked everywhere for her but could not find her.

My father was brought up by his paternal uncles, his father's brothers. After the war they came and lived in Sennar. I do not know my father's family well. They are many, in Sinja, Ramesh, Jebelein, I do not know exactly where. My father lived in many places. Once he was in Hasa Haisa, once in haj 'Abdallah. In the old days people did not have to work. Those who had goats would see a good place and move to it. But when he settled down, he came to Sennar and married my mother. He had been married a lot before my mother but he did not have a child. Only my mother had children, three girls, and at that point, he died. He had had no children from those other women. He had the right and they fooled him. Such was their state that when they did not become pregnant he divorced them. He was just looking for a child. When he had us three he thanked God and was satisfied with what God gave him but he was already an old man of over 50 years of age.

Although our tribe comes from the west I do not know anything about our family there. My father did not talk about the west, only about Omdurman. They were young when the war started. Everyone was in a terrible state and just ran away. They just left their goats in the desert and the families who were left took them and also ran. His father and mother took him and ran. His mother was a strong young woman but she only had the two children, Ahmad and Zachara. They had many brothers, however, the sons of their father's brothers.

I remember my father well. He was a mūezzin in the mosque. He used to talk to us and teach us al-Hamdu and all the verses of prayer. He would say, "Learn it so that you can pray." We were only young when he died. I was about 7 years old and my younger sister was very small.

My mother is Asha, the daughter of al-Tahir. She later remarried my uncle, Hamid, the father of my brothers. She had seven boys from him. Three died and four are alive. There is also a girl. We found brothers, thank God, and they have caused us no unhappiness. Two brothers work abroad and two are in Sudan. The two in Saudi Arabia are very good; they bring us clothes and send us money. They have appreciated my mother particularly and support her well. God willing, our children will follow them and become like them.

Asha's parents were al-Tahir and Howa, daughter of Muhammad. They are dead now, but I remember them both. They were present at my marriage. I did not know their parents. Howa's father was called Muhammad Batil, meaning a thin person, someone who has a light body without much flesh. [*Laughing*] You couldn't really call me "Batla," could you? I don't need all this fat.

I did not know Howa's mother's name. If she had told me I would have remembered. We did not forget things they told us when we were young. In ignorance, one remembers everything. People were illiterate in those days. They would tell a girl that if she went into the street and got lost, she should say she is the daughter of so-and-so, her grandfather is so-and-so, and everyone in the tribe would know her. They taught us all this when we were young. You memorized it: this is my mother's mother, my father's mother, my father's father is so-and-so. Now children just go to school to learn and come home. All that fuss we made is of no use. No one has time to learn about who they are. I do not tell my daughters. They know that I am their mother and Asha is their grandmother but nothing else. Can you believe it? If they were asked questions like we were, they would know nothing. In the old days, people were idle. They had no problems and life was beautiful; their hearts were happy and they were gay, not like us. Our lives are all problems. Then people were caring and kind. Life was a bit easier.

Howa had sisters. Khaltoum, daughter of al-Haj, is her sister, her paternal cousin. Their fathers were full brothers. Also she had a sister from her mother. They were all one family, sharing the same courtyard with my grandmother. Now my mother is alone. She does not have a father or a mother. Her old mothers have died. Only her sister Fatima, the daughter of al-Their, is still alive. Asha had only one sister and she had only one daughter, Khaltoum, the daughter of Omar. She is our sister. She married, thank God, and her daughters are doing well at university, still studying.

They all live as a family with my mothers. My aunt and my mother live together in one house though they have separate doors and a dividing wall in the middle. They both own their houses, they bought them themselves. My father's house is somewhere else and my grandmother's house is further down.

I had two sisters. The younger is called Teina and she looks just like me. She is married and has two children and lives nearby in al-Gul'a. Our other sister Husna died about twenty years ago. She left three children, two boys and a girl. The daughter lives with my mother and works at the council offices.

My children's father is Ahmad. We are relatives but not straight cousins. We were also neighbors, from the same area. His family is very kind to my mother and to me and the children. The divorce did not spoil things between us. I think of them as I did in the beginning. We don't have any problems because earlier we were neighbors.

Ahmad is now headmaster of the Southern Elementary School in Sennar. We were married for a long time, about twenty years. I had nine children from him. Then there was a problem. I was angry with him and I left the house. I would not go and live in the same house as him again. He did not have another wife but I was angry with him and refused to stay with him. My brothers tried to persuade me to but I refused. I said that I would not go back and that the question of my children was between my husband and me and, with God's permission, I should bring them up. Until they are grown up, as long as I live, I shall not begrudge them anything. Thank God, they have grown up well and are completing their studies successfully. After I had left him, their father waited for two years and then he remarried.

My mother begged me to remarry. My father's family comes and goes but I told her, "I won't do it. Don't get me mixed up with anyone. I don't like them anyway. Marriage is no good for me because I have children. The man wants the woman to stay home and I want to work." I will not keep my time free for a man and now I would not leave my work. This is why I did not want to remarry. All that is over. I married and had children; there is no further problem. From now on my children will marry instead of me.

Divorce did not confront me with any real difficulties. I am happy, thank God. Divorce is not a problem for a woman unless she then sits back stupidly doing nothing. If she does not work she will be tired and feel sorry for herself. She will not gain anything in life. When her children grow up they will find their mother was careless and did not do anything for them. It will be difficult for them. But for us, thank God, work is capital. The lack of a husband makes no difference. If you are working, you do not notice any lack. There are facilities you can provide better than your husband. There are things concerning you and the house that your husband cannot do for you. Yes, there are women who do not want this. They like being married. But if I married again, the man would only mess up my life. He would oppose things at home and bother my children and every day I would find fresh problems. . . . It is better to stay happy and relaxed and have my children come home happy with nobody to question them other than me, their mother. The new husband creates problems for the children and gives them a complex. For that reason it is better they are brought up alone by their mother.

When I first left my husband I did not have a house of my own and I was staying with my family. Then I applied to the town council and praise be to God, they gave me a plot of land in this place they called al-Gul'a. I had a little money and some gold. I sold the gold and with that and some of the money I built this house. It is in my name alone because I have five children. If I put it in one of their names, they would quarrel about it. The world is unknown. Maybe I will die and everything will fall apart. This way the house will be a heritage. If I die they can all stay in it and say, "We inherited this from our mother." Their father also has a house of his own, thank God.

At present my brother Tijanni lives with me. My sons were with me until they left home and then my brother and his family moved in. On my own, I am afraid of thieves. They say: "The midwife has money." It is better if a man is here.

Schooling and Training

I cannot read. I never went to school, but for a year just attended Quranic school over on the western side of town. At that time we entered at the age of 7 and I only stayed for the first year. I had not learned anything when my grandmother took me out. Before long I was married and then, thank God, I had my children. For all those years I did not work outside the home.

It was after I was divorced that I went to the school of midwifery. As I told you, midwifery was always my ambition. I went into it very enthusiastically, as if I knew it, because I was determined to do this work. However I was too scared to just go and deliver a baby without any training. Women would call me a rope midwife and say, "This is not a legal midwife." Women use the rope midwife only in an emergency, if there is no trained midwife available. If she comes and finds the baby ready, she takes a plain blade and cuts. She does not have a needle and thread or catgut to stitch with and she does not know how to cut an episiotomy. This is why I went to the school; there are many dangerous things to be aware of and without training you would be afraid. You must go and study. Take the lessons and then you know the right procedures.

I attended the school of midwifery here in Sennar. It took nine months until I graduated. Our studies were very good and the teachers appreciated us. By now the doctors who taught our group have all been transferred and there are new ones at the school. My sister-in-law was a student at the same time as me. Our husbands are brothers. Really it was too much of a coincidence. We were divorced at the same time and we studied together. For this alone I thank God, for our children were themselves brothers and sisters. We were in the same group. She entered the school a few days before me and I followed her, in Ramadān. We studied together and graduated together and got our certificates at the same time. It was a wonderful coincidence. Whenever our children came to see us, whether it was a lot or a little, we could feed them together. Thank God, our families were very good to us. Her mother especially, God rest her soul, was a very good, kind woman.

My mother was at first against my going to the school. She told me to go back to my children's father and bring up my children. She said it was better than school, but I refused and told her that my work would not affect them, that my work was for their own good and that it would enable me to do things for them, like build a house for them. Thank God I have succeeded but my mother and brothers were very good to me. When I was at school they came every Thursday and Friday. One or two of them came and brought me food and money and soap, everything I needed. Throughout my training I was never in want and I had no problems. I had a house here in Sennar that was rented out and every month I received the income from that. Yes, I completed the year without being in need and I was very happy there. If your family looks after your children and your belongings, you are relaxed. You can work well and do not worry. But if your children are unhappy and your furniture and things are uncared for in a rented house, you will be affected by this and become anxious.

The father of my children, well, he did not say anything. He kept quiet. He used to bring the children to me for a time on Thursdays and Fridays. They used to come and visit me and then go back to him and to school. He used to teach them and he kept them very well until I came back to them. Luckily I was here with them for the big examinations of junior and secondary schools. Thank God, they all studied well.

Now I am experienced in my work, I can undertake it all without any worry. But the first time I went into the classroom, I felt very scared, not of the lessons but of a big doll I found lying there. This was a dummy that they used to teach us, and it looked like a child. I thought it was a real child! In my heart I was very scared. What could this be? I looked closely at it and was even more frightened; what is this big doll-child with hair and shining eyes? "In the name of God, what is this?" I exclaimed. I thought it was a khalīja [spirit] lying there. Then I realized that it was only something normal and that they use it for teaching.

This was the only time I was afraid. I was not scared of the large doll, the full-size dummy they call Zarīfa. I went straight up to her as if I was ready for a delivery. The medicine of delivery is taught first and for it they use this plastic doll just like a nice woman: Zarīfa. They put her in the various positions of labor and

Student midwives (2001)

delivery and demonstrate the shapes you find in pregnancy. For example you can see when a baby will not deliver normally because its bottom is in the wrong position, on the side of its mother with its head on the other side. This type of case should be delivered by a caesarean operation. It cannot be delivered normally. They told us that you should transfer such cases immediately to the hospital. Sennar hospital is good, with its own specialist in obstetrics and gynecology. You should use it. Problems with deliveries spoil your reputation. If contractions are strong but there is no progress . . . , it is better to go straight to the hospital. There they make things easier for her right from the beginning.

In the hospital there are also midwives, nurses who have studied medicine as well as midwifery. They know how to administer medicines, tablets, injections by syringe, according to the hours and the doses. Something like that. They are not specialized in childbirth. Some of them are appointed to attend a course in midwifery and they learn delivery. But in nursing it does not mean that just because you are a nurse they let you deliver. They do not. You also have to study at the school of midwifery and complete the course before you can deliver. Our experience is greater and they cannot have it, just as we too cannot have their experience and know all about tablets and medicines. They are specialized in treatments and they treat the patients. After they have completed our course, they have two certificates and then they are able to deliver with a doctor. If a caesarean operation is needed, they assist. Something like that. There are nurses and midwives. They are not the same job.

At school they teach us that the law says we should not circumcise at all except for the Sunna form. Yes, at school they just show you how to cut the clitoris. . . . It is better if you do it this way because there is no danger, no hemorrhage, and no fear. This way a woman does not have a difficult time in childbirth and there is only the initial cut of the circumcision. They tell us not to do the bad pharaonic form. But in Sudan, people like a girl to be closed up below. It is not up to them, however. We see what is good and does not give the girl a difficult time and act accordingly. . . . half pharaonic, half Sunna, this form is good. The woman has an easier time in childbirth and when you come to cut her, it does not need a lot of stitching. . . . Now most people have stopped the pharaonic circumcision and we do only the Sunna.

Our teachers did not give us any rules for taking payments. They taught us that ours is a humane service. If someone gives to you, you thank God. If they do not, you also thank God. You behave the way you were taught. We cannot deliver and then ask the person to give us something for the delivery. They themselves may feel they want to give to us. If they do, you may accept. They are not forced to give. If they do not give, you thank them and the matter is closed. Thank God, they are under no obligation.

Graduation

The day you graduate, the teachers congratulate you and give you a certificate, a license, and a box [of equipment]. From the time you receive these, you go out and work on your own. No one goes with you.

The certificate is your right. You never give it back to the school and they can never take it away from you. If you make a mistake, they might come and take your box away from you for a while. For example, if someone dies in your hands through circumcision or a hemorrhage, these are the results of mistakes you have made. The authorities might come and take the box as a punishment, but they bring it back. They keep it for a short time so that you can improve your work and then they give it to you again. The box is owned by the school. You only get a box with your certificate. If you do not work cleanly and well, they can take it back.

You never have to go back to school, unless you want to go for a visit. You can always go to see other women graduate. Each group of students is sent out to study with practicing midwives. From each group they give me someone who may stay a month or half a month or even only a few days while I complete so many deliveries with her and she learns from me. If there is a delivery, I let her do it and just stand there and comment. She cleans the woman, cuts her, and performs the procedures she has been taught and which I also explain to her. She comes with me as the *pashdaiya* [senior midwife]. You watch her closely and the girl is left to you and your conscience. You must explain to her what you have learned and show her so that she carries on the right way. If you see her making a mistake you must say, "No, that is wrong. Do it properly because you are going to make a living from this work." The four girls I have had with me have worked well and now left me. On the day of their graduation I went and congratulated them on their licenses and boxes.

For my first appointment they told me they were sending me to a place called Hamadnallah so I went there as their midwife. Thanks be to God, I worked well but the work was not what I had expected. It was not like it is in Sennar and there was not much to do. Also I could see my children were in a mess so I came and applied to work in Sennar. When I first graduated, there was a midwife called Awadia working in al-Gul'a. She had been brought by the sheikh of the district but now she had left so I thanked my God and came straight here to my house in al-Gul'a. They transferred me immediately from Hamadnallah. I was only there for a year. I came home and, thank God, my children were pleased and I was happier too. Your home is never like outside. Also the work

Zachara heading off to work (1981), with box of equipment and kettle

in the town is better; the money is better, although I have to say that people in the country are very kind.

Midwife in al-Gul'a

I have now been in al-Gul'a for eight years and, thanks be to God, I have had no problems. Probably I have delivered two hundred to three hundred babies, I do not know the exact number. It is recorded in the [registration] book but I never actually kept count. Sometimes I deliver seven or eight or even ten in a month but then again I might only deliver one or two all month. Births are never the same. They have a sort of season. It is not simple. Sometimes for two months you will not have a delivery and you stay at home. You find the odd circumcision and you cope. You also get the monthly allowance of £S20 from the government so it is not too bad. But you have to make allowances for this. If you have a savings box you take from it and you manage because, thank God, the money does not stop altogether. You are careful with what you spend. If you have children who work, they help you in the house. My children are not yet working but, thank God, when they pass their examinations they will have good jobs.

If someone calls you, you have to go out at any time and under any circumstances. Even when it is raining, if someone knocks, you must go out and deliver and return in the rain. If you go and find it is not yet time for the delivery, you rest a while with them and then return home. This is like a law, that you should go and see for yourself. Only if you have a report from the doctor showing you are ill can you stay at home. You cannot be ill and stay home without informing the doctor, it is not allowed here. If a woman is hurt or something happens to her, and her family complains, you are in the wrong and they will make an investigation and punish you.

I usually work only in al-Gul'a. I just go outside the district if someone invites me to circumcise their girls. I refuse to deliver outside. For deliveries each district has its own midwives and the east has its own midwives too, like my sister [-in-law] Birkhita in Karima. I tell people: "It is better to go to the nearest midwife. There is no need to put the woman in danger if, for example, the dam is not working. Go to the midwife who is nearest to you." Circumcisions are a different matter; you do not have to worry about such things. If someone comes to me and wants my circumcision, that is fine. I can go in the morning and circumcise, stay a couple of days with them, and then on the third day, after checking the girl is well, return home. A circumcision presents no problems but a delivery is more difficult.

Deliveries

Delivering babies is simply work. If you have had a lot of practice at it you know much better than if you learned it from a book.

Yes, you learn the techniques best if you watch it or if you actually deliver. Books cannot teach you as well as experience. Watching and smelling, they say, teaches you more than the written word.

You do not simply go and deliver. When I go to a woman in labor, first of all I get information from her: Did they give her a card at the clinic? Where is it? How many times has she been examined? Has she been swollen? Has anything particular happened to her? I check her card and her answers. If I discover she has already borne six, seven, eight, or ten children, I do not keep her, even if her previous deliveries were straightforward. Something is sure to happen. In a woman who has had many children, the uterus is cool and the contractions are weak. She will not deliver quickly. You should take her straight to the hospital.

When you come to a delivery, always examine the woman properly. . . . You raise her on a bed on a plastic sheet and examine her, three times. The third time you do so, she should be ready. You should not examine her a lot as this can cause infection in the uterus. When the uterus is open, she is ready for the birth. The baby is ready to be born. You give the anesthetic and make the episiotomy. For deliveries, I always give an episiotomy for the circumcision scar. Make sure you keep the wound dry. Then the baby can come out. You examine her and make sure she is all right. You check below to see if she was torn. Then you stitch her. You check the baby. If it is a girl you find her bottom and if it is a boy you find his you-know-what!

In such a case, you have made no mistakes. You have delivered correctly and no one can report you to the doctor for any error. Your record is clean.

A normal delivery is when the baby comes head first. Even this way, distress can occur. You may find a woman's contractions are very hot but there is no progress. The contractions are so strong that she is shaking but the baby does not descend and the uterus does not dilate. This is dangerous, a sign of distress in the delivery. You transfer her immediately to the hospital because there they can help her. If they cannot deliver her from below, they can operate on her and she can rest. Also when it cannot be delivered both of you will tire needlessly and the baby might not live. If in doubt, it is better to transfer her.

There are many things we studied so that, thank God, we can recognize the different signs of distress. Hemorrhaging at any time is dangerous. If a woman starts to hemorrhage, you must let her rest, give her glucose in the vein and leave her resting on a sloping surface. If it stops, thank God. If it does not, take her straight to hospital. It can also happen that the placenta is presented first. This delivery is difficult but it is better you deal with it. This has happened to me. When I arrived they told me the woman had had a hemorrhage. I found the delivery very near and the bedding full of blood. I replied that when she hemorrhaged they should have taken her straight to the hospital. They said that they wanted me to see her because she was very uncomfortable and she was sweating. I found the uterus was fully dilated. I washed straight away and left her as she was. I just put the plastic sheet beneath her and started to bring down the placenta, gradually, until it came out. . . . I washed her, cut her, and delivered her. I did not panic, thank God. The baby came down and the placenta was still inside. While I was cutting the cord it fell out. It did not bother me after that.

Breech deliveries are also difficult. Only deliver the woman if the contractions are strong, the uterus is fully dilated, and the membranes are full. I have delivered breech babies with no particular problem but we are afraid of them. It is always better to take the woman to a specialist to be delivered either by caesarean or forceps because it can be dangerous. . . . If you see the bottom is coming first and the contractions are cold, there is only a small opening, and the woman is weak, take her straight to the hospital. These are signs of distress. Thank God I have not seen much of this. Even when I have had a breech presentation, the contractions were strong and the uterus was open. I helped the woman to rest and was able to deliver her. It has only happened two or three times, thank God.

Also difficult is the delivery in which the shoulders of the baby are by its leg and it has its back towards its mother's back. This you should transfer immediately to hospital.

Once I was confronted with the problem of a face-first delivery. I came and found that the woman's contractions were as strong as fire when I examined her. . . . If you find the uterus closed and the contractions are cold and the head far away, this is going to be a difficult delivery. She should be taken straight to hospital. If the contractions are strong and the head, the face, the mouth are coming, do not panic. I have delivered this quite safely. I found the uterus fully dilated. As soon as I inserted my finger, the baby sucked it. I waited, as they had taught us to, and recognized that this was a face-first delivery. . . . My things of course were ready and sterilized. I straightaway gave the woman the anesthetic and cut her. This type of birth can be very frightening. The face of the baby looks horrible, like the skull of a khalīja, we call it the face delivery in our classes.

This work of ours, as I have said, is an art, a skill. If you find something wrong and are able to do something about it, there can be no objection. This is something good that you have done to help the woman. There is nothing wrong with that. You must try to use all your skill to help. If you find a problem or foresee difficulties that will affect your work, however, try not to get involved because you will just get all the blame. It is better to tell them in the beginning to go straight to a specialist.

If a midwife is competent she will immediately recognize calcium deficiency [klubsh]. This is one of the most difficult cases we come across but it is easy to recognize. As soon as a woman develops klubsh her body changes. It becomes black, very black, and her face begins to tremble spontaneously. It shakes and she complains of a severe headache. After a while, she starts to hit out with her arms and legs. Then she goes into a very deep coma. Klubsh is like a mental illness that comes during or after delivery while the placenta is still in the stomach.

It happened to me when I was working out of Hamadnallah, in a small village near an irrigation canal. I forget the name of that place. I was taken to a girl named Sayīda. When I examined her I found the uterus fully dilated. Then she said to me: "Zachara, I have a bad headache." We had a doctor's assistant nearby. I told him that the woman had these symptoms and I was worried about her. He said that there was no problem, that if anything happened they could send her in a government Landrover to Sennar Hospital.

Then what I had feared did happen even though I had asked his advice. Just consider. It was a remote place and there was no one with me. Even her husband was not there; he came only after she had delivered. She gave birth to a boy but before I could bring down the placenta, she got klubsh. She was still conscious but I could see she was not right. I put the boy down and did not bother about him. I told a man to go and get me the car. The woman's daughters were screaming and shouting. I ignored them. I pushed them out of the room and slammed the door and told her husband to come and hold her down on the bed. Otherwise she would have fallen off and broken something. We have English salts in our bag and I gave her two teaspoons of that in her mouth, just before she went into a deep coma. I gave her another spoon of salts in her anus, drop by drop. The placenta was still in her stomach; I was holding it with my forceps, tied to her thigh. I got things ready and when the Landrover arrived we took her and her bedding gently and laid her inside. I told the driver to go carefully so as not to shake her or increase the coma. We set off immediately for Sennar hospital. As we reached the dam, she became conscious. Thank heavens, she was all right. "Zachara, why are you sitting next to me?" she asked. I said to her, "At last you have woken up!" You see, those three spoons of salts were good for her and shook off the klubsh coma.

When we got to the hospital, the first person we saw was Dr. Omar, a young boy, one of the new doctors. He took her from me as I gave him a report of what had happened. "Don't worry," he told me, "nothing else can go wrong. The placenta will come down and she will be fine." I told him that there would be no problem with the placenta but because of the klubsh I had been afraid to squeeze her stomach and bring it out. I thought that because there was no hospital near the woman's home and it was such a remote settlement, I should not follow my normal routine, I should just get her to Sennar. I could have brought down the placenta and have something else go wrong, a hemorrhage or anything. Then Dr. Omar at once removed the placenta and she recovered quickly. She asked me to telephone her family in Sinja and tell them what had happened. We chatted and she gave me messages for her children in the village. I went and told them and the next day I went to her again. By then she was fine.

If God wishes on you bad deliveries, you could meet with this problem a lot. I thank him that only once in nine years have I come across klubsh.

I have delivered twins many times, both normal and breech births. I do not really like to deliver them, preferring to send them to the hospital, but I usually find the woman is ready to deliver and it is too late to transfer her. This has happened several times. I do not like to do it but circumstances demand it. There was one case where a woman had already given birth to twins. I heard about her in the district. She was pregnant again and came to the examination clinic where they gave her a card. I said that when she came to deliver I would send her straight to the hospital. However she waited until her membranes were ruptured and then she sent her twin boys to fetch me. When I arrived I found the first baby was ready to come out. At once I delivered him and then the second baby. Later I asked her if they had not given her a card in the clinic that had instructed her to go to deliver in the hospital. She said yes, but she wanted to deliver at home and God had sent me to her house. I told her firmly that if I had found her earlier, I should not have delivered her at home and she should thank God she had delivered safely. To begin with, she had a card from the clinic that she hid from me. I did know about it, but when I went to her, it was not to deliver but to transfer her immediately to the hospital. This I was prevented from doing by her condition. She had concealed it on purpose. She should have told me about it in the first place.

I have never delivered triplets though I once delivered twins and the third was a bag of water. It was here in al-Gul'a. I went and found the woman was very ill. She was on the floor and had a rope midwife with her. I said to them: "I do not deliver on the floor. Bring a small bed." I organized the bedding and we raised her on it into the position we use in our deliveries. I knew there were twins because I had examined her on the floor. In such cases you find the stomach is very big and you can feel the babies' bodies; two heads and bottoms and sets of limbs. After I had raised her on the bed and washed her I realized the birth had started. As soon as I gave her the anesthetic and cut her, the first body came down. It was just a bag of water. It fell out and I dropped it straight into the basin. Then a baby's head came. I brought that out and then another body came, bottom first, and I was able to bring that down too. I was not at all scared because I had delivered twins before. This "thing" that came out first, I just thought was a baby with its legs first. I never expected a bag of water. Thank God the woman then delivered safely and her children are now growing well.

Circumcision

As I have already mentioned, if you want to circumcise, do not make the pharaonic circumcision because it often causes problems. When you meet Sudanese people they say: "You must do the Sudanese one," meaning pharaonic circumcision, but do not do it, it will adversely affect your reputation. You should do the Sunna form . . . I think this is better for you. Difficult work affects your reputation and something that does not make things easy for the woman is no good. . . . Nowadays most people have stopped doing the pharaonic form and we perform mainly this type of Sunna. But many men object to this circumcision. The father of a girl may come to us and say: "You must do a suitable circumcision," meaning the pharaonic form. So you half stitch her up, but not right down below. . . . The appearance of a girl with the pharaonic form is beautiful. People like it because the woman is all closed and beautiful. But the lips are too tight. Sunna circumcision is also beautiful. The woman looks closed, you see her closed . . . but this form heals quickly and the woman suffers no ill effects.

Many things can go wrong in circumcisions. . . . If you do circumcise messily and leave a vein bleeding, this will affect you and your work. There is a [legal] penalty for the midwife performing such an operation and the doctor will punish her as well. She will be in trouble both for the circumcision and for the hemorrhaging of the vein. Thank God, I have not had any such problem in the nine years I have been working, although it might still be to come.

There are many people who have not been circumcised. Uncircumcised women are also fine. I do not think that these people will circumcise their daughters either. They will leave them as they are because they say that circumcision is dangerous. Many girls nowadays are working and when they give birth they are only able to give their body a little rest before going back to work. Really, this is not a bad thing. I live according to the times. The people that God sends me are enough. I live well, yes, very well. But if one finds work one does not refuse it because work means more money. That is not a bad thing.

Recircumcision and Reinfibulation

If a woman is divorced and wants to remarry, she sends for the midwife. If she wants, we can recircumcise her. They call this 'adal, which means to be reconstructed. You just cut the circumcision scar as for a delivery, then dry the wound and cut a little from the sides of it . . . After this, they say she is 'adla. I do this a lot for women.

There is another problem for a girl. If her circumcision is closed, she cannot produce the honor when the bridegroom goes to her. The honor, sharaf, refers to the hymen. We were taught about the sharaf at school. . . . It can only be broken by a man, but if a girl is completely closed by her circumcision, there is no way he can break the hymen. In such a case you give the girl an anesthetic and cut her. You cut one or two of her circumcision stitches so that the opening is a bit wider. Then when the bridegroom goes to her, he will bring the honor. The hymen can be broken and the honor can come out. . . .

Examination Clinics

Every Saturday and Tuesday we have an examination clinic here in al-Gul'a in the medical center. On Saturdays I do the examinations and on Tuesday other midwives are on duty. The pregnant women are given cards that record details of their medical history and the number of examinations they have. As soon as a woman comes you find out how many children she has had and whether she had difficulties with the deliveries: how many hemorrhages, caesareans, miscarriages, or scrapings. We ask to see these cards when we go to deliver them. We also examine the women at the clinic and weigh them, keeping records of all this.

Women also come to me when they have pains and they have missed menstruating for two or three months and yet there is no baby. This is caused by infection. We give them a card from the examination clinic and send them to the gynecologist. He has to treat the infection and give her injections and capsules. He gives her them to swallow every six hours and some people are given treatment down below. Such problems affect menstruation and pregnancy and may cause pain. Her periods may stop and there is no pregnancy or if she does conceive, the baby is not able to hold on in the place of birth and she will lose it. This sort of case is for the specialist and he can cure her. We have nothing to do but refer her to him. When the woman is cured she will be able to hold a baby well.

Sudanese women have a lot of internal infection. This is not caused by the circumcision because that is done outside, to outside flesh that is not affected in such cases. Infections occur whether she is circumcised or not. No, internal infection is from the ovaries and the uterus and those inside places; the pain is inside. The pain, the infections, and the secretions are all inside the womb itself. It is like an illness and is not affected by circumcision. The best thing for a woman in any sort of pain is for her to go to the doctor, and then she will not become very ill. But some people become so ill they reach the limit and still do not go to the doctor. This is no good. Pain does not go away by itself. Some people get headaches and do not treat them. They grumble that they have had a headache since yesterday but are too lazy to go and get aspirin to cure themselves. Such a woman should swallow some aspirin, have a cup of tea, and cover herself for a while and then it would leave her. These things happen to everybody. If you go to the doctor you are cured properly.

Ear Piercing

Sometimes after I have delivered a baby girl, her family wants me to pierce her ears. Some people want it done after forty days, others bring the baby after a year, and I will do it. Other people just do it themselves at home. You only need a needle. You put on some anesthetic and pierce the ear. It does not need an injection, just a needle and thread and it is done. Then they insert gold ear-rings. We never ask anything for doing this. As I told you, I never ask for money, I just do it for nothing or as God wills. We do this whenever we are asked.

General Comments

If one of my children is ill, I sometimes treat him with an injection, but I will only treat people in my house. I will not treat people from outside. I refuse to give injections to people because they can cause a lot of problems. Many people get an allergic reaction from penicillin. You may have to take a woman with such a reaction in a coma to hospital. You should always get the nurse to give injections. If anything happens she knows what to do because she studied medicine. In school they did not tell us to give people injections so I work as I was taught. I only give women in labor the injection with the anesthetic and that is it. I will not give other injections at all. Only if someone is very ill and I take him to the doctor myself and medicine is prescribed that I get from the pharmacy, then I might inject it instead of bringing the nurse. But I would never take any risk of harming someone. The best advice is always to go to the doctor with any sort of pain. Then a woman will not get really sick. However once it happened that I was sick, and though I went to many doctors, I was not cured. This was a long time ago. I was depressed and unhappy and this unhappiness caused me pain. I had a temperature day after day and my eyes used to bleed. I could not sleep at all. I went to the doctor and he examined me and gave me eye-drops and things but the hemorrhaging would not stop. I had fever all the time and my heart used to thump: drub, drub, drub. I thought maybe I had heart trouble and so went to the hospital to be examined for that. They said that I did not have the right symptoms for heart trouble. Then someone said that maybe it was zār. I did not believe in zār but when I went to them and they burned the incense of burei zār for me, I recovered.

This first happened before I entered the school of midwifery. When I became well I began to believe in it. I said: "Thank God. This is the illness of the times. If the treatment is so simple I will make a Chair ceremony after I become a midwife. I will beat zār for seven days and I will be better." I did that and, thank God, I have had no difficulties ever since.

It was to the umīya Rabha that I first went and she later came to my house and beat the drums for seven days. I was working by then. I took a holiday for fifteen days and I beat the zār during that time. I had a savings box for £S400 and I used that money for the ceremony. Nowadays £S400 is not nearly enough to beat a zār. There is so much to buy and everything has become so expensive. There are Egyptian drinks: whisky, cognac, wine, and beer, as well as things I had never seen before. They [the leaders in zār] wrote the names on a piece of paper and the boys went and got them from the bar for us. Rabha is a very kind woman. She helped me and did not leave me to do it all by myself. I told her of my circumstances, how I had the savings box for £S400 and how I wanted to do all the things she needed for the zār, and thank God, it was enough. I beat for [the spirits] Bashir and for Rima Pasha and for Lulīya. I have a lot of zār and, thank God, I pleased them all. I did everything they wanted and brought all the things they needed: lots of things like two sheep, perfumes, incenses, food, and specially made clothes like the red jallabīya for Bashir and the dresses and firka al-garmasīs for Lulīya.

I still have zār. When people beat the zār, they sometimes come into my head and I go down. If they do not come into your head, you do not play. Yes, if the zār does not come into your head, you do not go down, you just sit quietly and watch. If a zār does come in your head, you go down. You are not shy in front of all those people. You play and get up again and dress in your tōb once more and then sit down. It is a very strange thing.

This work of ours, midwifery, is an art. You alone have pride in your heart. If you see people are talking rubbish, ignore them. Do not chat with them or bother about them. Just do the work you came to do. You find some people are no good and they talk in a way that is offensive to you. Ignore them. Only the pregnant woman, be good to her from the time she comes to you and you get to know her. If you find the people with her are only so-so, just stick to your delivery and that is all. You do not have any other business there and these people and what is happening to them do not concern you.

It once happened to me here in al-Gul'a that while I was delivering a woman, the electricity went off. The woman was ready to give birth. I had the scissors in one hand and the other hand was inside her, so I just cut her and brought out the baby. I delivered the baby with everyone in the house, including the mother, screaming. I paid no attention to them except for a woman who brought a lamp for us. I looked at the baby and found he was well. I brought down the placenta and everything was fine. If the electricity is cut off, do not panic. And if the woman is near to delivery, check that a lamp and matches are nearby. If the electricity goes off, people fuss and that can be dangerous. I said to those people: "Whatever is the matter? Why are you all shouting? The baby is well and the mother is fine and whether the electricity is on or off has nothing to do with it!" I reassured the girl, and she was fine. She had been scared about how she could deliver with the light off. Electricity cuts can be a bit disturbing, but you should not panic. Stay calm about everything that happens. Never be afraid because everything is according to God's will.

As I have told you, the government gives us an allowance of £S20 every month. It also supplies us, with Dettol, catgut, and pills. When I first started work, it was only £S5, then it was increased to £S10 and now it is £S20. But nowadays everything is very expensive. Life is very costly for us, and our children are still dependent. So we went to Dr. Yassin and told him that the money is not enough for us to live on. We asked that it be not an allowance but a salary and that it also be subject to increments like a salary. The doctor said that if they increased the midwives' pay elsewhere in the Sudan, then he would increase ours. But it seems unlikely that the principle of an allowance will ever be changed. To us, the idea of an allowance suggests something given to a poor person, a sort of charity. This is what we do not want. We want to have an official, permanent salary. If they could do this for us, it would be a great improvement.

But thank God, people do not leave us without means. If we had to live on just £S20 it would not go anywhere. Everything is so expensive. If a person has something extra in the house, like chickens and pigeons, then it helps a bit. You can slaughter them for breakfast and it helps. But in these times, not even an official salary is much use. It does not cover anything. What can we do? We work, and soon our children will be working as well, and after all their studies, they should have good jobs. I too will continue to work. I will not ask them for money, rather I will help them. I could not just sit here and beg my sons to support me and clothe and feed me. It is not possible. I must work until I grow really old and tired. I must help them because they will want to marry and have children. I must help them until my body refuses to let me work. Then I shall have to stay put and let them support me. But I do not want to have to rely on my children, I would rather help them. When they have children of their own, there is their schooling to consider, even though these schools are driving us crazy. If we are one family supporting each other and sharing our income, they will live well. They will have an easy time. We will be able to get a fridge and a television. We have never been able to afford such things.

My children are very good to me. They listen to what I tell them. None of them has married yet. They can marry after they have worked for a while. The girls must also work. Marriage is easy. Any young girl must marry, according to where her fate takes her. It is not necessary that they marry from the Ta'aisha people. Marriage is fate. My children are from fate and I will accept their marriages, whether they be close or distant, as fate. But now I want them to have schooling. After they have studied well and got their school certificates and worked for a while, then whoever wants to marry can do so and whoever wants to work can work. But I see work as more important. Marriage is not a problem. A girl should work, for one does not know what will happen. Her father and mother will not be here forever. If she works she will have some security. If her circumstances are bad like ours then she can support herself and her children. She will not be in a mess or need her mother and father. You never know if her husband will be present or if her circumstances will be like ours or even if death will intervene. Anything can happen. However much you stay with him, however good you may be to him, a man can change towards you. It is better all round if the woman can work. Then there is no problem at all.

Hajja Zachara the Midwife (2001)

In 2000, and again in 2001, Zachara was one of the first people we saw on our return to Sennar. She still lives in the same house, a few minutes walk from where I was staying and it was easy for me to bump into her on the street, to visit her and chat over coffee, and even, in November 2001, to make another long taped interview, from which I quote below. Her home is now one of the more prosperous in this area and she lives, very comfortably, with one of her married daughters and her family. Zachara continues to work as a midwife, though she is not as busy as when I last talked with her, partly from choice and also because of changes that have occurred in women's medicine in the Sudan.

All her children are now married and she has seventeen grandchildren. One son remains in Jordan where he has his own furniture company, making and selling furniture. He married two Jordanian women, cousins, who have each borne him three children and have adjacent apartments in the same building, raising their children as one family. Zachara visited them in Amman a few years ago and has also visited her other son in both Riyadh, Saudi Arabia, where he presently works as an engineer, and earlier in Syria where he went to work straight after graduating from the University of Khartoum. He married his first cousin, his father's sister's daughter, and they have two sons and a daughter.

Zachara's three daughters are also doing well. Two graduated from Egyptian universities. One now works as a tax inspector in Wad Medani, and the other is a high school teacher in Khartoum. They both married cousins and have children of their own. The oldest daughter, Someya, did not attend university but became an elementary school teacher, marrying a fellow teacher from outside the family and staying at home with her mother. They have three children to whom Zachara is very attached. All the daughters remain close to their mother and visit each other frequently.

Zachara at home with her family (2001)

All but one of Zachara's (half-) brothers are still alive, working in Saudi Arabia and Abu Dhabi and helping support their sister. So many relatives overseas have enabled Zachara to become quite a traveler. She commented:

I did not leave the country until after I became a midwife. My children took me outside for visits and my God did not forget me. My hope was to make the pilgrimage [Haj], to come and go to Mecca till I got tired, and my God has indeed taken me there. I have already made the Haj once, when my brothers were all there. I stayed three wonderful months. . . . A beautiful country, and the Haj was also beautiful, it was a wonderful trip and after that I had no need of anything else! Really, more wonderful than Paradise. . . . I did Haj and Umrah and now next year my son is taking me to Riyadh to make the Haj again.

I only went one time to Jordan, and also just once to Syria. . . . They [her sons] did not let me work or do anything. They had stayed there for more than a year, working and they knew the people, and did everything for me. They said there is no need for you to do anything. Just have a holiday! I was very happy with the Prophet Muhammad.

The only real sadness in her life was the loss of her mother, who died some years ago while making the pilgrimage to Mecca:

My mother was beautiful, she was not old or wrinkled [pointing to her photograph on the wall], she was healthy, too healthy. . . .

She also made the Haj and she died there, on the pilgrimage. . . .
My brother in Abu Dhabi sent her there, sent the money, did
everything for her. We were not together. I was in Sennar when I
got the news. . . .

When I went on the Haj my kids were scared and said, "You are
going to die there." I didn't feel happy on the Haj; they did not
congratulate my Haj. I went to Saudi Arabia and stayed three
months, came back safely, and thanked God.

I miss her [my mother] very much. She died there, and I went
and stayed three months but did not die. I said, "I am going to die
there," but death did not come to me. I did not want to come back
here, and said, "Please God let me stay close to my mother." My
mother is happier than me, she lies there in that good land, but
me, I came back to my hard world. What should I do? I am going
around till now.

We spent a lot of time talking about her work, and how it has changed:

I am lucky with my children as I get older and have health
problems, and work is not like it used to be. Work has become
little. Too many doctors now tend to childbirth, too many people
have opened special clinics for childbirth, and they have many
specialist doctors. But the people who don't have money, I still
deliver their babies, here in my home, in their home, whatever
they want. If they have no money, they come to me; if they have
money, they go [to the clinics]. But you know before this I used to
have too much work, I never stayed home. Now everybody wants
a different type of childbirth. Most people, rich and poor, are going
to the hospital to give birth. But I am not going to leave delivery
till I die or I get blind. Really! If I am blind, I can still cut unless
death takes me. Only when I get very old and can't move around,
I will leave it.

Today many nurses are also earning a midwifery qualification and work
in clinics or in hospitals, whereas midwives like Zachara do only home
deliveries. She also continues to provide practical experience for the
trainee midwives and helps women with reproductive issues, such as
menstrual cramps or birth control pills (though not condoms).

Women come to me more than a doctor. They see a doctor is
expensive and can't go, so they come here and I give them the
[contraceptive] pills and put things in order for them. I have to
sell the pills, for £S18,000 [approximately $7 U.S.). They are not
free. If they did not pay us for them, we would be working for
nothing. They [the medical authorities] give us this bag as help;
that's why they don't give us money. They have increased the
allowance of £S5000 to £S25,000 but they don't always give it.
Now the £S5 [given in the past] seems good. . . . If you wanted to
put them in the savings box, you could. Sometimes the women
also give us gifts, small sums of money, candy, oil, meat . . . it all

helps. Sometimes they just give you bread and that is enough. Sometimes they don't have anything—you just deliver their babies and you go.

She continues to make house calls after a delivery, for up to seven days after the birth, to check on the mothers and their new babies. As she sees them grow stronger,

Then you get happy, not sad, even if they do not give you money, because you feel the woman's happiness.

I asked Zachara what she knew about AIDS:

This sickness, hah, it was not there when we went to school. In the '70s we did not have any sickness like that. When we came here, there was no sickness, but now look at this rage: mosquitoes, sickness, AIDS, all sorts of bad things. Back then there was no AIDS; if there was they would have taught us about it. But now it is too much, it is everywhere, we start to be scared and if we see a woman is sick, we transfer her straight to the hospital. We don't touch her so we don't get sick. The doctors know how to treat her. I did not meet anyone with AIDS. If I did, I'd send them to the hospital. If a woman has jaundice I send her to the hospital where they know how to treat her and she does not get weaker. I cannot deliver their babies, they have too many problems.

Zachara's record as a midwife is not quite as spotless as it was in 1985, though nothing terrible has happened to her directly:

Well, no baby has actually died, but two women died after I treated them. One had already given birth when I arrived, and I found she had died. The other I sent to the hospital and she died there. . . . The specialist was not present, and his assistant pulled the baby with forceps [and injured her]. Only these two women, thank God, but not in my hands. Then there was another woman, about five days after she gave birth, she got a fever and died. Not many though.

We also talked of the escalating trend in Sudan for women to give birth by caesarian surgery, which was formerly very rare.

Now if we see a head high, they do surgery; and if it is breach, they also open her, in the hospital. If there are problems we send her to the hospital; they are too much for me. . . . They take her to the surgery room and open her up. Earlier we did not have this. We never heard about it till we saw it in Sennar. . . . They also did not teach us how to give the drip [IV]. It needs too much work, because if there is a vein broken, and there is lots of blood, you send her straight to the hospital. I never use drips, because they told us it is dangerous. Even when my son was sick, I brought a nurse to give him the drip, because I can't do it. If they taught me I would do it.

As for the most memorable births:

> Really, three times I have delivered sets of triplets. Three sets
> of triplets! They were easy. I found the mothers in their beds
> shaking, and right away I delivered their babies; it was not hard.
> With one of them I found at least one baby was breach and I sent
> her to the hospital, where they operated. The other triplets were
> easy and I delivered these babies at home. They are all still living;
> three of them are 22 years old, but none of them have had triplets
> of their own yet!

We also talked about female circumcision. This used to form the bulk of
her work, but no longer:

> Now people have left it. Since you have come to Sennar [over
> three months earlier] I have not done it once. The doctors said it is
> a harmful custom and people have left it, we have just stopped it.
> Our teachers said don't do it, but people wanted it. People on their
> own accord have left it, they don't like it any more. The govern-
> ment banned it and we stopped it too. Those who have light
> hearts, they go and do circumcision, some people still do it, but not
> as much as before. In one or two cases, the mother wants it, she
> does not want to leave her daughter uncircumcised, but there are
> not too many. Many teenagers today are not circumcised. I circum-
> cised my daughters, but they do not circumcise their daughters,
> and my sons' girls are not circumcised. The government did not tell
> them, they just left it on their own. If something is harmful, if you
> don't like something, you reject it.
>
> So people don't call us any more for circumcision. We used to do
> lots of circumcision, fironi, sunna, as the people want, but now the
> girl is intact, healthy, she has an easy delivery, and there is no cut-
> ting. In the past childbirth was harder, it took longer, but now it is
> easier for us to deliver the uncircumcised women. They are comfort-
> able, there is no tiredness, the woman is just lying down. But you
> don't stop helping the new mother. You go every day to clean the
> baby's cord with warm water and clean the scars. The uncircumcised
> woman can now do it by herself, but the cord, you need to clean that
> every day. Even if you have to go by public car, you go to her.
>
> Some people think that the girl who is open [uncircumcised] is
> not beautiful, but now the girl is relaxed and comfortable. She is
> not tired; there are no stitches. The baby comes down and you
> see it and catch it and get it out. This is beautiful, better than all
> that labor. Now if the woman in labor with her first child is not cir-
> cumcised, you just give her one cut if there is time, so you can
> stretch it for the baby to come out.

Although she must be in her mid-seventies, Zachara continues to enjoy
good health and is still active. She has all her own teeth and does not need
to wear glasses, despite her earlier eye problems. Her main difficulties are

from arthritis and from malaria, which has become increasingly trouble-some in this region:

> Once I went to my daughter in Wad Medani and got fever there. We all have these bed nets and yet we still get malaria. People have farmed by the river for a long time and never got it but recently we have had a lot. I hope the government solves the [problem of] malaria so we can get comfortable. This is our home, we were born and raised here and did not have mosquito or fever, just light headaches for which we took aspirin and got better and returned to work. But now this disaster has come to us. Fevers, fevers, fevers: it comes to us three or four times. We do anything, even quinine intravenously, to stop it. We go to the hospital and take seven shots, and malaria still comes again. Tired people, it kills them. Malaria is difficult. It never happened till they brought their planes to spray. I hope they can overcome it.
>
> [Laughing] I am happy now. I hope God gives us health. Thank God I had kids and they are grown now, because we got married young, very young. Not like our girls, who got married after they finished high school and college. Because of that we stay young. If you have your kids young, it does not tire you like these girls. They get tired of raising their kids because they are older.

She had little to say about zār. Once she had been to Mecca, Zachara no longer attended zār ceremonies.

> I was afraid I would dance with my head uncovered, jumping here and there, having a drink, falling down laughing, since they [the spirits] gave me things to drink and ordered me to "drink it." So I stopped going to the house of zār I was afraid because in zār one is doing something against one's will. You do what you're told because your head is not with you. When she is awake, a woman controls herself, but when the zār is in her head she jumps here and there, regardless of how she looks. It is unconsciousness with madness . . . madness [laughing]. God saved me from this, thanks be to God, and I decided not to go there after I went on pilgrimage. Before I went on Haj I beat the drums and I kept in mind all the zār threads.

Finally I wondered if there would still be midwives in Sennar twenty years from now. Zachara has no doubts:

> There was no midwifery building before my time, but then they built us a place for midwives at the center of the town. Previously midwives studied in Medani and Khartoum because there was no school here. Thanks be to God, there is one now. We are getting old and withered but we have worked and benefited from this and it is honorable work. Thanks to our teachers who taught us so well and we learned much from them, this career has supported us

and our children. Today there are three midwives in al-Gul'a—
though previously I was the only one.

We talked for about an hour and a half, then Zachara brought us a
breakfast tray she had prepared herself, and when that was eaten we spent
the rest of the morning, relaxing over freshly brewed coffee. We talked
briefly of the present government, which Zachara thought had brought
many improvements for the people, "though we still do not have any
money!" But mostly we laughed at ourselves and enjoyed chatting about
our long friendship. Zachara chuckled as she recalled how afraid she had
been of meeting me when Miriam first asked her to come and meet the
Khawajīya. Then I had just sat quietly because I did not understand much
Arabic, but she had liked me at once and has been happy to get to know
me more. She clearly remembered how she had been throwing the shells
when we met, and only now told me that then she kept seeing lots of trouble in store for me, particularly quarrels between Simon and me. She had
not told me until now because she didn't want to worry me, and thanks be
to God, everything has worked out well in the end for us all.

SERVANT OF GOD
FAITH-HEALER
AND SEERESS

part-time

We had heard about Bitt al-Jamīl long before I met her. Soon after we arrived in Sennar, neighbors told us about a woman in town with special gifts, who was able to tell what was in a person's heart without a word being said, who could look into the future, who could heal an illness when hospital doctors could not. Clearly this was a woman of some stature. I finally met her when I accompanied two friends needing to consult her. We took the public car into town, alighting in front of an imposing wall, which we were told surrounded Bitt al-Jamīl's grand house. We were fortunate that on this occasion few other people were waiting to see her. She greeted us warmly, as herself, but soon afterwards her possessing spirit came down to her and the visit became much more businesslike, to the satisfaction of both my companions.

Bitt al-Jamīl was a combination of holy woman, faith-healer, and seeress. She helped cure sickness and ease disorder, she forecast the future, and communicated with other dimensions in time and space. Her career was unique in late twentieth-century Sudan where no other woman achieved the same status. In content and methods, however, her work borrowed many traits from the roles of both the holy man (fakī) and the

131

Bitt al-Jamīl and her bridegroom Hissein (circa 1945). (Photograph courtesy of Suad Hissein and family)

leader (umīya) of zār, which is discussed in the next chapter. Indeed the work of the fakī and the work of the umīya also overlap, and they share many details of ritual. The service that Bitt al-Jamīl provided was similar to theirs but it also filled certain gaps. It was utilized by everyone, by men but particularly by women, and by those who were anxious to follow the conventional paths of popular Islam as well as those who accepted a wider spiritual world. She dealt with all types of problems, spiritual and physical, social and psychological, but she did not make great demands, either financial or otherwise, on her clients.

Sickness and disorder come in a bewildering variety of forms and there is an equal array of ways of dealing with them in the Sudan. In the case of the midwife, the medicine she practices is specific and technical. The symptoms she deals with are easy to recognize and the course of treatment easily prescribed and followed. Indeed she would argue that pregnancy is not a sickness but a welcome condition, and only certain aspects of its care call for medical attention.

All disorders are not so easy to pin down. Often they are manifested by psychological symptoms that obscure the underlying physical problem. Many of the parasitic and bacterial illnesses of the Sudan induce tiredness and apathy that lead to social and personal problems, and it is these that are then seen as the primary problem. The traditional medical practitioners in Sennar are often experienced in dealing with such matters, and to a person already emotionally and physically tired their methods are both more familiar and more reassuring than other more recent forms of curing.

When a person is sick in Sennar, however, he or she generally refers first to the hospital. Indeed, when poor urban women talk about why they have moved to the town from the countryside, a prime consideration is the more advanced medical facilities the town has to offer. Sennar has had its own hospital since the 1940s and it is one of the busiest spots in town. It has a full range of resident medical specialists and by the mid-1980s had its first surgery unit. At that time, however, it was also beset by problems, many of which related to inadequate funding. There was insufficient nursing staff so that a relative had to accompany inpatients to care for them. There were too few cleaning staff so that standards of hygiene were very low. As in the rest of the Sudan, there was a shortage of drugs so that prescriptions for illnesses depended largely on what was available at the time.

Furthermore the division between hospital and so-called "traditional" medicine should not be exaggerated. In a Sudanese setting, biomedical procedures frequently incorporate local therapies. Outside the hospital gates, vendors sell charms, seeds, roots, and amulets to aid a patient's recovery. Incenses are burnt in the wards, to soothe as well as to keep off

Selling remedies outside Sennar hospital (2001)

A Sennar fakī (holy man) (2001)

insects. Relatives of patients are encamped in the grounds, preparing meals and ensuring the obligations of visiting the sick are attended to. Occasionally the leader of the zār healing cult holds a brief fumigation ceremony inside a ward if spiritual disorders are thought to be complicating a patient's recovery. Consequently the hospital's rate of success does not differ greatly from that of other types of healers in town. For extreme emergencies, however, such as accidents, fire, problems in pregnancies, at that time it was the only institution capable of offering any viable assistance.

When hospital treatment fails to cure, this is accepted as a normal phase of the healing process and the patient reviews other options: the so-called traditional curers. Certain specialist problems may be dealt with immediately by the bone-setter and the barber. If the symptoms are not quite so specific then the patient looks for less prosaic explanations. With the family assisting and advising, the patient consults a local holy man, fakī, to determine the source of the problem. The fakī continues to exert a great influence in Sudanese life, urban and rural. For women at least it is through his role as a faith-healer and fortune-teller that he projects his status of religious leader. He is consulted about all sorts of problems: emotional, physical, social, psychological, and, if he is a famous man, descended from a line of holy men, he is often visited simply to share in his blessing or holiness, his baraka.

Many of the problems dealt with by fakīs are believed to be caused by magic or sorcery and are sometimes referred to as the "Three A's": *al-'ain*, *al-'ārid*, and *al-'amal*, categories that Bitt al-Jamīl repeatedly used. Al-'ain refers to the Evil or Hot Eye, the very widespread belief that a jealous person can cause harm to someone he envies and that a fortunate person is thus vulnerable. Al-'ārid is an obstruction, a sort of black magic that, when laid on an individual, renders her incapable of doing something—finding employment, becoming pregnant, making a journey, getting married. Al-'amal simply means a deed or operation and encompasses a wide range of consequences caused, for example, by performing magic on a piece of someone's hair, nail paring, or piece of clothing or by making an image of a person and damaging that. It is also used to refer to possession by zār spirits. The fakī is both the source of these problems (in that certain fakīs specialize in witchcraft) and also the means of preventing and curing them, by the practice of white magic or medicine (dōwa).

A good fakī employs at least three common forms of treatment. *'Azīma* is the mumbling of Quranic incantations and spitting after each verse to transfer the baraka. *Bakhara* (from bakhur, incense) involves burning charms, such as folded papers on which are written certain symbolic or religious signs. The patient then inhales the smoke with incense and fumigates himself with it. *Mihāya* is made by the fakī writing charms or religious texts on a wooden board, like that used by students of a Quranic school, washing them off with water, and then giving the liquid to the patient to drink. The fakī also offers ways of avoiding sickness and misfortune. Preventive treatment is largely by means of charms and amulets to ward off the Evil Eye and ill fortune. For example, weeds, roots, or squares of paper, on which the fakī writes Quranic verses and cabalistic signs arranged within squares, are wrapped in a cloth or leather pouch or drum and worn around the neck, on the arm, or below the waist as a safeguard against disease or harm. Their strength is derived from the baraka of the fakī who prescribed them.

Bitt al-Jamīl was a woman practicing very much a male profession. Though there is a tradition of female saints in the Sudan,[1] little is known about them and certainly there have been very few, if any, other women in the area of Sennar who aspire to such a position. In the 1980s, women could only think of one young woman, practicing faith healing and fortune-telling in the town of Sinja. They felt, however, that she was deranged and owed her power to jinn rather than help from God or even from zār. In 2001, I was taken to a middle-aged woman in Sennar, who also claimed to be able to see the future with the help of a spiritual assistant. The advice she gave to my friend, who was concerned that her husband had taken another wife, was not particularly helpful and she asked for a lot of money. Neither of the women was in the same league as Bitt al-Jamīl.

Possibly none of the holy men practicing in the vicinity of Sennar in the 1970s and 1980s, however, was quite so famous as Bitt al-Jamīl, who lived in the town itself. Her success was due mainly to the fact that in her work she remained very much within the local Islamic tradition. Despite being descended from a powerful and important family, with at least one known fakī among her forebears, she claimed that she did not inherit her powers, nor did people believe that she had done so. She did not belong to any Sufi order, and she made no claims other than she possessed certain favor from God. The fact that she was good at what she did, that people often recovered from the various disorders that troubled them, substantiated this claim. Her reputation was further enhanced and there was never a shortage of patients waiting to pay the small sum she asked for consulting with her and her divine connections about whatever was troubling them.

Bitt al-Jamīl never called herself a holy woman, preferring always to talk of her powers as a gift or "opening" from God. She was insistent that as an individual she was powerless; it was her dependence on God that enabled her to help people. Indeed I had great trouble convincing her that it was she, rather than her main spiritual assistant or intermediary, known as Bashir Fath al-Rahman, about whom I was interested in learning. On one occasion, I arranged to go and talk with her about her work, but soon after I arrived, she retired to another room. When she reappeared, Bashir had come to her: she was possessed. The "interview" proceeded at Bashir's insistence, but he was obviously waiting for me to ask for his help and was puzzled by the course along which I tried to steer the conversation. He was totally unprepared to discuss her (Bitt al-Jamīl), insisting on his pre-eminence as God's mouthpiece, although he enjoyed listening to tape recordings of Bitt al-Jamīl and was quite happy to show me the treatments used in his work.

Bitt al-Jamīl also did not adopt the full range of a fakī's methods and tools in trade. She certainly did not presume to philosophize, to expound Islamic doctrine, or to lead in prayer, solely male preserves in contemporary Sudan. Throughout her work she was conscious of her womanly dignity and modesty. In this she was very much within the local Islamic tradition: a healer who was endowed with very special baraka.

Like the fakī, Bitt al-Jamīl dealt with matters of fortune-telling and divination as well as of curing. She claimed to be unaware of the methods her spiritual assistant prescribed when she was possessed, but these were not unlike those used by a fakī. She had a rather fashionable "Holly Hobby" set of seven kitchen containers, a gift from Saudi Arabia, in which she stored cures of beaten incensed woods and roots. These were either burned as incense and inhaled or diluted with water and drunk by patients. At each public curing session, such as that described later in this chapter, there were also several buckets containing alternative cures. Some were filled with special roots that patients were advised to burn, while others held carefully concocted drinks made from boiling certain plants and roots, prescriptions for which were given at a small extra charge. Bitt al-Jamīl did not use the more esoteric techniques of the fakī, though she offered roots to be used as amulets. For divination she relied solely on spiritual guidance, and in a state of possession she often showed a certain clairvoyance.

In certain important ways the work of Bitt al-Jamīl resembled that of the leaders of zār (discussed in chapter 6). This she was familiar with since she herself had zār and regularly attended the local houses of burei zār for formal ceremonies, although she no longer became actively possessed by zār spirits. I only learned in 2001 from her daughter that she had a zār spirit, Shalabi, since she never spoke of him to me. Typical of zār, however, she operated through the method of possession. On her own, she stated repeatedly, she was powerless. Rather she claimed to be possessed by God himself, using Bashir as his opening or route. This was a totally different type of possession and spiritual contact from zār, as Sudanese Muslims would immediately recognize. The subordinate spiritual entities of zār, the red wind, can in no way be compared with an opening from God himself. Furthermore, the manner of her possession differed from that of zār. While someone in Sennar usually becomes possessed by zār through inhaling the special incense or, less frequently, in response to zār drumbeats, Bitt al-Jamīl emphatically stated that she attained a state of possession through a prescribed rite of prayer. After an early discussion with Bitt al-Jamīl about her powers, I wrote in my field notes:

> On the days on which the servants come, she lies down. Nearby, her husband (or an assistant) recounts the prayer beads. As he does, she becomes unconscious. When the "servant," God's opening, comes to her, her body trembles and her mind is once more conscious though she is later unaware of what she does or says. It is the servant who is speaking through her and using her. Many people come and ask the servant about their future, their families, their illnesses, and their problems. When the servant leaves her, she wakes, as if from a sleep.

On the other hand, many details in Bitt al-Jamīl's practice are also common in zār in Sennar. The routine organization is very similar. Bitt al-Jamīl was visited by her spiritual assistants three times a week, on Sundays and Wednesdays by Bashir Fath al-Rahman and on Mondays by a Doctora Roma (see below). Leaders in zār are available for treatment at all times, but they also hold special "surgeries" three times a week, known as coffee sessions *(jabana)* (described in chapter 6). As in zār special clothes are worn to welcome the spirits. On the days the servant Bashir Fath al-Rahman was expected Bitt al-Jamīl wore a long red jallabīya with a red kerchief on the head, knotted in front. For the female spirit Doctora Roma, she was said to wear a red skirt and white blouse.

The name Bashir is significant in burei zār as well as for Bitt al-Jamīl. On its own, it is simply a popular man's name. By 1970 Bashir was also a very popular zār spirit, the servant of the other zār spirits, a sort of intermediary between the more important zār and the human associates. He was treated less seriously than other possessing zār spirits and, significantly, was one of the few zār who talked, the only one who liked to chat, joke, and entertain. In addition, Bashir demanded remuneration for his time and advice. Women who went to drink coffee and stronger potions with Bashir on a Sunday or Wednesday did so because they wished to consult with him and expected to pay a small sum for the privilege. Drinking coffee and chatting with Bashir became a relatively cheap and easy way of seeking help with one's problem through zār especially if the hostess is a friend or neighbor. It is often the first step in trying to deal with a serious zār problem.

Bashir of zār, though a male spirit, is a male defined very much from a woman's point of view: a highly autocratic but very fallible and amusing being. Bashir Fath al-Rahman, on the other hand, the Bashir who came to Bitt al-Jamīl, remained a much more distant and respected element. Part of Bitt al-Jamīl's baraka stemmed from the fact that for so many years she was able to use and, in some ways, to control this spiritual messenger.

Bitt al-Jamīl's second spirit servant was known as Doctora (or lady doctor) Roma and was not unlike the female zār spirits, specializing in gynecological disorders, sexual complaints, and women's problems, which were often of a rather personal nature. Not surprisingly, perhaps, she was not regularly sought in public but usually consulted on a private basis.

In other ways, Bitt al-Jamīl's work was quite different from zār. She insisted repeatedly that "her" Bashir (and, by implication, Doctora Roma) was the servant only of God. He did not speak for any other spirit. He was summoned only by prayer and no incense, refreshment, or drum beating was used in his presence. Bashir of zār was regarded as a guest; Bashir of Bitt al-Jamīl was very much a consultant who came only to work, never to play or to entertain. While the cases brought to the fakī, Bitt al-Jamīl, and the zār were basically very similar, Bitt al-Jamīl herself repeatedly dissociated her "gifts" from both the leaders in zār and the fakī. Bashir Fath al-Rahman, she argued, was unique.

What sort of service was it then that Bitt al-Jamīl provided? Why was she so unique? And why was she accorded such widespread respect when the leaders of zār, particularly, were avoided by many women, as well as men? The reasons offered here are all somewhat tentative and I suspect may only touch on the real answer that is to be found embedded in the sort of belief system shared by many people in the Sudan but particularly by women.

Bitt al-Jamīl's gift was not inherited. She could claim that she was indeed chosen by God, the recipient of very strong baraka. The method of her "conversion" is reminiscent of the ways people discovered they had zār, but the nature of her beliefs and conduct of her work were very much within the broader Islamic tradition. She did not aspire to lead any path or way, and she discouraged people from regarding themselves as her followers. She only ever spoke as a servant of God. Yet it was because of her own personal charisma that Bitt al-Jamīl achieved such success, both financial and in terms of status. She attributes this solely to the favor of God and thus was very much in touch with the people of the Sudan. However she was undoubtedly a strong character, whether working through God's servant or not.

Still very much in keeping with local Islamic traditions, she did not approach God directly. He worked through her and she approached him largely through the agency of the male servant Bashir. The convention of Bashir himself may have been borrowed from zār but the total configuration of her practice was in tune with popular Islam. Through possession, Bitt al-Jamīl provided women, as well as men, with both leadership and guidance, but always safely within the conventions of popular Islam. Her intermediary was a male spirit, and it is evident in the conversations quoted later in this chapter that it was he whom the patients were addressing. Yet through him Bitt al-Jamīl expressed a caring and close concern for her patients, particularly women, that they did not always find within formal religion. Guidance from a fakī or an imam from the mosque was always in the formal manner that men and women adapt with each other in public and for a woman was often couched in patronizing terms. By contrast, for example, Bashir/Bitt al-Jamīl's remarks to the young woman whose leg was amputated (which appear later in this chapter) were warm and encouraging.

Bitt al-Jamīl's success was both material and spiritual. After she started her extraordinary career as soothsayer, healer, and holy woman she made repeated pilgrimages to Mecca; she bought a spacious modern house in one of the best areas of Sennar as well as several other properties that were rented out or occupied by family members; and she spent six months in a private hospital in London when she became ill and needed a coronary bypass operation. All this was apparently accomplished from small gifts rather than by exorbitant fees. Everyone was welcome to seek her help and was treated without apparent discrimination.

Unlike the other contributors to this book, Bitt al-Jamīl's work was part-time, in the sense that she only worked two or three mornings a week, with some additional private consultations. Furthermore, once her state of possession left her and she recovered from the mental fatigue it brought, she was able to relax and for the rest of the time resume her role as a middle-aged, middle-class housewife. Since she did not recall anything that happened when she was possessed, she encountered no apparent conflicts between the two dimensions of her life.

Despite her success, Bitt al-Jamīl remained a modest and caring woman. In keeping with her holy status, she observed her prayers and visited the local mosque assiduously. She also attended the house of zār for formal functions or if a friend was sick. Her home was always open to guests as well as patients, and Bitt al-Jamīl herself had a warm manner that contrasted with the gruff, sharp, wary way in which Bashir Fath al-Rahman spoke through her. In her daily life she was a very ordinary woman. Although she had servants and relatives to help with the housework, she went off each morning to the corner shop to buy the groceries and vegetables, and, one suspects, to use this opportunity of keeping abreast with what was happening in the neighborhood. She was conscientious about her social obligations and visited friends, neighbors, and relatives whenever her health permitted. This was much admired by women I talked with who felt that it made her one of them, unlike the leaders in zār who rarely made social calls. This was no doubt because Bitt al-Jamīl's spiritual assistants visited her only three days a week, while the leaders of zār have virtually no time off from their calling.

Bitt al-Jamīl is from the same tribe as Zachara the midwife. The two women were not unalike, and although their careers and lives were very different, it may be no coincidence that such dynamic women came from this particular ethnic group. The Taʿaisha people have a reputation for individuality, nonconformity, and for strength of character, and certainly their recent history suggests that they are ready to assume leadership. Significantly, there is also a tradition of holy women among the Taʿaisha people in western Sudan, although I know of no contemporary figure of stature equal to Bitt al-Jamīl.

Bitt al-Jamīl was also born in Sennar, though sadly her mother died when she was just a week old. Her daughter Suad recently told me:

> Her own mother, Sofiya, died seven days after the birth of her only daughter, the day of the naming ceremony. On that day the butcher was about to kill the sheep when the mother of Hissein [Bitt al-Jamīl's paternal cousin, whom she later married] came from the new mother's room, and said to the butcher: "Stop killing the sheep, Sofiya has died." Sofiya died suddenly, without suffering any illness. Bitt al-Jamīl's father had another wife, Soreya, who had given birth to a son on exactly the same day as Bitt al-Jamīl. The baby girl was given to Soreya who took care of her and fed her from her breast, with her own son. Bitt al-Jamīl was raised by her father's wife who treated her as if she was her own daughter.

Bitt al-Jamīl was married young and remained happily married to Hissein for over forty years. He sometimes helped her with her work and was very supportive of her. They had two children, their daughter Suad and a much younger adopted son Sofian. As already noted, their home was far grander than that of the other four contributors to this volume. An older house, it was spacious and solidly built, with large rooms and verandas, well furnished and with modern conveniences like a refrigerator (owned also by Naeima and Halima by 1981) and a television (owned by Halima and Zachara soon after we conducted these interviews, gifts from their sons who worked overseas). At the same time, chickens were running around the courtyard, in the corner of which were usually tethered a couple of goats or sheep. The impression was therefore not so different from that of the humbler homes with their clutter of livestock and human occupation. Like these, Bitt al-Jamīl's home was always bustling with activity. Though only her husband and son were living with her, she usually had various relatives staying or visiting.

Because she traveled widely, to Saudi Arabia and to Europe, Bitt al-Jamīl was more worldly and confident than the other women in this book. She talked knowledgeably about different countries and customs, of adventures she enjoyed overseas, and the people she met. She was also descended from one of the highest ranking families of the Ta'aisha people. Yet the minutiae of her life in Sennar were shared with her neighbors. When we met at social functions around the town, she was treated with the respect due to al-Hajja, but there was never any particular deference given to her as Bitt al-Jamīl.

There is no doubt that Bitt al-Jamīl is the most renowned character in this volume. Each of the other women is flattered and delighted to be included among the same pages. They lead ordinary, fairly typical working lives; her career was anything but typical. She is included here, however, because her accomplishments represent the ultimate ideal for many poor urban women who pray and wait for God to work his miracles in them. The fact that a local woman so pre-eminently became the receptacle for his mercy is justification of their ambitions and ideals. In her career are reflected the hopes, drives, and needs of many women in the Sudan.

The following account can be interpreted in many ways. At an immediate level it is an account of how a traditional practitioner works in central Sudan. It is also a testimony to Bitt al-Jamīl's success. There is no doubt that Bitt al-Jamīl believed in what she did and so did the many people who came to her for help. In the final analysis, that was what worked so well.

Bitt al-Jamīl (1981)

My name is Zachara though everyone calls me after my father, the daughter of Jamīl. I was born fifty-two years ago, here in Sennar. In those days we lived in another area of town, a second-class district. Then I became blessed. God blessed me with a special gift. I did not know anything; I was given it without knowing anything about it. God himself knows.

I am Sudanese. My tribe is Ta'aisha and my family is from the west of the Sudan. We are the people of the Khalīfa 'Abdallāhi Ta'aisha. The emir Muhammad Bishara was very close to us; he was my father, my father's uncle. He was my immediate grandfather, the emir of our district. He became the emir of Dongola, did you not know? We came to Sennar after the Mahdīya. My [step-] mother died a long time ago, over thirty years now. She never worked or had any gift like this. I have one sister, also living here in Sennar with her children. She is fine, she is quite happy but she does not have this gift from God either. I do not know of any woman in my family who ever had such a blessing. No one else has quite the same thing. It came from God and he gave it just to me.

When I was young there were no schools. I did not study then although later I went to the Adult Education Center for a little while. This was after I was married. I was married early, when I was 16, to my cousin, the son of my father's brother. After we married I just stayed at home as a housewife. My husband was self-employed. He works in the market here in Sennar with cars, lorries, and other vehicles. I gave birth to a daughter. By the grace of God we were all happy but I used to be ill a lot. I used to be very, very ill with fevers, always fevers, and I was always afraid. I was afraid that something was going to make me ill, that I was going to die, even before anything happened.

When I was first ill, people said: "Maybe this is caused by zār." I went to the umīya and they did the things of zār but I did not recover. They realized it was not from the zār. I went to the place of the umīya because I did not know any better. Then about twenty-one years ago, God blessed me with this gift. At the time, I was not well, I was ill in bed. They brought the umīya here and she was making the incense. Suddenly I sat up in bed and a voice said: "I am Fath al-Rahman, Fath al-Rahman alone." He spoke on his own. I did not know anything about it. This was the opening from God, *Rahman Allah*.

After I received this blessing from God, I became fine. I was able to do the housework and I was happy. I still used to get frightened but I was happy. I began to work through this gift. I started to have money from it. In the beginning it was not much but there was enough. Happily there was some, though not a lot. Now there is a great deal of income. I have made the pilgrimage to Mecca nine times and my husband has been fourteen times.

This gift of mine is not from the zār. It is from God. It is called the opening from God, Fath al-Rahman. I also have zār. I have an *'amal* [see page 135] which is nothing to do with my work, but I do not have the zār of the cross. The zār that I have belongs to Islam but is different from the gift of Fath al-Rahman. I am some-times possessed at the house of zār, but never by the cross.[2] I go to the house of zār sometimes, but I just stay in my chair and greet people. It is simply a favor to nice people whom I visit when it is Rajabīya, but I do not have anything to make me join them. I cannot refuse to go to places. I cannot say, "No, I do not want to." I have to go to all the places I used to. But when this blessing came to me, the voice said, "No, I am different, I belong to Work. That belonging to the umīya is different. It is good but it is differ-ent in every way."

The works of the zār and of the kujūr [black magic] are quite different. The work of the fakī is also different, nothing to do with me. I am an opening from God. God brought it to me, humble as I am, to work with. When God raises it, he raises it and when he accepts it, that is good. Thanks be to God.

I do not know of anyone else who ever had a blessing like this. It came from God and he gave it just to me. There are people who would like to be able to work just like me. They actually make the zār but they say they are doing it from Fath al-Rahman. That is all lies. Everybody says so. There are many Bashirs of the cross, of the umīya of zār, but there is only one Fath al-Rahman. Not just plain Bashir but Bashir belonging to Fath al-Rahman.

When this blessing came to me, twenty-one years ago, it was like I was blind, as if I was in a coma. I knew nothing. Since then, the same thing happens every Sunday and Wednesday. I do not know anything about it; it is as if I am not there. Suddenly when it goes, I find myself present. I never know who else is there or what they are doing, if they are talking, laughing, making money. I never know what is said until it is all finished and then my blindness lifts. While it is there, I would not know my own daughter. I am far away.

There is not just the voice of Bashir. On Mondays, Doctora Roma comes to see people who have problems with their stomachs. This is every Monday from ten o'clock. If she finds people here she starts work and if there is nobody here she leaves straight away. Bashir Fath al-Rahman comes only on Sundays and Wednesdays, no other day. This is different from the house of zār where the umīya is possessed by the Bashir of zār at any time.

If you come to see Fath al-Rahman, you do not have to tell him about your problem. You just take out 25 cents for me and remain silent. On his own Bashir will know what you are wanting in your heart. He will be working on his own. He will call the servants and tell them to do this, do that, do all the talking.

When Fath al-Rahman comes, you are in the house of Islam, in Mecca. Because I am old and al-Hajja I have to cover myself up for the house of God. It is necessary to cover my hair with a cloth and I wear a jallabīya that covers me up well. It is in red because he likes the color red; but it has no cross on the chest like the Bashir of zār wears.

We have ready the things Bashir uses. He brings the cures himself. No one knows what he or she will be; every cure is different. I know nothing about it. He brings them by himself and just says: "That is like that," or "This is so." If he says, "Beat it," the servants beat it, and if he tells them to put it in water, they do so. If he tells you to do something, you do it. If he tells you to wear something, you wear it. He does everything by himself. He can see all these things. The cures are all his. He brings everything he needs and divides them up on his own. He also brings the things for incense. He tells us to crush them so that he can give it to the people to drink. I have nothing to do with the incense. They might make it and use it in this house but I am not there. They might even make it here but I am not present. I am far away.

He also brings the medications from weeds and roots and crushes them so that people can drink them. They boil the roots in large saucepans and then afterwards put it in the big buckets. He brings all these things himself and does everything alone. If he needs assistance he asks for it. He does not ask me because I am not there. I know nothing about it. He does it alone.

God also protects people with his amulets. For this reason, he shows me special roots. Here in these seven tins I keep the roots of Bashir. They are all different and are to be used as incense. If a person has a problem and burns this as incense before he sleeps, then he dreams about the problem and sees the answer. One is for illnesses of the stomach, another for pain in the body. Then these others are for dental problems, skin diseases, eye complaints. I also have medicine in bottles. If a person is really ill, he takes that. If he is not so ill, he just takes the powders.

Even after twenty-one years, we know nothing about him. He does not want us to know anything about his work; he alone knows about it. He wants people to come to him. He counts the people who come and he even knows how many people will come tomorrow. I never know how many people are present. He knows there are a lot. Once the government came and counted the people. They made a survey of the people who came in just one morning. Over three hundred, 304 people, came that day.

When Bashir is here, I am not here. It is as if I am in a coma. He works on his own. I know nothing about it, whether he says good things or bad things. But he knows everything. He knows about cures and he also knows everybody's business. If you want to know about someone who is far away, he will find out for you. He himself knows every man and woman anywhere.

There is no special time for Fath al-Rahman; all the year is alike to him. He does not expect anything special in Rajab, like they have in the zār.

Some years ago, I became very ill. My vein got inflamed; it grew big from the heat. The doctors here in Sudan did not know anything. I needed to go abroad for treatment but did I want to go to Egypt? No, of course not. Where? Why, to London, of course. I went to London, just my husband and I. Thanks be to God, they found the vein and they changed it.[3] They took skin from the top of my leg and put it on my chest. Now, praise God, I am very well, though since the operation I am unable to work like I did before. I used to work from seven o'clock in the morning till half past two in the afternoon. Now I only work from ten o'clock till two o'clock or earlier if there are not a lot of people. If possible I try to stop at one o'clock. I cannot work like I used to. In the past I was very fit. Now, because of my vein, I need plenty of rest.

People come here from all over the place: from El Obeid, Khartoum, Port Sudan, Egypt, Omdurman, Gedaref, Nyala, everywhere, from all different countries. Yesterday everyone who came was from Khartoum. Everybody gives Bashir 25 cents. When I started work it used to be a dime but after I came from England, Bashir made it 25 cents. I felt rather weak and I was not able to work so much. There is also inflation to be considered. Everything has become more expensive. In addition, Bashir takes money for medicines. That used to be £S3 but it has now gone up to £S5 or £S6. Then anyone who is ill and recovers with Bashir's help brings a big sheep to Bashir.

Bashir is not the red wind. That just belongs to the zār. He comes on his own; he is different. He is good, praise be to God. I am always happy with Bashir and with his work. The poor, I do them good: greetings to them. Important people, I welcome them too. Rich and poor, they are all the same, I treat them all and go to them all. I never feel that because someone is poor I need not go to him. I treat everybody alike. When I am well I travel however I can. I used to go round on foot but since my illness I usually go by car.

My husband has never said anything against this work. In fact he is very happy with it. He saw that people who came to his house did so in an orderly way and were all quite respectable. They did not drink alcohol or smoke cigarettes or do anything bad. So he just said, "Greetings!" and welcomed them all. Now he also works for Bashir with me. He does this and that for him, my assistant in everything. He is his friend. Yes, he is very, very happy with Bashir.

Ten years ago I had a son. I just have two children, a daughter and a son. My daughter is now married with children of her own. We do not know if God will give this gift to my daughter or not. Maybe she will work after me. Only God knows.

I alone do not have anything, do you really understand? This is something God sent down, sent down with his strength. He gave me this to work with, and if he stops it, my work stops too. Only as long as he does not stop it can I continue working. I am just the means, may God find it acceptable. I do not have anything; I work only through God's strength. He gave me this to work with but it is entirely according to his will.

Thanks be to God. I am Bashir Fath al-Rahman, Bashir Fath al-Rahman, Bashir Fath al-Rahman. Let me repeat it three times so you can understand and so others who hear can understand properly.

I am Bashir Fath al-Rahman and God brought me down in mercy for the Muslims. With the work God enables me to do, I will help Muslims and I will help the whole of the Sudan for good, never for bad. I bring people help from God. Those who do not have anything, I give to them from God. I work with God's strength. God has brought me to help Muslims. If a man has money I take it. If he has none, I help him for nothing. I give and

God accepts so that the person can be cured. I am help from God and through me God brings happiness to all Muslims, not just to me. The mad person is cured, the sick is made better, the poor we give to, and God accepts this.

I alone am nothing. I do not have anything. I give and may God accept. I give for God and may he accept.

Nothing has been written about my work in a book. It is not easy to understand it. We never know what he will do, how he will act, what he wants. He could give this gift to anyone. If you want it, he could give it to you. Maybe he will give it to you. If you come here often you can become his friend. If he treats you well, he might give you this gift and you can help the people in your country. If you want to make a book about his work, come here when he is working. You can make a book from the tape of his talking. Come tomorrow at ten o'clock. Take the place next to me, put the tape recorder down and listen to his conversation.

Bitt al-Jamīl at Work (October 1981)

As Bitt al-Jamīl suggested, I attended her spiritual/curing session on the day following our interview and recorded the morning's events. In fact, I went on several occasions to see her at work and the account that follows is fairly typical. Taken together, the cases recorded on that particular morning provide a colorful description of the minutiae of Sudanese culture and the preoccupations of that particular period. They are also typical of other sessions with Bashir Fath al-Rahman. On the mornings he was expected, Bitt al-Jamīl completed her domestic duties quickly, attending to the shopping and supervision of the household as usual. She ate a light breakfast and by 8:30 A.M. retired to her room. There she dressed in the red jallabīya and headscarf favored by Bashir, lay down and recited her prayer beads. Sometime during the course of her prayers possession occurred. She claimed to know nothing from that time until she "woke up," being led back to her room when the curing session was completed and lying down quietly so that Bashir could leave in private.

By 8:30 A.M. people started arriving to consult Bashir, waiting in an outer courtyard till Bitt al-Jamīl either joined them or received them in the room she used for her work. Her house servants or relatives prepared everything. Mats were laid on the ground for clients to sit on, a plastic-corded chair was set in position for Bitt al-Jamīl, and nearby, on small tables, were placed her tins of papers, woods, roots, and seeds. An assistant had already put out the buckets of the medicinal drink prepared according to Bashir's specifications, and sat with these near the door, ladling it into bottles ready for designated clients.

On the occasion we taped the session, Bitt al-Jamīl held court indoors because (she had told me the previous day) she was recovering from a bout of malaria and needed to sit near a fan. Soon after 10:00 A.M. on a Sunday morning, Katie (then six years old) and I were ushered into a large, bare room in the front of the rambling house. It was furnished in minimal fashion with only a couple of rope beds against two of the walls and cheap grass mats on the floor. The shutters were closed to keep the room cool and a ceiling fan kept the air moving. Bitt al-Jamīl sat on her special chair at the far end of the room while those who came to see her clustered round her on the mats. It was evident that Bashir Fath al-Rahman had already "come down." Using the appropriate handshake, I greeted the holy woman as Bashir, addressing him by name. Without having to explain myself, I was waved to a bed nearby while he/she laid down my tape recorder on the small table in front of him/her, next to the tins of special wood, powders, and papers used by Bashir.

Bitt al-Jamīl had just taken her seat and through her Bashir was questioning his first client, a woman. During the course of the morning, approximately forty clients were seen. Almost 100 people came to the house but many accompanied a friend or relative and just wanted to see the great woman at work. Some simply came to chat with or give a message to Bashir, since this was the only place where he could be contacted directly. One elderly woman was sent by a third party (whom Bashir obviously knew since no name was mentioned) to reaffirm his promise to bring part of his harvest to Bashir. Through Bitt al-Jamīl, Bashir murmured piously, "God will help him." The woman replied humbly that this was only what Bashir was owed.

Bitt al-Jamīl's face was stern and impassive. There was a glazed appearance about her eyes that stared unblinkingly into the distance and rarely looked directly at anyone. The kindly expressions and the merry smiles of Bitt al-Jamīl herself were entirely absent. The voice was also different: harsh, guttural, somewhat inaudible. When I was addressed, for example, I was called "Chuchan," although Bitt al-Jamīl herself had no trouble calling me "Suzan." Everyone was clearly addressing Bashir rather than Bitt al-Jamīl, who in all ways other than physical was just not present.

Each patient in turn got Bashir's attention by handing over 25 cents. Waving this above her head and with no other form of acknowledgement, the possessed woman rolled her eyes upwards and called out:

Kura
La la lob, (de) la lo kun
Kunta laka, kunta laki
La la lo.

This call is obviously not Arabic and does not show any resemblance to Western languages, including Ta'aisha (R. C. Stevenson, personal communication). Nobody recognized it from visits to the houses of zār or fugāra but it was part of Bashir's unique ritual. Sometimes Bashir/ Bitt al-Jamīl exclaimed, "Yip! Oooh!" as she shook her head sharply before she turned to the next client. Often she called out something like, "I see the way" or "Which way shall I turn?" while she shook the patient's hand and lightly touched the person in the approximate area of the person's heart, as though to learn about the problem from the feel of the body. In harsh tones, she then proceeded to rap out questions quickly and abruptly at the person whose problem she was considering, giving him little chance to reply at any length. She usually suggested at least part of the problem without being told and is indeed credited with knowing exactly "what is in a person's heart." Not all her questions were pertinent and these were either ignored or quickly dismissed.

On this particular morning, thirty-three clients came to consult Bashir about substantial issues, and these are discussed here. The other seven clients I saw either brought messages that were inaudible or too obscure for me to know what the problem was. Of those I recorded, twenty-four were female and nine were male, a reasonably representative sample from my other visits. Of the women, only four were concerned with their own problems. By far the majority, twenty women, sought help for someone else. Six asked about their sons, four about their daughters, one about her children generally, three about their husbands, three about their sister or friend, and three about their brothers. In sharp contrast, all nine men who consulted Bitt al-Jamīl were concerned with their own immediate problems.

The types of problem taken to Bitt al-Jamīl vary but most fall into distinct categories. Overall, sickness is the most common. Ten of the women were concerned with illness, three with their own health, and seven with the health of other people. Seven men had health problems, all of them their own. The other two men had economic worries. Two women also had economic problems. Thirteen women, however, but no men, were concerned primarily with family problems.

By way of service, Bashir Fath al-Rahman offered various sorts of assistance. He never gave financial help though might forgo payment for people he knew were unable to pay, at least until their circumstances improved. Clients were usually offered a mixture of advice, diagnosis and prognosis, or clairvoyance. In cases of sickness, the following types of diagnoses were offered:

1. No diagnosis or cure, but some form of therapy, particularly incense burning, was suggested.

2. An explanatory diagnosis was couched in terms of clinical medical practice.

3. An explanation was given in "traditional" terms: usually either 'amal, 'ārid, or 'ain.

For most clients, not simply those who were sick, Bashir recommended some form of medication or treatment. The most common were:

- incense, incense burning;

- herbs/weeds/roots: (a) to be mixed with oil and used as ointment, (b) to be mixed with water and drunk, (c) to be wrapped in cloth/leather and worn as an amulet;

- prepared medicinal drink;

- no cure.

Everybody who asked for help was given some sort of prescription. In one case, it was rather refreshing when a man, who felt very sorry for himself, was told that there was basically nothing wrong with him, that he just needed some exercise and should find himself a job. Even here, however, Bashir supplied a special root for an amulet and some incense to make him feel better. The following account of this consultation is a good example of the combination of common sense, clairvoyance, and diagnosis that Bashir employed:

Bashir: This tiredness you get in your body and your nerves, have you had it a long time?
Man: I got it because I am always fed up. It is the result of always being fed up.
Bashir: You can't get up easily in the morning.
Man: Yes . . .
Bashir: You get headaches . . .
Man: Sometimes I do . . .
Bashir: And pains in your legs . . .
Man: Sometimes.
Bashir: You just need exercise. You don't need any medicine. I am going to give you something to find you a job. You don't need treatment. With God's help you will be all right and liked by everybody. I am also going to give you some weeds. Tie them round your arm and wear them. Also here is a little bit of incense. Burn some twice and it will help you. I want £S1 for the weeds; there are two here. You can wear them both or just wear one and give the second to someone else. With God's strength you will be fine.

Bashir clearly felt his treatments were incompatible with those of clinical medical practitioners. He only took a case if the person was not being treated by a doctor. Several patients wondered if they should go to the hospital as well or said that they had already seen several doctors. In each case Bashir commented abruptly that they should have faith only in God, or words to that effect. The following exchanges were typical:

> **Woman:** I wanted him to go to the doctor but he refused.
> **Bashir:** He has been to enough doctors. Now try my treatment. With God's help I hope it will cure him. If God does not want to help, it is out of my hands. We just depend on him.
> **Woman:** All right. We won't go to the doctor. We will depend on you and on God. God will help us.

And again (the patient was found to be suffering from a swollen stomach):

> **Bashir:** Have you been to see a doctor? If you haven't, I will cure it before the doctor can make a hole in it and empty the water from it. It will be easy for me to cure if you have not already consulted a doctor. If you have been to one, it becomes very difficult for me.

Bashir does not miss an opportunity to encourage clients to have faith in God and to trust his will. Through Bitt al-Jamīl's medium, the servant of God takes a personal interest in all those who consult him. Many are already known to him by name and their problems need little elaboration. This gives great comfort to everyone present, particularly those seeking help.

At times it appears as if Bashir is preoccupied with remuneration. Clients, however, do not feel that a consultation with Bashir is particularly expensive, and since his success rate is high, they are prepared to pay the sort of bonus Bashir expects once the desired results are accomplished. The following exchange shows the way such arrangements are made:

> **Woman:** How much shall I pay you?
> **Bashir:** Don't pay anything until your daughter comes back to you. Then you can bring what you like: £S15, £S20 or £S30. If the girl does not return, I don't want a single penny from you.

Even the tardy pay eventually. They never know when they might need Bashir Fath al-Rahman to intervene for them again. During the morning, a great deal of money was quietly deposited in one of the Holly Hobby tins. Everybody paid 25 cents at the start of a consultation and later a larger sum for the incense or medication they received. A few people simply handed over a folded note, usually £S5 or £S10, as they arrived. Although Bashir said several times that he would like £S50 if his help was effective I did not notice anyone paying so much. Yet people also told me that if Bashir helped them with a big problem they would not hesitate to pay that amount, whatever the sacrifice.

Women and Their Problems

Throughout the morning women easily outnumbered men as not only were there more female patients but also they were all accompanied by at least one other woman. Some carried small babies who were nursed and played with while their mothers waited to be called on by Bashir. Lots of other children played in the courtyard outside, peering in every so often to watch the holy woman or to call out to their mothers. No one was excluded and the atmosphere was casual, even though Bashir in Bitt al-Jamīl was regarded with a certain awe.

The largest number of women consulting Bashir that morning were concerned about their sons. Even where Bashir seemed more concerned about a daughter, women pressed their sons' problems first. The following is a good example:

> **Bashir:** Whom shall I see, the boy or the girl?
> **Woman:** See the boy.
> **Bashir:** Has the girl got married?
> **Woman:** No she hasn't, but see the boy for me first.

Problems ranged from a poor young woman worried about her infant son's health to middle-aged women in comfortable circumstances concerned by their adult sons' behavior. Bashir's advice first and foremost was to have faith in God:

> You cannot stop him and you only worry about him. Even I cannot stop him going the way he wants. Only God can take care of him and stop him from behaving like this. If it kills him that is his fate. No one can change that.

Yet Bashir also gives practical help. In the case just mentioned, the mother was questioned closely about her son:

> Where does he live? What does he do with his money? Does he save it? Is he married?

When Bashir learned that the son was not married and lived with three bachelors, the problem was evident:

> These three are bad for him. They take him to places of fun. But with the help of God I will take his mind off this group and put him on the right track. I will turn his mind to thoughts of marriage and of saving his money. If he does not save, it is no good. I will go around the country and do what I can.

As a prescription, the mother was given some incense to light for her son. Promised Bashir:

> After I have done my job and he has come around to your way of thinking and got married, you come and bring me what I

deserve. This is in God's hands. It is not up to you or me. I will give you this incense and you must do it for him. That is all I can do for him.

Another middle-aged woman was concerned about her son, who had completed university but had still not found a job. Bashir immediately got to the root of the problem, admitted only reluctantly by his mother, that the boy wanted to go and work overseas. This has long been a common ambition at all levels of Sudanese society because the opportunities for employment and remuneration abroad, particularly in the Arab States, are much greater than in the Sudan. The difficulty lies less in finding a job than in completing the necessary paper work for a passport, visas, and work permits, all of which are largely dependent on the good offices of a sponsor. Even if Bashir/Bitt al-Jamīl did not already know the woman and her family, the following line of questioning would not be particularly startling:

> *Bashir:* What is wrong with the boy? Has he got a car?
> *Woman:* No, he studies at the university . . .
> *Bashir:* So what is this thing about a car I can see?
> *Woman:* I don't know, really.
> *Bashir:* Did he get his degree?
> *Woman:* Yes, he did . . .
> *Bashir:* Where did he travel to now?
> *Woman:* Oh, he went away yesterday . . .
> *Bashir:* Yes, but he wants to travel abroad . . .
> *Woman:* I think so. He is preparing his papers. He wants to go abroad.
> *Bashir:* Who is this person abroad who knows you?
> *Woman:* It must be someone who was with him at the university . . .
> *Bashir:* You don't know what goes on in his heart, do you?
> *Woman:* No, I don't.
> *Bashir:* I can tell you. He wants to go abroad. Why should he want to go abroad when he has his degree? Why does he not stay here?
> *Woman:* Oh, he refuses. He wants to go abroad. He has been sitting around with his degree for a whole year not finding any work.
> *Bashir:* His uncle, who was supposed to send him a letter, did he answer him? He wrote to his uncle and his uncle was supposed to have replied.
> *Woman:* No, he didn't. That is why he is sitting around waiting for an answer to his letter.
> *Bashir:* Anyway, I will give you some incense and with the help of God, I hope it will do him some good. Where God wants to put his future, there it will be. So with God's help I hope everything will turn out all right. You light this incense for him, put his jacket

over your head and hold it over the incense. Don't sit anywhere
where there is a lot of draught. Do it every day. I hope this will
help and he will do what we want him to.

A third woman began to talk about her husband, but Bashir, who
evidently knew the family, broke in:

Leave that sick man alone. I am concerned about your son. Has
the pain in his chest gone? The pain in his legs? The shivering that
seems like a fever? Has the swelling on his legs and the pain on
his chest gone? Have all his pains, in his chest, his legs and body,
gone? And the bad headache that makes his eyes swell, has that
gone or not? And the shiver in his nerves, has that gone?

Murmuring, "Not yet," to each of these rapid questions, the woman kept
trying to have some control of the conversation.

He works in the bank in Sinja and . . .

she interjected at one point. Bashir appeared not to have heard.

With God's help I will cure him for you

he pronounced. Again the woman tried to explain.

My son works in a bank in Sinja and on his way to work one
day, something happened to him that caused him pain in one leg.
I want to travel to him to see what has happened.

Bashir ignored the interruption and added:

This is an 'ārid or an 'ain. An 'ārid is like a bad omen or maybe
he has passed something. It is like an Evil Eye. You think it is
some sort of 'amal, something which people do against you but it
is not that. This is just an 'ārid or an 'ain. He got this Eye near a
water hole [khor]. With God's help I will cure him for you.
Although he works in the bank this thing happened to him at
night, not at the bank. It came to him as he was crossing the khor
leading to the bank. He walked over some urine and was hit by
this Eye. Nobody has made a bad 'amal for him.

The prescription in this case was also incense to be burned for the young
man. The woman persisted that she wanted to go and see her son but did
not know when she could travel. Bashir repeated that she should take the
incense and light it for him at her own home.

With God's help it will help him until God lifts your leg up and
you can travel and take his medicine to him.

The same woman was also having trouble with another son who
lived with her. The complaints seemed endless and she was obviously
very unhappy with his behavior. He had promised to make improvements
to the house but so far had done nothing. He still had not built a dividing

wall between her and his wife's parts of the house, nor had he yet bought the doors for the toilet or even fixed the toilet. He had started to buy tins of equipment but he hadn't really done anything. . . . Bashir was firm but encouraging and obviously had earlier knowledge of the family problems:

> **Bashir:** Listen here! This son of yours will finish the house.
> **Woman:** When?
> **Bashir:** He repaired that other house of his, the one he had to get the people out of, and that is why he does not have any money left to repair the house you are living in. When he gets his salary, then, with God's help, he will finish it for you. You just wait. Give me some time. All I have got is God's help and strength.

The woman detected Bashir's impatience, adding apologetically that she herself was ill.

> If it wasn't for the worry over my son in Sinja, I would not have come. Every part of my body aches and hurts me.

Bashir was not entirely unsympathetic. Certainly nobody left the house dissatisfied with the response they had received from him.

> You go to your son and I hope he will be well. With God's help I will cure him.

Problems with schools came up several times. Women generally feel that a good education, or at least a school certificate, is important for their children and try very hard to keep them in school for the necessary qualification. Schooling is largely free for students who pass their annual examinations. Those who fail, however, have to pay to repeat the year. Not all students want to do this. In the following exchange (where Bashir apparently did not know the family in question), the student's refusal to return to school was the issue:

> **Bashir:** Where is this boy?
> **Woman:** He has left school and he won't go back.
> **Bashir:** So you have come to see me about getting him to go back? With God's help I hope we can get him back into school. There is nothing wrong with him except that someone gave him the Eye. An Arab [nomad] gave him the Evil Eye. He has got some sort of allergy in his body, an itch and a pain in his neck and he has got headache . . .
> **Woman:** And sometimes he leaves home . . .
> **Bashir:** He has got nothing wrong with him except this 'ārabi Eye. Is he the first son or did he come after the girls?
> **Woman:** No, he is the second son and the girls came after him.
> **Bashir:** I will give you some incense to light for him. How long has he stopped going to school?
> **Woman:** He has not been back since the 'īd holiday. He just refused.

Bashir: All right. With God's help, I will let him go back to school.

Schooling is a problem for girls as well as boys. One woman was concerned about her sister who seemed to be working too hard at school and had just completed her school examinations. Bashir told her not to worry.

She has studied very hard. But I will give you a little incense. Burn it two days running and God will help her to pass.

Girls' academic problems are often exacerbated by social problems. Until the 1970s a high school certificate was regarded mainly as the qualification for marriage with a successful man. Although this has changed as increasing numbers of women achieve professional careers, some girls who fail their examinations are still taken out of school and married rather than given the same opportunities as their brothers to try again. Once married, few women return to school or follow any further training. The next young woman was not simply suffering from pre-examination nerves, and in talking with her, Bashir showed that he held far from traditional views on the place of women:

Woman: She is scared of her examinations.
Bashir: I will cure her of her fear and with God's help and strength she will pass her examinations. After she has succeeded bring her to me again.
Woman: Her father has taken her out of school and married her off. The husband is not around and we want her father to agree to let her go back to school.
Bashir: Did you have a weed from me?
Girl: Yes.
Bashir: Just put it on your father and he will automatically tell you to go back to school. Here is some incense. Light it and call your father's name. God will help.
Woman: What about when she goes back to her husband?
Bashir: Oh, he will take no notice. He will let her do exactly as she likes as long as she is wearing this weed.
Girl: I want to go back and repeat the year at school.
Bashir: Even if your father knows you want to go back to school, he will not pay for you, especially if you are going to repeat. I am going to do something for your husband to make him pay for it. God will help us and you will pass your examinations.

In several cases, women were simply concerned about the health of their children. One young woman with an infant son of nine months was a neighbor of mine from al-Gul'a who told me later that she goes to see Bashir regularly about health and family problems. She finds his treatment much more reliable than that of the hospital. On this occasion, Bashir quickly established the problem:

Bashir: Has the wind in his chest gone?
Woman: Not yet.
Bashir: Has the allergy covering his whole body gone?
Woman: Not yet.
Bashir: This is not from him but from his mother. He gets his allergy from his mother. It covers him completely. Has it come up on his head?
Woman: Yes it has.
Bashir: And on his face?
Woman: Yes.
Bashir: And it has come out on his back and chest?
Woman: Yes.
Bashir: I will give you some weeds to rub all over his body. It will cost you £S1. Mix it with the yellow motor oil and rub it on his body. Then wash it off with carbolic soap. When God has cured him, you can come and pay me what you like: £S5, £S6, or £S10, it is up to you.

Another woman obviously had family problems, but Bashir dealt with the immediate problem, the health of her son. It is interesting to note how again the woman's sympathies are so obviously with her son, 'Abdallāhi, rather than with her husband:

Bashir: How is 'Abdallāhi, now? And how is his father with him?
Woman: Oh, his father has turned really nasty and is always shouting at him to get up in the mornings.
Bashir: He really should get up in the morning. Because he is ill, however, he can't. He has a big swelling in his liver and that is why his urine has turned yellow. I am going to give you some of the medicine that you gave your daughter. It cured her.
Woman: Yes. She took some of it but the rest got lost.
Bashir: I will give you some extra medicine without payment so she can finish what she started. Use the same thing for the boy. It is made from weeds. After he has completed the treatment he should come to me and I will give him something else to drink that will get rid of all the blood in his liver.

In another case, a young mother was worried about her daughter's cough, and Bashir's diagnosis has an alarming ring to it. He obviously has seen the patient on an earlier visit:

She has a cough that was caused by a bad fall on her back. The cough is not harmful, but rather like asthma. She gets heavy breathing that is the opening of her back. I did not give you medicine before. This time I will. I will give you some incense and some weeds that you tie together for under her arm so that she sweats on to it. Take all these medicines and pay me £S6. After she has taken all of them, bring her back to see me, in about three weeks.

Several of the problems revealed social tensions inherent in Sennar society. The following discussion about a daughter's marriage difficulties, for example, throws light on local family organization and the problems of arranged marriages. The daughter stayed at home with her parents after an apparently unsuccessful marriage. Relations between a mother-in-law and son-in-law are never easy, formally characterized by restraint and respect, even avoidance, but even so, ill feelings such as this frequently surface. Again, Bashir had a typically positive approach and, in this case, tended to support the absent son-in-law:

> **Woman:** He hasn't sent us any money or any help. He didn't bring us anything.
> **Bashir:** Did he come and see you?
> **Woman:** Yes, he did but he didn't bring anything, no money or anything.
> **Bashir:** Yes, because he didn't get his pay. He will come soon and will bring you all you want and you will be very happy.
> **Woman:** We don't want very much. But we worry about his bad temper and his nasty language.
> **Bashir:** I will catch all that and give you some treatment for him. Do you still wear my weeds around your arm and neck?
> **Woman:** Yes. Do I wear it or should I give it to my daughter?
> **Bashir:** You could take one for yourself and give one to her, or simply let her wear it since it is her happiness we want.
> **Woman:** He even came for the 'id and did not bring her anything, any gold or even sugar.
> **Bashir:** Don't worry, I will cure that for you. With God's help I will make him bring as much as possible.

Three young women, aged about 30 and with bright eager faces, had obviously come together, a first visit for two of them. Possibly they were from outside Sennar for they did not seem to know anyone and kept a little apart. The first woman handed over 25 cents and waited expectantly for Bashir to speak to her:

> **Bashir:** You came to see me about your children?
> **Woman:** Yes . . .
> **Bashir:** Where is their father?
> **Woman:** Somewhere . . .
> **Bashir:** And how many children do you have? Two?
> **Woman:** No, three.
> **Bashir:** And you only have two living with you?
> **Woman:** Yes . . .
> **Bashir:** How old is the girl?
> **Woman:** She is 5 and the boy is 7.
> **Bashir:** The father will keep the son but I will let him give you the girl.

Woman: He has taken them far away.

Bashir: Don't worry. They are only in El Obeid and I will make him bring your daughter back. But the boy is better off with his father. Once he is 7 years old he is better off with his father. Now you have another husband it is not right that the boy comes to live with a strange man because his Eye is very strong. He will be very jealous. Anyway now that you have another husband, why do you want to bring the children to this man? You should be satisfied. But you are not really well in yourself, are you?

Woman: I am all right.

Bashir: I will help to bring the little girl back but I will not do anything about the boy. He had better stay with his father. I will give you some incense to take with you. This vest you have with you, who does it belong to? Your first or second husband?

Woman: This is my second husband's . . .

Bashir: That is no good. When you light this incense, say the name of your first husband. With God's help, I hope he will send your daughter back to you. I will do my best. If you want any treatment for yourself, come whenever you like.

Such problems are common for Sudanese women of this age. Bashir usually suggested to young women that they have come with problems about their husbands or children, often the same thing, if their appearance does not indicate serious health problems. Bashir invariably recommended the Islamic solution that sons over 7 years of age stay with their father while daughters live with their mother but he never sounded much more optimistic than in the previous interview. Divorce continues to be difficult for most Sudanese women, despite the positive examples of Halima and Zachara, recounted earlier in this volume. Frequently women lose custody of their children and are unable to see them at all in practice, regardless of the divorce settlement decree.

The second young woman had similar problems, which Bashir quickly determined and about which he adopted an equally firm position:

Bashir: As long as you have put your problems in the hands of a judge, he has been told by God to give you your rights. Don't worry, you should get everything. It is no good trying to be tough. You have to try and deal with your problems the quiet way. No need for pulling and tugging.

Woman: Yes, I understand. Now he has left me to my family.

Bashir: No, he hasn't. He has left you to God. So you have to try and make it up.

Woman: But all I want are proper rights for my daughters and myself. The problem is that he made the case.

Bashir: Go and take the advice of your family. If he accepts that, fine. If he does not, then come back to me.

Woman: All right.

Bashir: As long as you have the children between you, you really have to try and make it up.

Woman: You know what he told the judge, Bashir? He told him that I leave the house and I go out shopping. He said I just leave my daughters dirty, with lice in their hair, that I do not watch what they are doing and I let them go out as they please. He also said that I send them to the market to buy onions and things. Is that wrong? Should I not send my daughters to the market, Bashir?

Bashir: What did the judge say to him?

Woman: Nothing. He didn't talk to him. Oh, I think he thought it was useless. He told him to go and get some witnesses and treat it as a family problem.

Bashir: Did you tell the judge that he doesn't pay you, that he doesn't give you any money and doesn't look after his daughters?

Woman: Yes, I did.

Bashir: All right. Just be patient and God will help you. The best thing is still for you to make it up.

Woman: I don't mind making it up but I told the judge, I don't like to be treated badly and to be pushed around.

Bashir: I will give you some incense. Some of it is free, some of it costs 25 cents. If you don't have the money now, pay me later.

The third young woman was concerned about her husband's health. Hers was obviously a return visit and she had probably persuaded her friends to accompany her to consult Bashir about their problems.

Bashir: What did you do with the drink I made for your husband?

Woman: We didn't do it the right way.

Bashir: What do you mean, not the right way?

Woman: The first day I made it, he drank it and nothing happened. Then the second day I made it too hot and when he drank it, he vomited it all.

Bashir: Did he vomit anything with it?

Woman: No, just that and it was just like he drank it, it hadn't changed at all. Then he felt much better.

Bashir: You have to make it and let it ferment a little in the beginning. Then you warm it and give it to him to drink. You give him half and you boil the other half so that it does not go bad.

Woman: We have a fridge but I think he vomited because it is sour, fermented.

Bashir: You have to crush some ginger in the evening . . .

Woman: I did that. I crushed the ginger and prepared it and gave it to him.

Bashir: Put it away and give half to him today and half tomorrow. Can't he come and see me himself?

Woman: No. I asked him if he could and he said he couldn't, his legs are too swollen.

Bashir: Maybe with God's help he can come on Wednesday. Tell him he has a bad swelling in the middle of his back and it is causing the pain in his chest.

Woman: Yes, I know. It has even divided his back.

Bashir: The only way to get rid of this pain in his back is to let the blood out of it.

Woman: He really has pain in his chest, like a constriction.

Bashir: I knew about his back pain before you came to me.

Woman: Yes, I didn't have to tell you. You knew about it.

Bashir: So I'll give you something to put in a bottle with ginger and you give it to him. Either add ginger or cinnamon or cardamom and warm it in a bottle, far away from him. Don't let him see it. Give it to him to drink, the weeds and the spices. It should be warm, not hot, maybe warmed in the sun. It is better if you leave it all night in either ginger, cardamom, or cinnamon, whichever he prefers. Cardamom is best. In the early morning, warm it and give him some to drink. Put the rest in the fridge and next day do the same thing; warm it and give him some to drink. The third day the same.

Woman: Do I have to give it to him every day?

Bashir: Yes. You shouldn't miss a single day because his stomach will be soft. He takes it the next day and it will loosen him and empty out his stomach. Then when you get the money, come and pay me.

Woman: Today is the 23rd . . .

Bashir: No it isn't, it's the 25th.

Woman: When I get my salary I will bring you some.

Bashir: God will provide. I want you all to be happy, that is all I care about.

Family problems kept recurring, closely tied up with economic and personal problems. The following case was a woman worried about her brother, but even Bashir could not see straight through to the core of her problem:

Bashir: I am going round and round. Who am I looking for?

Woman: My brother. He is far away. Where is he?

Bashir: Doesn't he send any money to his mother or to you?

Woman: No, he doesn't, only to his wife.

Bashir: Where is his wife? Is she with him?

Woman: No, she's not.

Bashir: Do you want him to bring his wife to stay with you?

Woman: Yes, we do. She is not divorced and he is not living with her so we want her to come to us.

Bashir: All right. I will give you some incense. You burn it and with God's help I will hope to bring her back to him. I will also give you some incense for his mother. When she lights it, she should say his name. With God's help I hope to bring him back to you with his wife, and then, when he comes back, you can bring me £S50. If you cannot bring £S50, don't lie to me.

Woman: I won't lie. If he comes and brings his wife, I will bring the money.

Consulting Bashir by proxy is common but is obviously not as good
as a personal meeting. A woman came about her sister in Sukki who has
various health problems, and though Bashir made a diagnosis, he obviously wanted to see the patient for himself:

> **Woman:** She is really not well at all. She has pain all over her
> body, in her legs, her body, her head . . .
> **Bashir:** She has got an 'amal. Somebody has written some-
> thing against her. Have they moved from their house or are they
> still in the same place?
> **Woman:** It's the same house they have always lived in, in Sukki.
> **Bashir:** All right, leave it to me. I will make her some incense
> and you can take it to her. You do it for seven days and then she
> must come. I do not tell anybody not to come to me. She must
> come and see me herself. People come from all over the place.
> She has to come. Do you have anything more? Here is some med-
> icine. Mix it with grease and rub it on her body and her legs to
> help the pain go away. Pay £S1 for that. Divide the medicine into
> two and use it twice.

One of the saddest cases to come before Bashir on this particular
morning was also brought vicariously. A young woman had had her leg
amputated and since then had felt very bad. Her friend told Bashir how
nothing had gone right for her after that, and how she was having a really
hard time. She just lay on her bed feeling depressed. Bashir was immediately alert and offered his usual positive philosophy:

> **Bashir:** Don't let her do that. She should not give in to depres-
> sion. She has to depend on God and have faith in him. God will
> help. I will give you some incense for her for which you pay 25
> cents. I have another weed; take it to her for £S1. It will help her
> and make her way easy for her.
> **Woman:** What about her garden?
> **Bashir:** Take care of her and that will be successful.

Economic problems ran through many of the cases that came before
Bashir: there was just not enough money to go around and simply thinking about this induced headaches and various other physical problems. In
a few cases women came with specific needs. Some obviously wanted
ongoing support from Bashir in order to be able to cope with their practical problems and demands. The following woman was reporting back to
Bashir on a long-standing problem she was having in getting her papers
in order.

> **Bashir:** Did you go and have your papers stamped?
> **Woman:** Yes, I took them . . .
> **Bashir:** And what did they tell you?

Woman: They asked me to take them to Medani . . .

Bashir: You should go yourself, not send them with anybody else. You should travel yourself. Go on Saturday. There are a lot of people there on Saturday. You will find people you know there.

Woman: Can you give me some incense to help me on my way?

Bashir: This is for 25 cents. Take it.

A newcomer to Bashir had difficulty deciding what she most needed help with: her health, her divorce, or her search for a job.

Bashir: What did you come to see me about? Are you not well?

Woman: Yes . . .

Bashir: The heat you feel in your stomach, have you still got it?

Woman: Yes . . .

Bashir: The pain you feel in your legs, is it still there?

Woman: Yes . . .

Bashir: And the bad backache?

Woman: Yes . . .

Bashir: And the pain that causes you great headaches?

Woman: Still there . . .

Bashir: How many years have you not had a baby?

Woman: I have never had one.

Bashir: Aren't you married?

Woman: Yes, but my husband divorced me.

Bashir: There is another man who wants to marry you, a merchant. He has spoken about you but he hasn't come yet . . .

Woman: I haven't heard anything about that but I do not want to get married again.

Bashir: You have come to me with a problem and with God's strength, I will see what I can do for you. You have got some old 'amal and it is causing some numbness in your right leg. With God's help I can get it out for you. What is this headache you keep getting, has it gone or is it still there?

Woman: I still get it sometimes . . .

Bashir: Are you going somewhere for something?

Woman: I am looking for a job.

Bashir: I will get it for you, I will find you a job. But this 'amal, this was a bad thing done to you. It has been following you for a long time. Wherever you went, you could not get rid of it. With God's strength, I can remove it. Do you want treatment for that and the job?

Woman: Can you treat me?

Bashir: Yes. I need £S6, for treating you and for getting you the job. Do you have £S6?

Woman: No, I don't . . .

Bashir: I will give you some weed to wear, which will make you liked by everybody and be sure to get you your job. Which job do you want?

Woman: In an office in Haj 'Abdalla . . .

Bashir: You used to work at sewing, didn't you?

Woman: Yes. I had a machine and everything but I never made enough money from it.

Bashir: People never paid you enough. I think it is better if you work in an office. For £S1 I will give you this weed to wear. Go and meet the man in the office and it is certain you will get the job. After you have got it bring me what I deserve. What I am giving you now is just to get you the job. After that, pay me £S20. I will give you some incense as well. Don't tie this weed up in leather, wrap it in a bit of material and sew it and wear it. Then take the incense and burn it for yourself before you go and meet the man about the job.

Only three women came to discuss their own health problems. The first whispered her problem to Bashir and was told that she was suffering from an 'ārid, though as yet Bashir did not know what caused it. She was given incense and told that she should burn it in private and then ask Bashir what was wrong with her. Only at that time would Bashir Fath al-Rahman learn what was troubling her.

A second woman was afflicted by the Evil Eye (which Bashir found was troubling three patients altogether). She complained of a whole range of symptoms, several of which were dismissed by Bashir and most of which seemed quite unrelated:

Bashir: The allergy you have in your stomach, has it gone? Is it still there? And the pain you have in your stomach like a cramp, has that gone? And the tiredness in your legs, is that still there? And the pain in your kidneys that causes heavy bleeding in your periods, is that still there? And the pain in your back that causes a pain in your right side, is that still there? And the shiver you get in your nerves that makes you shake all over, is that still there?

The woman nodded to all these complaints.

Bashir: The problem with your nerves is now nothing. But when you take a smoke-bath, do you get a rash all over your body?

Woman: Yes.

Bashir: Then this is an 'ārabi's Eye, the Evil Eye, which has touched you. With God's help, I will get it out for you. Do you have enough money for the medicine? The cure is very costly but with God's help, I will remove this 'ārabi's Eye. You will suffer very severe itching in your ears from the removal of this Eye. With God's help I will also remove the pain and allergy you get from the smoke-bath. I will give some incense to help but this will not make it better. If you have £S6 I will give you some medicine which will cure you completely.

Woman: I do not have £S6.

> *Bashir:* I can give you incense for £S1 and I will give you this medicine for another £S1. Rub it in your mouth and it will help your eyesight, which you are also complaining about.
>
> *Woman:* I will come back again with the £S6 for the other medicine.
>
> *Bashir:* I hope that with God's help you come back for the rest of the cure.

The following case sounded particularly serious and painful, and Bashir offered a diagnosis with caution. He was also reluctant, however, for the woman to seek help elsewhere, particularly in Khartoum, the capital, where the best healers in the country are reputed to be found:

> *Woman:* I have this white rash on my eyes. It peels and itches, like an allergy.
>
> *Bashir:* I can give you a medicine to collect it all in one place, or I can give you another medicine that will let it go gradually. It will cost you £S1 for me to remove it straight away.
>
> *Woman:* What if I go and do it in Khartoum?
>
> *Bashir:* No, I can do it for you here. I will get rid of it. You put this medicine in at night and something will come out of your nose, like cotton wool. When this comes out, you will know it is your eye disease coming out.
>
> *Woman:* Sometimes I don't see with this eye. It's as though there is water over it. I get very fed up with it.
>
> *Bashir:* With the help of God, I hope everything will improve and your illness will go.
>
> *Woman:* All right. I will come back and see you on Wednesday.
>
> *Bashir:* Tell your husband to come and see me as well so that I can remove the bag he has got on his back. This is causing the swelling in his leg and the pain in his heart. Tell him to come and have it removed.

Men and Their Problems

Men's problems, and the solutions proposed for their problems, sounded altogether more complicated than those of the women. For the most part, they consulted Bashir about tangible physical or economic symptoms and he treated their problems with the seriousness that they demanded. The dozen men who visited Bashir during the morning were generally younger than the women. Two were very young: one a Fellata, the other a nomad, dressed in ragged jallabīya, could not have been more than 20 years old. Another was a few years older, smartly dressed in trousers and shirt and obviously better off. Several were middle-aged men. One was accompanied by his wife and both had health problems:

> *Bashir:* You came before and brought some money. How much did you bring?

> *Man:* I brought £S6 for the medicine.
> *Bashir:* Did all the medicine you took from me cost £S6?
> *Man:* Yes, that's right.
> *Bashir:* And you are feeling much better now, aren't you?
> *Man:* Yes.
> *Bashir:* But you have got something wrong with your back . . .
> *Man:* Yes.
> *Bashir:* And you get nausea when you eat. You don't digest your food properly.
> *Man:* Yes.
> *Bashir:* You have some dirt in your stomach, some discharge or something that has not come out. I will give you a bottle of something to get it all out and then you will feel much better.
> *Man:* I also get nightmares . . .
> *Bashir:* After you kill a sheep you won't get any more of these nightmares. This is what they call *kabbas*. Have you seen a black snake?
> *Man:* Yes.
> *Bashir:* I will give you some herbs and some incense to get rid of all your ailments and also something to drink. Take half now and then the other half another day.

An older man was told he was suffering from worms. His treatment was down to earth and cost nothing:

> *Man:* Should I not eat anything?
> *Bashir:* When you eat or drink you do not feel much in your stomach. Drink only red tea and warm water till the sun is high in the sky and then drink a custard of flour and warm water till it is afternoon. Then you can eat what you like.
> *Man:* Should I eat beef?
> *Bashir:* Repeat my treatment for two days, then for two days more. After those four days you can eat meat. The first and second time you go to the toilet, you will get rid of the worms from your stomach. This is your problem; you have worms.

The young nomad was also told he was suffering from worms, though his condition appeared to be much more serious. His cure also appeared to be rather drastic, and confirmed my impression that men were diagnosed more rigorously and more elaborate remedies were proposed for them than for women:

> *Bashir:* Have you been here before?
> *Man:* No, it is the first time.
> *Bashir:* You have a swelling in your stomach. Have you had it just recently or for a long time? Where have you been and what water have you drunk?
> *Man:* I have drunk water from a well and from a water container [*birka*].

Bashir: This has made a large swelling in your stomach. You have got worms and your intestines are in a very bad way. This causes the very high swelling. What you have got is something like liver cancer. It is caused by water that is not fresh and has been lying around. When you go to the toilet, your urine is very hot and comes out slowly, in spurts. Instead of it all coming out you do not get rid of it; it goes back into your stomach. Do you still vomit?

Man: Yes.

Bashir: Do you get pain between your shoulders? And a hot sensation and heaviness in your lower abdomen?

Man: Yes.

Bashir: Do you still get pain and swelling in your legs?

Man: Yes . . ..

Bashir: And the very severe pain in your back, do you still have that? The heaviness in your eyes, is that still there? The headaches, do you still get them day and night?

Man: Yes . . .

Bashir: And the stabbing in your kidneys, do you still have that?

Man: Yes . . .

Bashir: If God helps me, I will cure you. You will have to take a lot of medicines from me. Count the bottles! Every time you finish one you must come back to me and take another, just like the first, which costs £S6. Start with one medicine and take it for about twenty-three days and then come back to see me.

A man with stomach problems had a similar range of symptoms but was given a different, rather elaborate diagnosis:

Bashir: You keep vomiting? You have nausea and a lot of phlegm?

Man: Yes . . .

Bashir: And you have a lot of heartburn? Your heart beats heavily? Do you still have a lot of swelling in your legs or does it come and go? This heartbeat you get, when you drink a lot of water, it presses hard upon your diaphragm and your heart and it causes palpitations. You feel you cannot breathe very well. When it presses on your heart you feel a tightness and this is why it causes the swelling. When you take these white tablets and you urinate, then you feel relief and the diaphragm goes down so that you don't feel the tightness in your chest. When you feel easier your heartbeats become normal and the swelling becomes less. The itching in your ears is from your breathing. When your heart is pressed, your lungs feel very heavy and they cause this heaviness and itching in your ears. You get very bad headaches and become fed up and restless and cannot sleep. This is all because of the water that rises to the heart, pushing up the diaphragm. This medicine will make you want to urinate a lot. Take this bottle and drink from it for nine days. Then take the tablets for fourteen days, making twenty-three days in all. Take it all.

The young Fellata had become ill after consulting some nomads:

Bashir: You went for treatment to some 'arab and they made you some medicine that you took the next day to cure you. After you took the medicine you got this very high fever. What is the fever?

Man: I had a fever and my body was aching, but now I am a bit better.

Bashir: When you come home you are very tired and your heart is beating, tuck, tuck, tuck. Do you pray?

Man: Sometimes . . .

Bashir: You must continue to pray and ask God to cure you.

Man: When I am at work, I am very bothered. I have something on my mind all the time and I don't know what is wrong.

Bashir: Yes. When you are at work you are fed up and you wonder when you are going to finish, what time it is and so on. I will give you some incense to bring you some peace. Pay me 50 cents. May God help you.

A middle-aged man was making a revisit about his bad leg:

Bashir: How are you?

Man: I am still not too good. It's my leg.

Bashir: This leg is really stiff and it is making your whole right side stiff, even your arm and your eye. Even your heartbeat is not normal. I will have to do something about it. If I don't, it will be no good. I gave you some weeds to rub on your leg. Did you use them?

Man: You gave me some to drink.

Bashir: Oh, now I will give you some to rub on your leg. The medicine is just starting to work on your body. I will also give you these weeds. What you do is to mix them with oil from the car, the yellow oil. Put them in a tin together and then add some sesame oil. Every night rub it into your leg where it is hurting you most. Now the medicine is entering your body it will loosen your muscles and your nerves, with God's help. There is also a drink to loosen your stomach. That will cost you £S1. Drink half tomorrow and the rest the next day. Take it for two days. Take the medicine now and if you don't have the money with you, pay me another time.

Several of the men tried to talk to Bashir privately. They leaned forward and spoke too quietly for their words to be overheard. One young man had financial worries, which he tried to explain to Bashir. Even he was offered some reassurance and a course of action:

Bashir: Don't worry. I will give you some incense to light. Mention the money when you light the incense and you will have enough money to finish your building.

Bashir's advice was on the whole practical and did not invite self-recrimination or blame, as in the final case. The well-dressed young man had come for some sympathy and some horticultural advice. It was apparently his first visit and at first Bashir mistook him for a merchant:

> *Bashir:* What sort of work do you do? Are you a merchant, buying and selling things?
> *Man:* No, I have come about my allotment [*hawāsha*]. I have been planting tomatoes.
> *Bashir:* Tomatoes? Which? The big sort for £S50 or the smaller ones for £S30?
> *Man:* I can't tell you really because it didn't work out. My project failed.
> *Bashir:* Oh? Was it eaten by worms?
> *Man:* No. It just burned out. Nothing grew . . .
> *Bashir:* The people who put down the insecticide must have killed the crop. They put down too much. You have to go and water it a lot.
> *Man:* Yes . . .
> *Bashir:* When you go back now, go and give the crop a lot of water to get rid of all this insecticide that is destroying it. They have given it too much salt . . .
> *Man:* Yes . . .
> *Bashir:* I will also give you some incense to light for it. Just light this and place it in the garden. You don't have to cover the trees or anything, just light it and leave it there on its own. Give the land a lot of water in the beginning and then stop the water and let the land dry out, till it gets thirsty. Wait till it becomes green again. Then next time you plant it and start making a profit, don't forget to bring what I deserve.

It was just after 12:30 P.M. Helped by her house-servant, Bitt al-Jamīl left the room, indicating that Bashir was ready to go. All the problems had apparently been dealt with and those of us who remained were chatting together. For Bashir it had been a busy morning though the work had not been uninterrupted. Periodically he took time off for a chat and a joke, though he remained in Bitt al-Jamīl the whole time. Not all patients treated him with awe. Those who were regular visitors adopted a friendly, sometimes teasing attitude that contrasted with the distinctly aggressive, defiant manner of those who owed a lot of money or the apprehension of newcomers. Several times when there was a lull in patients, Bashir turned to me and asked me to play back some of the recorded session to which he listened with great interest. At one point, he asked me to play some of the tape I had made the previous day "with that woman," Bitt al-Jamīl, which is largely transcribed in the middle section of this chapter. This we listened to attentively, while Bashir held up a hand solemnly to maintain quiet. He apparently approved of what had been said and was happy that the rest of the world should know about his work. Certainly since that time he never indicated any misgivings to Bitt al-Jamīl about this project and she remained concerned that people in other countries should know of Bashir Fath al-Rahman and the gift of help and healing God bestows through him.

Zachara Jamīl (1929–1998)

In 2000, I was saddened to learn of the death of Bitt al-Jamīl, which occurred in 1998. Despite her heart problems in the early 1980s, she had enjoyed relatively good health and continued to work in Sennar until the time of her death. When I returned to the town in 2000, however, none of her close relatives were living there and it was not until the following year that I heard from her son and daughter and was able to learn about her later years. Her son, Sofian, who now works in the market in Sennar, heard about this book and contacted me to talk about his mother. He also put me in touch with his sister, Suad, who is living in Khartoum with her children. During Ramadān I spent a couple of very pleasant days with them all, talking about their mother and about their own lives.

Particularly moving was Suad's account of the events surrounding her mother's death. The months between 1998 and early 1999 were bleak for all of them. Suad's husband had become very sick, with prostate problems, probably cancer. No doctors had been able to do anything for him, and in June of 1998 her mother went from Sennar to see if she could help him. At that time she was in reasonable health, still holding her healing sessions two or three times a week. On the morning of July 13, however, she felt tired when she woke. "I am very tired. My whole body aches," she repeated at least twice to Suad. Then she said she wanted to take a bath. Suad went to the bathroom with her and waited outside the door with a clean jallabīya. Bitt al-Jamīl came out of the bathroom but instead of pausing to dress, hurried straight to her bed and lay down. Concerned, Suad followed. Her mother slowly opened her eyes and then stretched, as though she was preparing to die. Suad urged her to repeat the Shahada (the Islamic confession of faith). This she did, and repeated other Quranic verses. Then, very quietly, she died. Suad called her daughter to bring water. She closed her mother's eyes and mouth and washed her correctly. Meanwhile wailing from others in the house announced their great disaster. When Suad went to explain to her neighbor what had happened, the woman immediately asked, "Did something happen to your husband?" "No," Suad replied, "worse than that. My mother has died."

Bitt al-Jamīl had prepared her coffin and all the perfumes and oils needed for her funeral in Sennar, but she died in Khartoum. Some people offered to transfer the body to Sennar, but Suad said no, she wanted her to be buried close by, in Faruq's graveyard. Then, not long after the funeral, tragedy struck again, twice. Suad's husband died just over two months later, and in March 1999, Suad lost her father, Hissein.

People like my neighbors and me, who saw Bitt al-Jamīl's house in Sennar, assumed the family was very rich, but when she died, Suad said, her mother had no money. Towards the end she was earning as much as £S3–4 million a month (then about US$1200–1600). However she and her husband gave all their income away to the poor, particularly to orphaned children. She left her children two houses in Sennar, but these are now rented out to provide some small income for them all. Suad's own apartment in Khartoum is rented for her by her son-in-law, a doctor in Saudi Arabia.

People had come to Bitt al-Jamīl for help from all over Sudan, Egypt, and Saudi Arabia. Sometimes they sent her tickets to go to them. Accompanied by her husband and Suad, she went several times to Saudi Arabia, where she successfully healed a young man with severe psychiatric problems. Later his brother developed the same symptoms. The family again sent for her and she was able to cure him too. Generally Saudi people do not like to have foreigners heal them, said Suad, or have them to stay in their houses, but Bitt al-Jamīl and her whole family were welcome guests in this family's home. When they heard that she had died, one of the men immediately came from Saudi Arabia to give condolences to them.

A year before her death, Bitt al-Jamīl's spirits came to her husband and said, "If Bitt al-Jamīl dies, we want to go to Suad within a year." Hissein promised to talk with Suad, but she refused, saying she wanted to raise her children. She felt that if she agreed all her time would be devoted to the spirits. After her mother's death, the spirits—Bashir, and the zār spirit Shalabi—came directly to ask her herself, but she gave them the same answer: she needed to raise her children. Suad described the spirits in detail. Bashir was small in size, while Shalabi looked like the joker in the pack of cards, with a big curled moustache, wearing white clothes and riding a white horse. However she has never seen Roma.

In July 1998, Suad's eldest daughter went to Sennar to have her first child, not knowing her grandmother was already in Khartoum. Suad had to phone her and tell her of her grandmother's sudden death. She was very upset and almost immediately went into labor with her first child who was thus born in Sennar. Before her forty days rest period was complete, the spirits came to her, three days running, and asked her to work for them.

She told them, "I am busy. I have a husband, a baby, a house. I cannot do it." Since then, nobody has seen the spirits again. But whenever she is in the house in Sennar, Suad often finds strange roots in the oddest places. Nobody knows where they come from. One day a man named Abu Zaid came and gave her a large number of roots. "These are your mother's roots," he said. She didn't ask him where he found them.

Even when her mother was alive they used to find roots suddenly appearing in the house—on top of cupboards, in corners they knew they had recently swept. Suad claimed Bitt al-Jamīl never bought the roots for her cures, only the herbs she mixed with them, and for these she sent to a certain trader in the market. Many people used to help her by going to the market or mixing the medicines, but they were not really assistants. Only her husband could really be called that.

Suad knows her mother's treatments for some illnesses. She had special cures for toothache, for breast cancer and other malignant tumors, for all sorts of things. People still come to her for Bitt al-Jamīl's cures and her ilba (box of equipment) remains in the house in Sennar. A woman once came to her, crying that her son was in prison on a criminal charge: "Give me from the cures of Bitt al-Jamīl." She treated her and after twenty-one days her son was released, innocent. The guilty one had confessed.

Suad told us many stories of how her mother healed patients. Once a man came from Chad suffering from water in the abdomen *(stizza)*. He went to many doctors, without success. Bitt al-Jamīl treated him several times and at last he recovered. There was also a woman from Sennar who had her first baby by caesarian delivery. When she learned she was pregnant again she was very afraid of another operation. She went to Bitt al-Jamīl who began treatment, which lasted a long time, once or twice a week. When she came to give birth, she had a normal delivery. Said Suad repeatedly, "I saw this with my own eyes." People were unconscious, could not work, yet when her mother treated them they got back their health.

Suad also talked about her mother's life. For example, before she began to work with the spirits, a handsome man had come to Bitt al-Jamīl and asked for money. Bitt al-Jamīl had said, "The breakfast is cooking, I didn't yet prepare it." The man replied, "Just give me the beans in your hand and I will wait. *Allah aldik*, God will give to you." When she came back from getting the breakfast, he had disappeared. Three days later she became very ill, and lay in bed, unconscious. Her hair, her mushāt, all fell out. People said "We should try zār," but her husband, a farmer and very devout Muslim, refused. "No, no, no. No-one knows zār or beats zār in this family. Let her die but no zār will be beaten here." They let him go out to the farm, and then they brought the equipment and incense and Bitt al-Jamīl became possessed. However this was not zār. Fath al-Rahman appeared to her and said, "I am from God and Bashir is my servant." They brought the incense to Bitt al-Jamīl, her eyes opened and she recovered. When her husband returned from the farm they sent her to meet him at the door. He asked, "Did you do the zār?" and when they nodded, he was so happy he agreed they could do it again. When Bashir first came to her, he was non-Muslim. Her husband told him, "No, no, no, you will become a Muslim" and Bashir agreed. Sometimes when Bashir stayed the whole day, she could not recover to say her prayers, so her husband told him, "You must leave her at the time of prayers." After that when Bashir came, he left at the call to prayer. She would stop and say her prayers and then Bashir would come back again later, as her husband had told him.

When Bitt al-Jamīl went to London for heart surgery, her surgeon was Egyptian. As Bitt al-Jamīl was coming round from the anesthetic, he told her that something very strange had happened while he was operating: he had heard a voice. At first he thought it was her, but how? She was unconscious. He was very frightened. Bitt al-Jamīl replied that this must have been Doctora Roma, the Greek spirit. She told the doctor about her work healing the sick, and gave him some of her treatments.

Suad had other stories to share about Doctora. Once the spirit told Bitt al-Jamīl that she would sleep from 3:00 A.M. one day to 3:00 A.M. the next. Bitt al-Jamīl told her husband and said there should be no disturbance, no cars outside, the place should be quiet. Her father told all the cars to stay away. Everyone in Sennar knew that Bitt al-Jamīl was to sleep for a long time. She wore Roma's dress: white blouse, red skirt. In the room where she slept, her husband brought wood to fasten doors and windows to keep out the noise. Everybody expected her to die. Even her husband told her to "lie in the *gibla*." For a long time she slept, behind the locked door. When people came close to it, they heard a strange noise: "Umm, umm, umm." After that there was no noise until 3:00 A.M. in the morning. They heard her moving, opened the door, and found her very, very tired.

All the relatives, educated people, came to ask her what had happened. She said she had been to Greece and was very tired from being with Roma and her children. Roma had twin girls plus another son and daughter, and they had been walking together, all over Greece. Bitt al-Jamīl described the beaches, trees, flowers, buildings, yes, even the color of the buildings she visited, in great detail. People who knew the country agreed it sounded exactly like Greece, right down to the windows on the buildings.

Bitt al-Jamīl's family today (2001)

"Did you eat?" they asked her.

"No, they did not give me any food. I did not even see Roma and her children eat any food or drink anything while I was there."

Unlike the spirits in zār, none of Bitt al-Jamīl's spirits ate while they were with her. Even when Bashir came she never ate nor drank, yet when he left, she did not feel hungry or thirsty.

Bitt al-Jamīl's family still mourns the loss of their grandmother, grandfather, and father but are getting on with their lives. Suad's six children are all doing well. Her oldest daughter and her husband now have three children, and live in Saudi Arabia. Her second daughter is a lawyer, presently doing graduate work. She is divorced with a 2-year-old daughter and lives with her mother. Suad's youngest daughter is a student at Afhad University. The oldest of her three sons lives in England, where he originally went to study computer science in London and where Suad once visited him. The others are still in school. None are married. Sofian is not yet married, but works in the market, like his father.

Some of the family's proudest possessions are the medals and a certificate Bitt al-Jamīl received, personally, from then President Nimeiri in January 1985. These recognized the contributions made to the nation and the Mahdist state by Bitt al-Jamīl's grandfather Emir Muhammad Bishara (1861–98), governor of Dongola until he was killed by the invading

Anglo-Egyptian armies. However, Suad and Sofian assured me that the knowledge their mother's reputation also lives on, not just in their own lives and hearts but in a book read by people outside the Sudan, is a source of equal pride.

Endnotes

[1] For example, as described in the *Tabaqat* of Wad Daif Allah.

[2] I.e., a Christian spirit.

[3] She had heart bypass surgery.

6

AL-UMĪYA
OF TOMBURA ZĀR
LEADER OF A SPIRIT
POSSESSION/HEALING
GROUP

Within a few months of my arrival in Sennar in 1979, I heard the drums beating insistently to announce the activities of burei zār. Soon I was taken to their ceremonies and to the houses of the leaders by my neighbors in al-Gulʿa. Halima, Fatima, Zachara, and Bitt al-Jamīl all attended zār burei ceremonies with varying regularity, even though they were busy and well-adjusted individuals and did not suffer from any chronic health trouble. Women who do not have any problems with zār may attend ceremonies just to enjoy the drama and excitement, and certainly if a friend, neighbor, or relative is hosting a zār ceremony it would be a discourtesy not to attend.

Tombura zār is more elusive than burei and less popular. I had been in Sennar for well over a year before I was aware of its activities in the town. Significantly I met Naeima, a leader of tombura zār in Sennar, during the annual thanksgiving or reaffirmation ceremonies of Rajabīya when she was making an honorary appearance at a house of burei zār. Later I was called (or invited) to attend the house of tombura by Naeima and was able to accompany one of my neighbors who needed fairly regu-

Naeima welcomes guests to her sister's zār ceremony (1985)

lar support from the group. From the beginning, Naeima welcomed me warmly and was concerned to help me learn more about the spirits.

Zār, the belief and ritual associated with a certain type of spirit, continues to play an important role in the lives of many Sudanese women, though the past fifteen years of Islamist government have both affected many women's attitudes toward such beliefs and have witnessed attempts, largely unsuccessful, to suppress zār practices. In 1980, all those I knew and worked with in Sennar accepted knowledge about zār with varying degrees of confidence. Many did not like it, and some claimed not to have ever suffered any problems from zār spirits. The majority, however, had had some personal experience when their symptoms or problem had been diagnosed as being caused by a possessing zār spirit. For the most part zār was an everyday topic, a diagnosis or explanation suggested routinely for a disorder. Confirmation of a zār problem by a recognized leader, however, was more drastic. It is rather like being told one has an incurable but controllable disease. On the one hand one feels relief to know definitely what is causing so much trouble and discomfort. On the other hand there is a feeling of trepidation at the thought of the lengthy and often elaborate attempts to control the disorder before it affects one's whole way of life. In zār, however, there has always been something more: a sense of spiritual elitism, a feeling of being singled out. This may not compare with the real elevation of being chosen by God, as in the case of Bitt al-Jamīl in the preceding chapter, but it still leads to a feeling of advantage that is evident in those who talk about their zār as though they belong to some exclusive club.

In Sennar, as in much of contemporary Sudan, there are two main types of zār: burei and tombura. Although distinct origins have been hypothesized for them and there are certain differences that will be discussed below, they are basically the same phenomenon. While their clientele are for the most part distinct, members of each group occasionally visit back and forth and enjoy comparing each other's ritual. This may be a relatively recent rapprochement in Sennar, but it is also evident from older women's accounts of zār in their youth that the two have always been close. Fundamentally they are an expression of the same set of beliefs and satisfy the same needs in their participants, though their methods and ritual differ somewhat. As noted in chapter 1, it is possible to see burei and tombura as different "paths" within zār.

Zār is both a category of spirit and the practices associated with possession by those spirits. Such possession can cause problems or illness, usually a form of mental illness, and these are also referred to as zār. Much of the ritual of zār ceremonies is directed at controlling such disorders. In both burei and tombura, essentially healing rituals are enacted through possession by certain distinct spirits. Under the guidance and leadership of a woman known in Sennar as the umīya, predominantly female patients become actively possessed by well-defined spirits. While in this state, they assume the characteristics of the possessing spirit, in behavior, dress, movement, and sometimes speech. The whole procedure is carefully controlled and orchestrated by the leader, who derives her knowledge and power from traditions and paraphernalia that are symbolically stored in a large tin box, *al-ʿilba*. Patients may experience mild forms of possession in their home, and sickness is sometimes diagnosed as an expression of possession, but it is only under the strict control of the umīya, usually in the more formal setting of the house of zār, that the full enactment of zār possession occurs. Here spirits are summoned by the leader, according to the powers and knowledge she has either inherited from a close female relative or acquired by apprenticeship. Those zār spirits are also controlled through her exercise of those same powers. The aim is always propitiation, never exorcism.

Tombura is the name of a Zande town in southern Sudan. The term also refers to a musical instrument, a sort of *rabāba* or small lute, a six-stringed instrument that is played during the formal ceremonies of tombura zār and that is also commonplace in daily life in southern Sudan. Naeima keeps her instrument in the room reserved for zār, where it leans casually in a corner among the other equipment. When it is brought out and played on rare formal occasions, it is decked with ribbons and cowrie shells and treated with distinct respect. Each tombura instrument, as well as its six strings, has a name that was bestowed by its original owner.

Tombura has a smaller clientele than burei zār and is generally regarded with greater trepidation. While women may attend a burei ceremony simply to enjoy themselves, tombura is taken much more seriously. In the literature available on Sudanese zār, tombura is far less known and understood than burei, and I also found that I was only allowed to carry my inquiries to a certain level and then politely blocked, in 2001 no less than 1985. A recent ethnography of tombura in Omdurman (Makris 2000) has partly remedied this gap but many questions still remain. Tombura is regarded as a more esoteric and demanding form of zār and, until recently, has been less popular than burei among women. There is always a certain tension apparent in tombura, which I certainly was not aware of at the house of Bitt al-Jamīl or (to a lesser extent) at the house of burei zār. Yet significantly, tombura is continuing to expand in Sennar and attracts a wide range of followers, including some from burei zār. This seems largely due to the charismatic personality of the present umīya, Naeima. She is much admired by women outside the tombura group for her very powerful zār and for the strict discipline with which she manages the zār in others; for her successful control of the spirits, which is manifested both in the organization of the group and its material improvement; and for her own attractive appearance and personality.

Naeima is now one of only two female leaders, *umīyat*, of tombura zār in the district of Sennar. A second elderly umīya lives in Kabbosh where she has a regular group of followers, but she no longer devotes much time to zār activities. A third leader who was practicing in the 1980s died some years ago, and nobody has yet taken over her work.

Exact numbers of devotees in zār are impossible to give and largely irrelevant. No membership lists are kept and there are long periods when individuals' zār are passive. The number of participants at regular sessions varies enormously from one week to the next. The size of the group at a formal ceremony depends largely on who is hosting it and whom she invites. In Rajabīya, however, a thanksgiving rather than a curing ceremony at which members are expected to support their leader, numbers in tombura continue to be large. In 1985, I noted that almost a hundred people participated in Naeima's house of tombura. By that year, several old friends from burei zār told me that in addition to their burei spirits they also had some of the tombura spirits, particularly Shirumbay, the servant in tombura zār, who is described in greater detail below. I was unable to attend Naeima's celebrations in Rajabīya 2001, but she told me that over a hundred women came, a not improbable figure as on the more routine biweekly healing sessions of Shirumbay I counted an average of forty women.

The majority of the participants in both burei and tombura are female. It is difficult to estimate how many men are suffering from zār as, for regular treatment in either house, men prefer to seek help privately. Rarely are they seen at public ceremonies, such as the regular coffee sessions in each house of zār. They avoid the social side of zār, the casual entertainment that it affords and that is attended only by women. In this sense men seek only the spiritual aspect of zār.

Many women who attend the house of tombura zār are described as Malakīya, even though I discovered this was far from the case. The term Malakīya refers to people descended from the ex-soldiers who "colonized" the area of Sennar in the early twentieth century, largely detribalized peoples from southern and western Sudan who were taken in slavery to Egypt where they were converted to Islam and enrolled in the Egyptian army in return for nominal manumission. Malakīya literally means civilians and distinguished the colonists from the local military and business districts in the areas where they were settled. The whole history of zār in Sennar is intricately tied up with these ex-soldiers and their families and supports the theory that it was the nineteenth-century Ottoman armies that were responsible for the dissemination of zār beliefs throughout a wide area of North Africa (Constantinides 1972). There are also recurrent themes and terms in zār, which appear to have been derived from the army: titles for male tombura officials such as *sanjak* and *brigdir*, the hierarchy of officials, rituals associated with the processions and meals, or special foods such as *bulbif* (bully beef).

Yet Naeima herself is a Mahas woman, which is significant in that the Mahas have a long tradition of holy men. Though her mother also held strong zār beliefs, Naeima claims to have succeeded to her position in zār through a sanjak of Turkish background. Her followers today come from a wide range of ethnic backgrounds, and many of the old stereotypes about tombura seem to be largely disappearing.

The similarities in zār burei and tombura are many. People say the zār are all one, the spirits are the same, although differently named individual spirits are dominant in each group. These spirits are regarded as guests and as such, welcomed with respect and generosity when they possess someone, to avoid upsetting them and risking their punishing the hostess by bringing her sickness or disorder. However, zār spirits are not simply guests. They are foreign guests or at least outsiders. There are no zār of familiar or local people, but rather zār spirits represent the various foreigners important to Sudanese history. Although there are some colorful individual spirits, they are organized into distinct groups. The Derewish (Sufis) is nominally at least the most important and on formal occasions leads in the possession of all the spirits. Foremost in this category, recognized by both groups, are the spirits of Sheikh 'Abd al-Kadir al-Jilani and Sheikh al-Badawi, Sufi teachers who are important in Sudanese Islam. In tombura, a third major Derewish spirit is recognized: Sayīd Bilal. Bilal was the Prophet's slave who was freed and became the caller for prayer, a significant choice for a leading zār figure.

The Khawajat, pale-skinned foreigners, and Pashawat, officials of the Ottoman period, are both important categories in tombura zār, possibly residual from earlier periods when such foreigners had a greater influence on local lives. Pashawat spirits like the color white (as in burei) and include such characters as Hakinbasha and Khallinbasha, titles of official statuses or positions under Turkish rule rather than individual names. The category Khawajat, in both burei and tombura, is described in terms of seven boats, *sabaa marākib*, which represent, nominally at least, seven subgroups of foreigners. In Sennar, these are not particularly elaborated. One colorful character in the tombura Khawajat group is named Nimr al-Kinda. Constantinides (1972:95) noted the same name in Omdurman burei zār in the late 1960s and wondered, only partly fancifully, if it could possibly represent the intrepid nineteenth-century explorer Samuel Baker, who traveled extensively in Sudan and was active in the attempted suppression of the slave trade from southern Sudan.

The category of Sittat, the Women, is more elaborated in Sennar tombura than burei zār and includes several individually named spirits such as Mary the mother of Jesus. The Habbashi, Ethiopians, is equally popular in both burei and tombura zār in Sennar. Jodulla is the name of an Ethiopian tombura zār who is believed to like a red jallabīya and needs to have a red sheep sacrificed for him, reminiscent of the demands of the burei spirit Bashir.

The final category of spirits, the Sudanese, is most individualized in Sennar tombura. Distinctive spirits range from Osman Digna, the famous military leader from the time of the Mahdīya; Jamalli, an 'arab who likes those possessed by him to carry a sword and to wear a white wrap tied round their waist; and Banda Azrag, Black Banda, who demands black clothes and a black goat (for sacrifice).

The number seven dominates the ritual in zār. Besides the seven categories of spirits, the preferred length of a formal zār ceremony is seven days, referred to as a Chair, *kursi*, in both burei and tombura. The number seven is very significant in Sudanese culture at large, particularly in ritual associated with birth and death (El-Nagar 1975:249).

The power of the umīya is felt to be derived from her tin box, her 'ilba, which is stored carefully in the house of zār, a place Naeima also refers to as "Shirumbay's room." When the umīya is carrying out a treatment it is said that she is "opening the box," a phrase reminiscent of that used for the fakī's method of treatment by "opening the Book." The 'ilba holds, among other things, the various incenses used to summon the zār spirits, together with a couple of decorated cigarette boxes used to hold both cigarettes and written messages to the zār. Cigarettes are important in even the simplest form of treatment.

In both houses of zār, the spirits are summoned by the same particular incenses. Throughout zār sessions, an assistant (usually an apprentice umīya) keeps the incense pot burning and ready to fumigate patients as they need and for which they pay a small sum. Such fumigation does not necessarily summon the spirit and result in active possession, but it is believed to make a person and her possessing spirit feel better. Although I was told that the same incenses are used in both houses, an umīya takes her own incense with her when visiting other houses of zār.

The organization and ritual of the two groups is almost identical. The umīya is available much of the time for "opening the box," for consultation, help, and fumigation by special zār incenses. There are thrice-weekly curing sessions, when a woman with strong powers becomes possessed by a particular spirit and is available for consultation about a range of problems, not unlike those dealt with by Bitt al-Jamīl. On Sundays and Wednesdays, a male spirit is summoned. Women possessed by him are served strong, sugarless coffee, at the ritual known simply as jabana, coffee (party). In burei zār the spirit is known as Bashir and he has the most highly developed profile of any contemporary zār entity. As a Christian Ethiopian he wears a cross on his chest (which thus distinguishes him from the Bashir who comes to Bitt al-Jamīl), likes the color red, drinks alcohol (when available) as well as coffee, talks a lot, and is loud and entertaining. He is described as the servant of the zār in that he takes messages to and from the bigger zār. While therefore rather lowly in the burei panoply, he is by far the most popular zār in Sennar today. Women who are possessed by other zār are hopeful that Bashir will come to them too. They claim this is because holding a jabana for Bashir offers a potential source of income, although it is evident that the spiritual status it confers on the hostess is also an important consideration.

In Sennar tombura zār, a similar session occurs every Sunday and Wednesday but the spirit who comes is known as Shirumbay, a name with Turkish associations, but which I have come across in no other context. He is neither so entertaining nor so well known as Bashir. He is said to be half-Ethiopian (Habbashi), half-Italian (Khawaja). His Italian father, also a zār, is called Bashugi, while his Ethiopian mother is unelaborated. He is said to like the color brown and Western-style male clothes. Naeima showed me the outfits she had collected for him: a smart man's suit in a heavy brown fabric with a jacket, and trousers cut off rather dramatically at the knees. These are worn with a white shirt and a sort of trilby hat. The full outfit can only be used occasionally. I saw Shirumbay possession on many occasions, including the more formal tombura ritual of Rajabīya, in 1985 and 2001, but I only saw the hat worn by Shirumbay. He also likes meals of chicken, eggs, and fruit and eats with a knife and fork. Those possessed by him were said formerly to drink beer, gin, whisky, and sherry. In fact, before Sharī'a law was introduced in 1985, I saw them drink only the local home brew and coffee; since then I have not witnessed any alcohol consumption. I never saw Shirumbay eat.

When I was attending the house of tombura between 1981 and 1982, Shirumbay's room, in which was stored all the tombura paraphernalia and where the regular coffee sessions were held, was a simple semi-enclosed veranda. Formal ceremonies were held largely in the courtyard outside, but it was from Shirumbay's room that proceedings were organized and directed. In 1983, largely through devotees' contributions, Naeima was able to build another room, more modern and much-admired, for Shirumbay, with cement walls painted pink and a tin roof, complete with door and windows, curtains, and red linoleum on the floor. Henceforth this became the headquarters for tombura in Sennar. There was another smaller room, however, to which Naeima, possessed by Shirumbay, retreated when she/he wished to consult privately with clients. Small and bare, it had a dirt floor and no furnishings other than a simple mat. It was purely utilitarian and provided no comfort or distraction whatsoever. By 2001 Naeima had expanded this room, with an additional hallway where petitioners could wait, but it remained very plain. The contrast, between the spaces where Shirumbay did his real work and where he relaxed to meet socially with his followers, was dramatic.

The two spaces symbolize the two related needs that zār provides. Health problems may appear to be the most urgent, but the social needs are also important. To be sociable is an important attribute in Sudanese society. "She likes people, she likes to chat," is one of the ultimate accolades, for spirits no less than for humans. While those possessed by Shirumbay appeared to me to be inarticulate and uncommunicative, devotees in tombura admired his sociable nature. Most tombura spirits remain aloof and do not talk at all. Those possessed by Shirumbay, on the other hand, sit with the people and communicate directly, albeit brokenly. This is a major reason for his increasing popularity and for the success of tombura in Sennar today.

On Tuesdays, a female spirit sometimes comes to offer a similar sort of consulting surgery, but for gynecological and obstetrical matters. Women consult her with problems of pregnancy or getting pregnant, childbirth and miscarriages, stomach pains and sexual problems. The resemblance to Bitt al-Jamīl's Doctora Roma is of course immediate. In tombura, she is called Habbashīya, the Ethiopian Woman, or Bitt al-Habbash (Daughter of the Ethiopian) and is said to be the sister of Shirumbay. In burei the spirit with the same function is Lulīya, a name found in popular Sudanese music and culture since the 1970s. Lulīya is also believed to be the sister of Bashir, and her profile is almost as highly elaborated as his. Habbashīya is less commonly seen or known. She likes sweets and sweet drinks but does not eat meat, so there is no need to sacrifice an animal for her. As with Doctora Roma in the previous chapter, women prefer to seek a private consultation with her.

It is this informal aspect of zār ritual that is the most important for many women today. Although descriptions of zār invariably focus on the formal ritual, the kursi and the sacrifices, it is in these less dramatic "coffee parties" that women derive their routine support for zār. It is also here that the processes of change and modernity in zār are most apparent. For both these reasons, the tombura coffee party is described in greater detail below.

The formal ritual in zār, on the other hand, is better known. Organized largely by women, it follows a carefully prescribed program, similar in burei and tombura. The ritual is most elaborate in the thanksgiving ceremonies held during the month of Rajab or in the curing ceremonies, hosted by a patient who is advised that this is a major step towards alleviating her symptoms.

The first day of each ceremony (or part of a day in a one-day event) is traditionally referred to as the "Laying of the Mats" or the "Opening of the Box," an introductory ceremony in which the house of zār is made ready. Mats are laid on the floor for guests to sit on; screens may be raised round the courtyard to afford some privacy, the umīya cleans and prepares all her paraphernalia; and the gifts for the karāma, food and clothing, are shown to the zār. Music and dancing is brief. The second day is the "Day of Henna" in which the "bride" of zār, the patient, is carefully decorated and prepared as a bride and both she and the animal for sacrifice are decorated with henna. The third day is the "Day of Sacrifice," culminating in a torch-lit procession at sunset, which leads the animal to be slaughtered. An intensive evening of spiritual visitations invariably follows. On the fourth day is the elaborate ritual known as the "Opening of the Head"

Ritual procession of Pashawat spirits in zār burei (2001)

(fath al-ras). After its slaughter the previous day, the head of the animal is boiled. It is then placed on a large round tray and with special drumming brought into the center of the expectant assembly. The tray is raised seven times by the umīya, a drink of a glass of water is offered to the head, the mouth of which is then pried open to allow the zār to depart. Finally the meat of the head is shared by those present.

This sequence of events is basically repeated for a seven-day ceremony, allowing for more zār to be honored. At a one-day ceremony, no animal is killed and events are compressed into a single evening's ritual.

It is possible to pinpoint differences between zār burei and tombura although they are not as startling as the similarities. For example, there are small differences between zār spirits like Shirumbay and Bashir, Lulīya and Habbashīya. The use of music varies in burei and tombura. In tombura music is used only on the most formal occasions when the tombura instrument (the 6-stringed rabāba) is accompanied by small, barrel-shaped drums covered with hide and beaten with sticks and rattles *(kush-kosh)*. Banners are important markers in tombura, not found in burei. In Sennar, two sets of flags, one green for Sheikh 'Abd al-Kadir al-Jilani and one red for Sayīd Bilal, are raised before the beginning of a formal ceremony and left to mark the place of sacrifice *(mayanga)* for the duration of the ceremony. This use of banners or flags on ceremonial occasions bears a resemblance to zikr as well as to the army.

Having visited houses of zār in other parts of the Sudan, I find today that these differences are no more significant than those between any two local groups of zār, at least of burei. Each group hands down different details of rituals, traditions, and experiences but they all share a common set of beliefs. It may be that in tombura there is greater uniformity than one finds in burei. I was told that each box ('ilba) of burei is separate while all tombura is related to the main 'ilba, which is in Khartoum North.

Whatever the comparisons, however, everyone agrees that there is one vital difference between burei and tombura. Tombura is masculine while burei is feminine. All differences stem from that opposition. Thus we find people saying that burei is cool while tombura is hot. Burei likes to play while tombura is harsh, tough, demanding. Terms are used here that are hard to translate exactly. Spirits in tombura do not come and go, as in burei. Once they actively possess a person they stay with that person until they have completed their business, even if it takes all night. In burei, on the other hand, spirits are more considerate; a zār will depart temporarily just to let its hostess go to the toilet, an example frequently cited. Spirits in tombura demand more of a person, physically, mentally, and financially, than in burei. Yet possibly they give more too. I was told glowing accounts of the generosity of Shirumbay by people who had gone to him for help, and certainly I found his generosity somewhat overwhelming.

Reinforcing the male symbolism in tombura is the nominal male headship vested in the sanjak. Unlike in burei zār, in which all the leaders are usually women, in tombura zār the highest position can only be held by a man. He is referred to as the sanjak, a common term for a military officer in the nineteenth century. His presence is necessary for all formal tombura ceremonies, when he plays the tombura lute and leads the singing to summon the zār spirits. There is no parallel position in burei zār. The sanjak also has a male assistant, whose main duty is to prepare and slaughter the animals for formal zār ceremonies. In 2001, the son of the sanjak I met in the 1980s was taking over from his father, and the two men generally worked together.

Yet it is the umīya of tombura who is the visible leader in contemporary Sennar. She works closely with the sanjaks, who visit her home regularly to consult with her but who play no part in the routine running of the group. The elder sanjak is a quiet, withdrawn man, who says little and seems to have no contact with patients other than on the few formal occasions when he leads the music, but even on those occasions he is now assisted by his son, who is the major performer. As far as the women who regularly visit the house of tombura are concerned, Naeima is the real leader of zār.

Sanjak and the equipment of tombura: drums, lute, and incense

Naeima was born and raised in Sennar and comes from a close-knit family with a strong tradition of zār. When we did the interviews, her mother, a well-known midwife, lived nearby. When young, she had suffered from several kinds of zār: burei, tombura, and nugāra. The latter was a more violent form of tombura that came to Sennar directly from southern Sudan but has been lying dormant in the town for the past fifty years. By 1985, she had let them all go and simply attended Naeima's ceremonies without becoming possessed. Naeima's younger sister, a midwife in Sennar hospital, also had very strong zār but it was that of burei. Her possession was nowhere as powerful as that of her older sister but gave her a great deal of trouble. In 1985 Naeima hosted a nine-day burei ceremony in the house of tombura to try to help. A large crowd of both burei and tombura devotees gathered, and though the attending spirits were all burei and the ritual leadership was provided by the two leading umīyat of burei, it was Naeima who was a most gracious hostess and who helped ensure the event's success.

A third sister died some years ago and her son, an adult now working in the Gulf States, is treated by Naeima as her own child. In 1982 he was married from her house to a Ta'aisha woman (also a midwife but no relation to either the groom or to Zachara in chapter 4), and Naeima had a room especially built for them in her compound, next to the room for

Shirumbay. After he returned to his job overseas, the bride stayed with her mother-in-law, Naeima, until after the birth of their son. She later returned to her mother's home and was divorced by her husband.

Naeima has a large circle of friends and relatives who support her in zār. She also has two older women who work with her closely and are obviously learning more about the esoteric detail of tombura. Hajja Miriam helps prepare the house of Shirumbay for guests and administers the incense. She does not become possessed for curative sessions although she too possesses strong zār. Hajja Asha, on the other hand, sometimes summons Shirumbay and takes the Sunday coffee session. By 1985 so many people were attending some of these sessions that Naeima and Asha worked together, becoming possessed simultaneously and talking with patients. I was happy to meet Asha again in 2001 at the house of Naeima, but surprised that she had not undergone the ritual necessary to become an umīya herself. Apparently she is content to remain Naeima's assistant.

Naeima's working day varies. She does not have any houseservants, seeing to the shopping and cooking herself, though sharing the chores nowadays with her nieces, the children of her recently deceased sister. She still has an allotment on the outskirts of town and, though she does not work in it herself, visits it regularly to supervise the cultivation. In the past she had a stall outside her home from which she sold processed foods, but by 2001, her income from zār seems sufficient for a comfortable living. The days on which Shirumbay is expected are completely taken up with zār. She rests as much as possible, for she never knows what demands he might make. By the middle of the morning, her mind begins to drift off into a rather vague, other-worldly state and she gives the appearance of one dozing. Shirumbay never actively possesses her, however, until he is summoned by the appropriate incense. He often stays until well into the evening. On other days, Naeima might also be working with zār all day, as people come for incense and advice or she may have resident patients, particularly men who do not care to attend the more social occasions of the women. They sleep in the house of Shirumbay and receive intensive therapy from Naeima, much of it through possession.

Each box of zār brings some income to several individuals. In the case of this box of tombura, only Naeima regards it as her main livelihood. Women pay what they can for her to "open the box" for them. In burei, as with Bashir Fath al-Rahman, 25 cents sufficed in 1985, but I noticed that in tombura larger sums were offered. Occasionally women made gifts to the zār as large as £S50, a sum more than double the midwives' monthly allowance at that time.

Besides Naeima, the sanjak is paid for his ritual services and the woman who serves coffee is given a small sum by each participant. She is someone who leads a clean life and who herself has strong zār. Finally the musicians are given something for their performances, by the audience and usually more generously by possessing spirits (that is, by the women who are in a state of possession), who slap notes on their foreheads in expansive and typically manly gestures.

Despite such help, Naeima is very much alone in dealing with tombura. It is she who makes decisions and she is very much in charge of what is going on, both in her home and in her business dealings. She is certainly outwardly a much stronger and more worldly character than the sanjak. In 1985, I noted that she was relatively young for such a position of responsibility, though by the time I met her in 2001 she was in her early sixties, approximately the same age as the other contemporary leaders in zār in Sennar. By that time she had suffered arrest, imprisonment, and harassment for her activities, experiences that ultimately only strengthened her commitment to zār. After we conducted the interviews in 1985, she had also been very sick with heart problems. She was hospitalized in Khartoum, undergoing extensive surgery, and spent many months recuperating. Certainly zār never claims a monopoly on sickness. Basically it deals with cases that have not responded to any other form of treatment, and the most difficult cases are taken to tombura rather than burei zār. These it provides for with a long-term, even lifelong, form of therapy.

Naeima was a willing informant at first and a helpful and welcoming friend throughout my stays in Sudan. When she first invited me to talk with her about tombura, I suspected it was because she had heard of my interest in burei zār and did not want to be excluded. Later, however, she obviously had second thoughts. While still agreeing to contribute to this volume, she changed her mind about using her proper name and was never able to make any follow-up interviews to the original hour of taping. The same thing, interestingly, happened in 2001, when she insisted that I should use her proper name in the new edition of this book and wanted to give me full cooperation. Even though she promised to do so several times, some other problem always interfered. On several occasions when we started to talk she wafted off into what seemed like a state of possession, whispering gibberish into the tape recorder. Tombura spirits do not talk much, and it was obvious that discussion was at an end. My interpretation of these occasions was that she felt the zār themselves were preventing her from adding to what she had already told me, although it is also possible that she was simply tired of the pestering foreign anthropologist and found in this manner a polite form of withdrawal. Or maybe the zār actually were making a silent form of protest. Meanwhile Naeima continued to welcome me to the house of tombura and sent for me to join in their various activities. It was only at a verbal level that information was at an end.

The following autobiographical extract is therefore less complete than the other contributions in this volume and certainly contains as many questions as answers. I include it because zār activities are obviously important in the lives of poor urban women. Since so little is still known or recorded about tombura zār, this chapter is a significant document in itself. Hopefully, it will inspire further research. Elsewhere I hope to describe in detail the organization and history of burei zār in Sennar. It is hoped that in time our awareness of tombura zār will be as full, but meanwhile the following section helps to remove some misconceptions of this type of healing cult and serves as a basis for future understanding.

Naeima al-Umīya (1981)

My name is Naeima Muhammad, though most people know me as Naeima Silga, after my stepfather. For seven or eight years now I have been working as the umīya of tombura here in Sennar. I was held by the zār long before I took the 'idda, but I did not like the zār; I did not like it at all. When I was ill they told me it was zār but I completely refused to do the things they wanted. I went to hospitals, I went and consulted fugāra [holy men], but I would not bother with zār. Then finally the zār appeared in my head and I recovered. They brought the things of zār to me and I became well. Then they beat the zār and did all the things of zār, the slaughter, the *meiz*, and so on, and I was completely well.

Later the man who was the owner of this tombura zār made me the head of these 'idda of his. Before he died he said to me: "If I die I entrust these 'idda to you." So when he died, I became umīya. I started working in zār. Shirumbay comes into my head and I work. The girls come and beat, and if someone is sick with zār we go and beat in their house. In Rajab, we make the Rajabīya here. Rajab is our Big 'īd when all the people gather from Wad Medani, Khartoum, Kosti, everywhere. Many people come to our tombura, people from all over the Sudan. Only Fellata people do not come. They prefer to go to burei.

I was born in Sennar, but my father's family is from Wad Ramli in the north. We are Mahas people. My mother is Bornu. My father met her here and married her in Sennar. They gave birth to us, my brother, sisters, and me, and when my father died, we stayed here with our mother. We were married here, and my brother and his family share this courtyard with me and our mother. I also had three sisters, although one has died. Altogether we were five. We who are left are all here in Sennar. One sister is not yet married.

I went to school for two years but they took me out early and had me married. I was married very young, from the third year of the elementary school. My breasts had not even developed. He

Beating the drums of tombura (2001)

was from outside my family. We did not agree so he left and went away. We had no children. After he left I stayed here in my house and worked. I used to sew all the time, from morning until night: sheets, clothes, turbans. I bought this house from the proceeds of my sewing. Now with zār there is no way I can do it, but then you would find me sewing from dawn until dusk. I would make sheets by the set and sell them. God really favored me. Now that we are so busy with zār, all that is finished.

My mother has had zār for a long time, although recently she has let it go. Her mother, my grandmother, did not have zār. They say zār is usually inherited, but her mother did not have it.

I became ill after I was married. My husband said nothing. Of course, when I was ill it was my brother who was looking after me. He did not leave anything undone. They brought Yusuf, the sanjak of tombura here, to me and he gave me the incense of zār. After they had done that, the zār of tombura came and spoke. There was Sheikh 'Abd al-Kadir al-Jilani, there was Sayyid al-Bilal, Sheikh al-Badawi, Halanbasha, Jerahīyin, Osman Digna, the Khawajat, the Hawanīyin, the Nemanīyin, another one whom I forget. . . . There was the crocodile and the people of the river. There are a lot of people in zār. The river itself has many zār. Then there are the people of the desert, the zār of the tigers and so on.

The zār of tombura is different from that of burei. I have never taken the incense at the house of Rabha, umīya of burei. Tombura is not like burei. Burei plays for a bit and then the person who has it has to go off to the toilet; then he goes off again to drink water and to eat; then he comes back and plays again. Then he leaves again to go to the toilet and returns. In tombura if the zār comes into your head, it just stays there the whole time. If it stays for five minutes and then goes, it will not come back again that day.

Yusuf Ahmad al-Sayīd, the sanjak of our tombura, came from Turkey. He was white-skinned and very *miskīn*. He inherited tombura from his father, from his family, and he brought it with him from Istanbul to Sennar. He came here to join his brother, the son of his mother's brother, but he never went back again to Turkey. He stayed in Sennar and married here, although he never had any children of his own. He worked as a painter until he became very old and could not see. Before he died he put me in charge of his equipment ['idda]. I took them and became the umīya of these 'idda.

There has been tombura in Sennar for a long time, since before we were born, but each sanjak is different, each one is quite separate. Today in Sennar there is just one sanjak, Hassan, who lives at the village near the airport. His wife Sara is the other umīya of tombura in Sennar today. Hassan is the only one able to slaughter, but he has an assistant, 'Abdallah, who lives not far from us. They all learned tombura from Yusuf. Before Yusuf came there had been another sanjak, but his zār was different. He was a sanjak of the nugāra of the Fertīt. That is really nugāra; it is neither burei nor tombura proper. In nugāra people go outside in the street and beat the nugāra drum. They wear the *rahat*, a skirt like that of the southerners, and they have a kind of rattle, kushkosh. They beat their nugāra and they play with fire. Their play is very difficult. They have slave veins. If they want to get rid of somebody, they beat the vein and harm him. They might also hit him with the vein and kill him. That type of zār is very harsh.

It is a difficult thing to be entrusted with tombura. Only if someone is very patient and can endure a great deal can he be given it. Yusuf himself decided the place where he would leave the box. We, his girls, his daughters in tombura, were many, but he chose only me. After he died, I put on the belt of tombura. When the sanjak died I took off his belt. I held the special ceremony for girding the belt, with a sheep slaughtered for Sheikh 'Abd al-Kadir al-Jilani, another sheep for Sayyid Bilal, and a third sheep for Suliman al-Badawi. I had already sacrificed many times in zār when the sanjak had carried out the actual slaughter for me. During the lifetime of Sanjak Yusuf I had slaughtered many times, and now with these three I took the belt. Everyone came, including all the important people of zār. They did the girding and handed over the 'idda to me. I took them and started to work. Now I too have girls working with me. They enter Rajabīya with me. Hajja Miriam is one, and next Rajabīya she will slaughter her fifth sheep.

Tombura does not have the same zār as burei. There are many zār in tombura. There are Muslims and there are Christians; there are Derewish and there are Nubans. The people of the river and the people of the desert are all quite different. Yes, tombura has a lot of people [spirits]. If you took the tombura from six o'clock in the morning until six o'clock in the evening of the next day, you would not be able to get them all to be quiet. There are many, many people [spirits]. The important people of zār are quite different from Shirumbay. He is just their servant. They send messages to Shirumbay to serve them. They cure the ill, they deliver babies; anyone who wants something, they do it for him. But these important people do not like to talk. They just come and drink coffee and water and they do not do anything else.

Shirumbay is different. He comes and drinks plenty [of alcohol] before he leaves. While he is in my head, I do not know anything. You saw how he likes to drink. Does he not drink a lot? I do not drink, ever. When he leaves my head, I do not drink. He drinks, but when he finally leaves my head, I do not even have any taste of drink in my mouth. He just takes it and goes. Look at this supper [meiz] of his. When he makes a supper he has cognac, whisky, gin and wine, beer, sherry, every sort of alcoholic drink. They [the zār] come and fill the table. They all come wearing their official dress. They bring the *din-din* to one table, they bring *romi* cheese, bully beef, sardines, different types of cheeses, raisins and dried fruits, all sorts of canned fruits. There would be three full tables. They bring Pepsi and lemonades and the chairs are all lined up around the tables. Shirumbay wears his special dress and hat and goes out to his tables. They drink all the drinks. They are there from six in the morning until eight at night. When the zār is in my head and I have a supper for it, it does not leave me all night. It is nonstop. The music plays, he plays until the sun comes up and then it finishes. Then it finally leaves my head. I am very very tired. All my body, my arms, my legs, are aching. Look how long he has been in me. I get up and go and have a bath and then there is nothing. Shirumbay is very difficult, very strong, and very harsh. He is much more demanding than any zār in burei.

I have learned to do many things in tombura. When someone is sick, we make a ceremony—a Chair, half-Chair or *tasbīra*, or a one-day event. The tasbīra is the same as the half-Chair but they do not bring a sheep for it. They bring six pairs of pigeons, six pairs of chickens, and beans. They treat the woman as if it is a half-Chair. They do henna and the silk ritual for her, they beat the music for her for three days, and they keep her shut up for another three days. On the seventh day they take her to the Nile and make a karāma for her. This is the tasbīra. It is done with chickens, and they also make a dinner of sour milk [*ghadah bayad*] for her.

In the half-Chair ceremony they wake on the second morning and sacrifice a sheep. On the third day, they "open the head." Then they shut her in for three days. On the seventh day they also take her to the river.

The whole Chair takes seven days. For seven days the sick woman takes the music. Then for seven days she is shut in. There is incense fumigation and perfume for her. That is it. When she has completed fourteen days, she goes out. They make a karāma for her and take her to the river, and she is cleansed.

For all these ceremonies the sanjak must come. Only he can beat the drum. He comes and beats the music, and he takes the letters. When a message comes from the zār he takes it. We spend the seven days there, at the house of zār, then collect our things, and we come home.

This tin box of 'idda is always being used. Every day people come to fumigate themselves, all the zār. Three times a week, people who want to be cured come. Shirumbay does not come to my head a lot, just once a week on a Wednesday, when he usually stays all day. On Sundays he comes to another person, Hajja Asha, and she opens the box.

When they beat the tombura, many people go down. Did you see this instrument, the tombura, being played? When we come to play it, we tighten the strings and tune it and then we can play it. I learned to play the tombura after I learned all the customs of zār. We play it in Rajabīya, and I also play it outside when we go to beat the tombura for someone who is sick.

We are going to build a new room for Shirumbay here in my courtyard. The people who come to us bring money to Shirumbay. That is not for me. Shirumbay has his own safe, and we are building this with his own money. I want to build myself a room, and he also wants to have a room built for him separately. When it is done, we will hold a big meiz for him.

Extracts from Sennar Tombura Zār: Visits with Shirumbay (1981)

In the six years I lived in Sudan I often visited the Sennar house of tombura: in Rajabīya, for curing ceremonies, but most commonly for the regular coffee sessions held twice a week for Shirumbay. These continue to form the core of Naeima's work, and I attended several while I was back in Sennar in 2001. While it is in the ceremonial form that the full ritual of zār is enacted, for women it is in this routine work that the real nature of zār and their relationship to society is best expressed. Even within the routine work, there is some variety and ceremony, as the following account indicates. This is drawn from my field notes for October 1981, telling of three consecutive visits to the house of tombura.

Last week, Sharma told me that Allawīya Jineina was ill again. She has pains in her arms caused by zār and probably needs a new watch. (She actually said, "the zār needs a new watch.") I went to visit Allawīya to commiserate. She said she had been ill for a long time and needed to go back to the umīya's house for treatment. She plans to go on Sunday and because of my concern invited me to accompany her.

On Sunday I was at Allawīya's house soon after eleven and waited for her to finish getting ready, taking a little incense and perfume myself to make me feel a little more presentable. Allawīya herself was carefully perfumed and manicured and looked splendid in a fashionably orange tōb.

We arrived at the house of zār about noon and stayed a couple of hours, although I learned later that some women were there until after 7:00 P.M. We entered a large corner courtyard by the side door and found half a dozen women gathered under the shade of a lean-to [rakūba]. A plump, attractive lady with a brilliant smile came forward to welcome us very warmly. This was the umīya, Naeima. We greeted the other women, all of whom Allawīya obviously knew well, and one of whom was her mother's sister. Some were from Naeima's family. An older woman, with the same smile as Naeima, I knew immediately was her mother and recalled meeting her a few months ago at the house of the midwife. Another young woman, with a small child clinging to her, was the wife of Naeima's brother who shares in the compound. She was squatting in front of a stove, stirring a large pot of stew, occupied for most of the time with domestic chores.

Naeima invited us inside and led me into the room behind the lean-to, with mudbaked walls on three sides and on the fourth open to the rakūba with which it shared a thatched roof, supported by a crooked house post in the center of the room. The dirt floors were being covered by ordinary straw mats. Against each wall was a bed covered with a brightly colored sheet. We slipped off our shoes and were invited to make ourselves comfortable on the beds. This I did, though the other women, who followed us in to chat, sat straight on the floor. Iced lime juice was brought to us and an electric fan was set up close to my bed.

Hajja Miriam, a slight, older woman wearing a scarlet scarf casually around her head and shoulders, was getting things ready at the back of this room. She had laid the mats on the floor and was arranging the incense pots near the center of the room, close to the house post. There are usually two pots, one of which burns only coals, and these were already glowing. Hajja Miriam added fresh coals to the pot and, from a small can nearby, loosened some incensed wood, ready to add to the fire. She extracted incense powder from a round tobacco tin, touched another tin that held small pieces of paper as if mentally checking that it was in position, moved a cigarette box against the house post, and refolded a kerchief that lay on top of it. Finally she set a small wood and rope stool in the center and stood back to make sure all was ready.

One of the women came and joined me on the bed. She told me she was Khadiga, a childhood friend of Naeima from Khartoum. Divorced, with a teenage daughter in secondary school, she has an important sounding administrative job that involves a great deal of traveling, and she has recently spent six months in London and traveled in both North America and Europe. She became personally involved with Naeima's zār a couple of years ago when her father, who lives in Sennar, was very sick. She took him to a famous fakī near Sennar who burned incense, looked in the Book of Islam, and gave her an amulet for him, but it did no good. Then she came to talk to "Shirumbay in Naeima's head." Naeima put a paper in the tin, burnt incense, and performed some other things for him. Khadiga gave some money and promised to bring £S100 if her father recovered. He did so, quickly. Khadiga now hopes to have finished saving the £S100 for Shirumbay by next month. She does not attend zār in Khartoum but likes to come and stay with Naeima and visit her house of tombura whenever she can. She pointed out the tombura regalia, tucked under a table in the corner. Walking sticks and a stringed instrument poked out casually. These were part of the umīya's equipment, but they played no part in what followed. I gathered they are used only on formal occasions, but they are always present.

It was some time before anything happened. We sat around chatting, largely on mundane topics such as the ever-rising cost of sugar and where it was available; or plans for the Big 'īd which approaches next week and who will be traveling where. Khadiga continued to tell me her story and the others talked quietly together.

Today, Sunday, is the day that Hajja Asha becomes possessed or, as Khadiga put it, Shirumbay comes to the head of Hajja Asha. Hajja Miriam finally put more fresh coals in the incense pot, added to them some very heady incensed wood, and helped Asha to fumigate herself. Asha, clad in white, sat on the floor next to the house post, facing us. She leaned over the incense pot, breathing in deeply, and her eyes became large and glazed. The rest of the group fell quiet. Shirumbay has arrived, someone said. It had happened so quickly and imperceptibly that I was barely aware of what had happened.

Asha picked up the folded kerchief from the top of the cigarette box and tied this round her head, knotting it firmly on her forehead. In turn the women got up and went to shake hands with the spiritual visitor, clasping thumbs in the ritual way of zār. I felt strange regreeting someone with whom I had not long before already shaken hands, but the different handshake and the clumsy, almost inaudible way in which Hajja Asha now responded made me aware that some changes had occurred. Until this time, Naeima had been sitting quietly on the corner of the mats with the other women. After greeting the zār, she announced she was going to wash and change her clothes. She returned a little later wearing a short jallabīya in red and black material, with a black scarf over her shoulders, and resumed her place on the mats.

Several children were running in and out. One small girl, aged about 4, was told to come and greet Shirumbay. She refused and started to scream with fright. Her mother scolded her and even smacked her, but she continued to scream until another woman took her and soothed her. In a very real sense zār is inherited. From an early age, small children attend such gatherings and learn to accept the spirits. Allawīya later told me she has been coming with her mother and her aunt since she was a baby.

The situation was defused when coffee was served by Naeima's sister-in-law. On a tray held aloft she brought in twelve small cups and a large coffee pot, used only for Shirumbay. Shirumbay-in-Asha was served first and then the rest of us were handed a small cup of coffee, unsweetened as Shirumbay demands. When our cups were refilled we were offered sugar. After the coffee ran out, cigarettes were passed around to everyone and, rather self-consciously in many cases, they were lit and inhaled. A little later a jug of 'aragi was produced. Asha poured a little of this into a single shot glass and ordered each of us in turn to drink it (which was usually accomplished in a single slug). Allawīya protested that she couldn't. She was told it was medicine and was then able to toss it back. I refused as politely as I could, and a little while later Naeima returned with a cold can of Bavarian beer for me. She smiled and said that she knows what the Khawajat like.

Most of the women were middle-aged, but it was the two young women present who showed obvious signs of sickness. As soon as the coffee had been served, one went up to Hajja Miriam and crouched over the incense pot. Miriam held the incense for her to fumigate herself and sat her to face Hajja Asha. Not much was said, and Shirumbay-in-Asha obviously knew the problem. Khadiga explained that the woman has been suffering from severe stomach pains. She has been to several doctors in Khartoum, but they were unable to help. Finally she came to zār, and she is now much better. She left immediately after receiving the incense and her brief consultation.

Her glass of 'aragi seemed to give Allawīya the courage to go for treatment. Hajja Miriam helped her to incense, steaming her body, including her feet and head, under her tōb and letting the incense soak into her. She then moved over beside Asha and tried to ask her about her arm pains. Asha, however, just rolled her eyes and gave the appearance of joking about it. At this, the atmosphere suddenly tensed again. Allawīya's aunt, who is a regular visitor, broke in angrily that Allawīya was a young girl who is very miskīna. She has been in pain for a long time, but this is the first time she has asked Shirumbay for help. Everyone started muttering sorry, *maalish*, and Asha grew more serious. She told Allawīya to return on Tuesday to see the zār Habbashīya. Allawīya picked herself up, nodding curtly to me to indicate that it was time to go.

Naeima saw us out. On the way, she took us over to her own house at the other side of the courtyard. Here she has two rooms, with solid mud-baked walls and screened windows. After pausing on the enclosed veranda to drink iced water from the refrigerator, we were taken through to her bedroom, where Naeima proudly showed off her amply furnished room with its double bed, satin bedspread, and closets bulging with china and bedsheets. She showered me with oils and perfumes and pressed us to stay and eat lunch with her. Regretfully we declined. Allawīya had to get back to her baby.

We went back again the following Wednesday. Allawīya said she had not gone to see Habbashīya as she had no time to prepare herself with the appropriate smoke-bath and henna, but she was hoping Shirumbay-in-Naeima might help her today. When we arrived, we learned that Habbashīya had come to the head of Khadom the previous day and stayed for a long time. Many people had come and a lot of beer had been drunk.

It was not yet 1:00 P.M. but Shirumbay had already come to Naeima. She sat on the floor in Shirumbay's room, close to the central post, dressed in the same jallabīya she had worn on Sunday and with the red and black scarf knotted across her forehead. Presumably on Sunday she had been prepared for Shirumbay to possess her, either spontaneously or if someone specifically wanted to consult her Shirumbay. As we walked into the lean-to, I went and shook hands with her in the usual manner of zār. Naeima rolled her eyes in my direction and rasped to the others: "Who is this?" They explained that I had been on Sunday and come back today because I wanted to meet Shirumbay in Naeima's head. Naeima showed no sign of recognition. In soft tones she asked me if I like the Sudan but gave me no further attention. I presented her with a packet of cigarettes. She waved them round at the others, explaining where they had come from. They were not shared out, though only seven women, including Naeima, were present at this stage.

Soon another woman, also middle-aged, squatted next to Naeima. They shook hands and Naeima passed her the incense pot, which she held under her tōb, inhaled, and emerged stiff-faced and wide-eyed. This, I was told, was not Shirumbay but Bashir, a visitor from burei zār. The woman who was newly possessed was from our district of al-Gulʿa and had been

Shirumbay (2001)

directed by Bashir to go and see what it was like at the house of tombura. Solemnly everyone got up and went to welcome Bashir.

The ritual with unsweetened coffee followed. The woman possessed by Bashir grimaced at the taste and grumbled about it. Shirumbay tried to mollify him: "Don't be angry. You can have sugar in your second cup," and the audience, as we often seemed to be, tittered. The woman with Bashir seemed a little concerned about me. She and Naeima chatted and laughed quietly together but when she caught me watching them, she stared at me with such intensity that I felt uncomfortable.

A little later, Hajja Asha arrived. She greeted us all and apologized for being late. Quickly she knelt in front of the incense, inhaled deeply, and suddenly she too was possessed by Shirumbay. On this occasion, she was much more relaxed about it. She sat beside the woman from al-Gul'a, smiling a lot, and frequently asked me if I was alright: "*Qwaysa?*"

Conversation was desultory. More women drifted in, and by the time we left at 2:30 there were seventeen present. For much of this time, the three women possessed by two zār (two Shirumbays and one Bashir) sat side by side facing the rest of us, chatting and joking between themselves but in a way that suggested a performance. There was no doubt that they were the center of attention and their actions, impersonations, or simply behavior of foreign male spiritual beings seemed part of an act to entertain the rest of us. Little actually happened. One young woman came up to Naeima, knelt in front of her, and handed her a piece of paper with writing on. This Naeima scrutinized carefully and dramatically before putting it in a cigarette tin in front of her, next to a pile of money. The woman went back to her place without anything being said. Khadiga whispered that sometimes people prefer to write to Shirumbay about their problems rather than talk about them. He deals with what he can and passes on the rest to the other zār. The money is given to Shirumbay, rather than Naeima, and it will be used for his work, either to help patients or to purchase equipment and supplies for the house of Shirumbay.

For much of the time, the women talked among themselves, throwing out joking remarks or questions to the zār in a casual way that elicited almost monosyllabic answers. Suddenly the atmosphere changed when a young woman went forward and quietly asked Shirumbay a question. This provoked a long monologue in reply from Shirumbay-in-Naeima, who in broken Arabic complained that the woman had not followed the advice she had been given. Khadiga explained that the woman was a nurse at the hospital and had been ill for a long time. When she had consulted Shirumbay earlier, she had been advised to take regular smoke-baths, use lots of perfume and henna, and then return to Shirumbay to say how she was. She had not come back until now, when she complained that the treatment had been no good. The other women kept interjecting *"Inti dastūrat,"* "You are possessed." It did not seem to be directed at her specifically. Maybe it was simply to defuse the tension.

Shortly afterwards, Hajja Miriam came and whispered in Naeima's ear and Naeima/Shirumbay, followed by Asha/Shirumbay and half the women present, got to her feet and left the room. The woman possessed by Bashir remained behind and indeed left soon afterwards. She seemed simply to have been making a rather difficult social call. Naeima, still possessed, staggered out, awkwardly crossing the threshold backwards as she entered the small room next door. Inside it was dark and bare, containing no window or lighting other than that from the doorway and no furnishings other than the mat laid on the dirt floor. This is Shirumbay's consulting room. On this day Shirumbay stayed here with Naeima and Hajja Asha until well after sunset, dealing with patients and taking messages for other zār. Sitting cross-legged on the floor, the women faced each other across the incense pot and the assorted cigarette boxes, while Hajja Miriam guarded the entrance. Patients were admitted one by one, sitting to the right side of Shirumbay while they outlined their problems. The agitated nurse was summoned in first but left promptly, as soon as she had talked with Shirumbay. Most of the women sat outside in the courtyard on beds, waiting their turn to go in and talk with Shirumbay. Some took in letters; these Shirumbay scrutinized and put in the tin, to forward to the appropriate spiritual quarters. Some problems were dealt with immediately. Asha and Naeima sat with their heads forward, their faces serious as together their guest spirit advised those who came to consult them.

Allawīya was one of the first to go for help. She was fumigated again and had her chance to speak. The women I sat with knew that her problem was not just in her arm. She had been married four months ago to a man from western Sudan, a stranger to Sennar, and it was not a happy relationship. Their baby had been born before the marriage, an extraordinary state of affairs in al-Gul'a, no less than in Sennar society generally. Allawīya was told to return again to the house of Shirumbay in a week's time when we were both invited to lunch, a karāma to mark the big 'īd that begins tomorrow.

We stayed chatting with the other women for a while, but Allawīya was restless to leave. She and her husband share a house with another family, the mother of whom was looking after Allawīya's young daughter. I knew she did not expect us to return early, but Allawīya now recalled all the preparations she still had to make before the 'īd tomorrow, and reluctantly I too took my leave.

On our third visit we were invited for noon but it was almost one when we arrived, since Allawīya's cosmetic procedures took even longer than usual. Nothing was happening when we arrived, however, because a neighbor of Naeima's had just died and Naeima had taken lunch to the bereaved family. With a few other women we sat round until almost 2:00 P.M., chatting lightheartedly, about the 'īd, their families, and who had traveled where over the holiday. One woman roasted the coffee beans ready for the karāma and another ground them in the mortar. Guests were arriving steadily, several of them carrying contributions to the karāma lunch.

Naeima returned. Quickly she changed into a short plain jallabīya with a white tōb draped across her shoulders. Without more ado, she sat cross-legged in her usual position on the floor of Shirumbay's reception room. The ritual built up as Hajja Miriam came with the little stool and placed it nearby. She brought a couple more burning coals and deftly placed those in one of the incense pots, adding a pinch of incense powder on top.

The mats in the enclosure quickly filled up. Naeima sniffed loudly, drew her tōb over her head so she was completely covered, and pulled the incense pot under her tōb. At first she just held it there, letting the smoke fill the space under her wrap and gently seep through the soft material. Maybe it was not strong enough; her hand stretched out and took another pinch of incense from the tin. As that burned, she sighed again and began to move the pot up against her body, holding it against her chest, her arms, close to her face, and inhaling deeply. While it was still under her tōb she laid the pot on the ground again and began to shudder a little, to toss her head quickly. Finally she sat upright and pushed her tōb off her shoulders. There was a certain expectation in the air, but certainly no sense of reverence at the occasion. Some women watched her while others continued to chat, to greet more newcomers, or to wander around. Naeima's tōb fell to her shoulders and her head began to roll languidly. Her eyes, stretched wide open, also began to roll. Her head tilted slowly from side to side and viewed the women . . . and then very slowly she closed and reopened her eyes, wide, and tilted her head to the other side to look at the rest of the group. Her mouth pouted slightly, her expression was solemn. Hajja Miriam leaned forward and handed her the kerchief, a red and white striped one, laid ready on top of the cigarette box. This she tied slowly and carefully round her head, knotting it firmly in front of her forehead. "Dastūra," someone breathed. "She is possessed. Shirumbay has come."

Hajja Miriam moved first. She got off her stool, moved around in front of the incense pot, knelt on the ground in front of Naeima, and touched the ground in front of her with her forehead. She stayed like this for a minute or so, bottom in the air, a position of true obeisance. Still kneeling, she leaned forward and kissed each of Naeima's shoulders once and the top of the head, three times. She moved back to her usual position on the low stool and let others come forward.

"Come," said Allawīya, usually not very communicative at the house of zār. "Get up and greet Shirumbay." I waited a while as everyone pushed forward to salute the new guest. Some bent over and put hands on Naeima's shoulders and kissed the top of her head; others simply shook hands vigorously in the special zār grasp. No one else knelt. Usually Shirumbay just grunted in reply to the women's greetings. Sometimes, as when a woman who had been absent a long time came forward, he articulated throatily: "Ooh, aaah." Eyes widened, and a beam spread over Naeima's altered face. This happened when an attractive woman, about 30 years of age, came up to greet her: Khaltūm, a friend of Allawīya's family from Kosti who had not been to tombura for several months. I learned later that she has relatives in Sennar and frequently comes to visit them. She told me they do have tombura and Shirumbay in Kosti but not like in Sennar.

When I finally went up to shake hands, Naeima responded very heartily, staggering to her feet and again shouting, "Ooh, aaaah," with apparent delight. I had once more taken a present of some cigarettes for Shirumbay and when these were presented to him, he waved them enthusiastically. One of the women called out: "Ah, Shirumbay, when you are getting presents from abroad, it is the end for us Sudanese women. What can we do?" Everyone laughed and Shirumbay-in-Naeima beamed.

For a while, the women just talked quietly among themselves. Khaltūm from Kosti came and sat down next to Naeima and, in a sociable sort of way, began talking quietly with Shirumbay. Meanwhile, an elegant, assured young woman came and sat down calmly on the mats. From a fashionably slim handbag, she pulled a packet of cigarettes and lit one, looking relaxed and thoughtful. Other women greeted her shyly. Many of them look uncomfortable with cigarettes and certainly lack her air of poise.

Two women came in carrying coffee. One I had seen several times at the house of tombura, and it is she who hosts the spirit Habbashīya on Tuesdays. The other was her mother, a close friend of Naeima and her associate in tombura. They laid the tray, the large coffee pot, and a dozen small cups in front of Naeima. They do not usually serve the coffee but this karāma was being offered, at least partly, by them to celebrate the younger woman's recovery from a long illness. The fact that the Big 'īd has just finished makes it an auspicious time to hold it.

Outside sat a small boy, about eight years old and wearing a white jallabīya. Broad-featured and black-skinned, he was improbably nick-named Doctor. "How is Doctor?" someone laughed. His mother retorted, "He wants to come and greet Shirumbay. His father says it is a long time since he saw Shirumbay." With that the child was dragged reluctantly, crying, towards Shirumbay. He hung back, apparently in great fright, but was forced up to Naeima who very gently took his hand and spoke to him, quietly and brokenly, with many nods of the head but eyes less staring than before. He calmed down and watched her, fascinated, as gradually she began to joke, to roll her upper body about a little in comic fashion. The onlookers began to laugh with her. Doctor did not stay long. Is this a future sanjak, I wonder?

We drank coffee, first cup unsweetened and accompanied by the usual protests, the second full of sugar. A woman who was later possessed by Bashir started shouting at us, at Allawīya and me, that we must pay our share. Foolishly I had thought that we were guests and therefore need not contribute. Apologetically I now laid down 25 cents on the tray as I had seen the other women do and the lady of the coffee murmured, "thank you." Allawīya obviously hoped that was sufficient for her too, but the women kept telling her that she should pay as well. Reluctantly she untied 10 cents from the corner of her tōb and handed that over.

All this time, more women were coming in. Today is a special day, said Khadiga. Everybody is invited to come to see Shirumbay. At the most crowded point, more than forty people were present, with women coming and going all afternoon. There was great variety, of ages, of skin colors, and of facial features. Several were elderly, but even more were young women. Some were dark-skinned, large-featured women like

Allawīya and her relatives from the Malakīya district of town. There were even more women with triple scars on each cheek, Sha'igīya markings, that I realize are also commonly found on people formerly associated with the army. No men were present, though usually on more formal occasions one or two are there, either patients or friends of the house of tombura.

As we sat drinking coffee, large sums of money were being handed over to Shirumbay. A young woman laid down £S50. Her mother later told me that she had been sick for over two years and had consulted doctors and fakīs all over the place. No one had been able to help her until Naeima had "opened the box" for her. She improved immediately and is now well. Several other women handed over one or two £S10 notes; these Naeima laid carelessly down in front of her. No one was about to steal from the zār. Hajja Miriam later removed the money.

A procession of women came and knelt before Naeima, as we sat chatting. A middle-aged woman, dark-skinned, dominant-looking, with smudged facial scars, came up and greeted Shirumbay so effusively that she spilled the latter's coffee. Undeterred, she knelt in the brown liquid and stained her tōb. She bowed in front of Shirumbay so that her head touched the ground, then slowly raised herself up, kissed Naeima's shoulders, and touched the top of her head. As she leaned back on her heels, she ritually shook hands with Shirumbay. Later I heard her telling the other women how ill she had been but how much better she felt after seeing Shirumbay.

She was followed by a rather sad-faced woman, with quiet manner and a brown tōb. "Really, Shirumbay, I am tired, so tired," her voice trailed away as she outlined her complaints: headaches, heart palpitations, pains in arms and legs, nausea, lack of appetite. "So tired, Shirumbay, so tired," she finished. Shirumbay raised his eyes to the ceiling and rolled them. He made a sort of gesture of dismissal and just disregarded the woman, who sat there quietly for several minutes before she realized that she was being ignored. A few minutes later she moved back to her place, obviously uncomfortable about her treatment and wondering what she had done wrong. She should have waited until later to talk with Shirumbay, I was told. On occasions such as this, Shirumbay is just being sociable. Treatments are made later, in private.

Shortly after the coffee was removed, Shirumbay/Naeima staggered to his feet. As he had earlier when he was greeting his long absent friend, he moved heavily, arms out-thrown as though he was extremely obese, his movements clumsy. In this way he waded out. Followed by half the women present, he paused at the doorway, turning and passing through it backwards, to the small room next door.

This happened at about 2:30 P.M. We left just before sunset, and during this entire time, Shirumbay-in-Naeima saw a steady stream of patients, without a break. She worked alone today, Hajja Miriam helping only with incense fumigation. This, I was told, was because Naeima's possession by Shirumbay is extremely powerful and, at a special karāma, everyone wants to bring their problems to Shirumbay-in-Naeima. She had nothing to eat, though I suspect she drank alcohol and smoked cigarettes. It was apparent that she would be there for at least a couple more hours. I was told that, a few weeks earlier, Shirumbay-in-Naeima had been busy with patients for thirteen hours without a break.

Soon after Naeima moved to her consulting room, Khadiga beckoned Allawīya and me to lunch on the veranda outside Naeima's room. We joined Naeima's friends from Khartoum and Kosti, together with the wife of a local sheikh, whose name keeps recurring in zār because of the strong spiritual powers this family has passed on in Sennar. The latter talked solemnly, unhappily, and quietly all through lunch, apparently about family problems. It is said in town that her husband has been neglecting his zār and that is why several of their children have severe problems, mental and social. She was obviously a very unhappy woman. There seemed to be a feeling, however, that her problems were not of this world. The rest of us sat in silence, unsure of what to contribute, but she seemed not to notice our unease. Meanwhile, the food was delicious: hot spicy pumpkin stew, stuffed peppers, barbecued meat, and salad, which we mopped up with bread. We washed it down with cold water from Naeima's fridge and then with hot sweet tea.

Afterwards we rejoined the women in the lean-to. By now Hajja Asha was possessed by Shirumbay and another woman by Bashir. They sat together, facing out of the enclosure, chatting and providing entertainment while Naeima continued to see patients next door. A bucket of ice-cold beers awaited us, my treat from Shirumbay, I was told by Hajja Miriam. I was given a can for myself while the coffee lady poured small tea glasses of beer for the women, which were swigged back in a single gulp and often followed by a grimace, like a dose of unpleasant medicine that the patient is sure will do her good. There were also several bottles of 'aragi, contributed by the women present, which were shared out by Shirumbay in the same way, using just one small glass and directing the intake in a very specific way.

Allawīya sat with her aunts for most of the time. She did go to talk to Shirumbay-in-Asha about a pain she has in her upper abdomen that has worried her for some time. Shirumbay asked her if she was pregnant. She said no, because her baby is only six months old and is still being breast-fed. She was directed to talk directly to Naeima's Shirumbay, but she did not do so today.

Before I left, I went and sat with Shirumbay-in-Naeima for a while and chatted to him rather platitudinously. I knew that he expected me to consult with him about something and he kept prodding me gently: "Qwaysa?" "Are you well? Is everything all right?" I rambled on about how we are moving to Nyala next week and how sorry I would be not to come and see them again for a while. Maybe this was what they expected me to ask about? I had been talking to my neighbor Suad a couple of days ago, and she asked me why I never asked the zār for anything. Such as what? I had asked. "Such as, for example," she had replied, "that you do not want to move to Nyala, you want to stay here in Sennar with us. The zār can certainly arrange that." They probably could. I realize I am just not ready to try them.

As I got up to leave, Shirumbay (people are definite it is not Naeima talking) insisted I take four cans of beer for the Khawāja, my husband, and then thrust £S10 in my hand: a present for me. I protested loudly, but Naeima carelessly dropped all the other notes through her fingers. "Look at how much I have," he/she said. It was at least £S100.

We had to leave at sunset because Allawīya grew anxious about her baby. Many women had left; those still at the house of Shirumbay were washing and preparing to say their prayers or relaxing on beds around the courtyard. Apart from the fact that Shirumbay-in-Naeima was still busy, one got the feeling that the karāma, whatever it had been to celebrate, was over.

Allawīya was not surprised by Shirumbay's generosity towards me. She said that he had been helping her regularly since before her baby was born. When she first went to him, before her marriage, he gave her three dresses, £S5 for the tailor, and some slippers [shib-shib]. He is strong, she said, he is rich, and he offers real help to those who go to him.

Naeima, Umīya of Tombura (2001)

When I returned to Sennar in 2000 for just two weeks, none of my old friends knew what had happened to Naeima or Allawīya Jineina. Indeed many of them were at pains to explain to me that they no longer went to zār, either burei or tombura, as they had learned it was contrary to the tenets of Islam as it is now promoted in Sudan. In 2001 I learned the situation was not quite so simple. While some of the women I knew in 1985 have left zār as they have grown older, there are still many others who continue to participate in zār activities. Allawīya had indeed left town—my neighbors told me that she had been divorced and now lives in Khartoum. Naeima, on the other hand, is still living in the same house. I arrived in Sennar shortly before the beginning of the month of Rajab, when thanksgiving ceremonies are held for the zār, and at the first ritual I

attended I met several of her followers who were happy to take me to her.
Over the next few months I was able to visit her several times, to attend
her coffee sessions for Shirumbay as well as an elaborate thanksgiving
ceremony in the village of Kabbosh at which she played a leading role. At
first glance, Naeima also appears to have prospered in the decade or so
since I last saw her. Shirumbay's room was much the same—but is now
used only as a guest room, since Naeima finds it too small and too hot to
work in. In the past few years new rooms have been built for the zār, dom-
inating the compound and overshadowing all the older rooms. Shirumbay's work is now carried on in a large enclosed veranda, which easily
holds fifty people—with room for more on important occasions. The
veranda leads to two other new rooms, where Shirumbay meets with
patients, with plenty of space to store all his provisions and equipment.

However, the intervening years have not been altogether kind to either
Naeima or the zār. In 1993, after several years of increasing pressures from
local and state government to stop zār ceremonies and to close her house,
the police burst in on a tombura healing ritual. Naeima described how:

One day I went to beat zār for another woman, in her home.
The men were sacrificing a sheep outside, while the women were
inside the house ready to start beating the drums. Suddenly police
rushed in. They seized all the men and women, as well as our
equipment, and forced us into their car. One policeman who did
this had a certain problem with women who beat the zār. We were
all taken to prison, to await the court's judgment. They said that
the men are homosexual and asked me who are the other umī-
yas? I said I am the only umīya, I don't know any others. The
women were all lashed 25 times each, then allowed to leave. The
two men and I were kept in prison for a month. They would allow
me to go, but I refused to leave the men. After two days the same
policeman was caught with a woman in a compromising situation,
and they were put in prison with us. When I heard about it, I
insulted him greatly, and said, "You were arrested for a moral
crime but we were not." When his colleagues brought him food, I
insulted them too and after that he had no visitors.

My friends came from all over Sudan: Wad Medani, Sinja,
Khartoum, and Sennar, bringing food, and some gave me money
and cigarettes. Every day my food was enough for everyone in the
prison, even the police. Moreover I always gave the police
cigarettes and money. The arrested officer also ate my food. He
and the girl wept and asked my pardon. I became a friend to
everyone in prison.

We spent a month there. On the last night the women in the
prison wanted to say good-bye. They got permission from the
prison authorities, and each woman put in her share to make a
tea party for me, with singing and dancing. The police ordered

them to lower their voices, asking, "What will people say about us? We represent the law and are supposed to prevent such things." In the morning we were taken home in their cars. When we reached home we found that people had killed a sheep to celebrate our safe return and prepared breakfast. I told them to take it to the police at the prison. Since then there has never been a day when the police came to my house, never.

Now when I want to beat zār, I send a man to bring a permit. One day someone knocked on the door, and I went and found the police with my 'idda, the basket and twenty *tarbush* [hats for the Egyptian spirits]. One asked me, "Are these yours?" I said, "Yes, haven't you broken them?" They said, "We have broken all the 'idda except yours," and gave them to me. My 'idda had frightened them very much because snakes kept appearing in them, so they want to get rid of them.

In the years since we last met, Naeima has lost her beloved mother and, shortly before I arrived, her younger sister, so I found her in mourning. The rest of her family, however, remains close by. She no longer shares her compound with them but has been able to buy neighboring houses for her brother, her last surviving sister Awadia, and their families, making sure that the properties are registered in their names so that if anything happens to her they will be secure.

Her compound is now shared only with the people of zār. Her work remains the same: three times a week people come to her and she gives them incense. Shirumbay comes to her and she opens the box, incenses people, and then examines them to see what is wrong. If it is the illness of tombura, she sees that:

They will not recover if they go to the hospital or see any number of doctors—and vice versa. Tombura cannot heal all illnesses, only those caused by the zār themselves.

Tombura treatment differs from that of burei. Ours is the best. If a person is ill and given the treatment in tombura, he will instantly be cured and immediately stand on his own two legs. If he has zār, our treatment will make him completely well. Then he must beat the zār.

Naeima agreed that now she has more work than ever in zār. Soon after Ramadān in 2001 she was planning for two full ceremonies. The first was for her old friend Khadiga, whose commitment to zār has strengthened, despite the death of her father many years ago.

After Ramadān, I will make a Chair ceremony for Khadiga for nine days. She will sacrifice one sheep, a white one, for Sheikh 'Abd al-Kadir al-Jilani, another two for the Pashawat. She will also hold two suppers [*sofras*], one for Bitt al-Habash and another for the Pashawat. Then they make the procession with the sheep before it is killed. This will take nine days, after which we take her out to the Nile, cleansing her and giving the Nile its due. After that she will go to her work.

We talked at length about the nature of tombura zār:

Zār is not *djinn*, it is rīh, wind. It lives between the ground and the sky. It is not above nor beneath. It will not go down except in heads. Some are found in deserts, some in seas. Also there are *al-Suakniya, al-Nuba, al-Banda* . . . Sometimes you find them in the shape of snakes, and this can startle you. Sometimes Shirumbay is present . . . in many places [at the same time]: Khartoum (though not in Halfaya), Kober, Medani. In Kosti you find the great sanjak of tombura called Abbas and there too you will find Shirumbay.

Shirumbay may be a lowly spirit, but Naeima emphasized that he has powerful attributes:

Once, on the fifteenth day of Ramadān, while Shirumbay was present, a snake came out of a hole to the place of incense, with its tongue out. Everyone was frightened and crouched up on the beds, but the snake also climbed up, onto the back of the woman Daro. Then Shirumbay said, "Leave her alone!" Daro also cried, "Leave me." Slowly the snake got down and went over to smell the incense. Then it went into its hole but came back out carrying sandalwood in his mouth, throwing this near us. It didn't bite anyone—all the people were astonished. Another day it appeared near the water pipe. Aziza's children saw it and ran crying for help, calling for me. I held the whip and told them to have nothing to do with it. They went to their mother and told her, "We saw the snake of aunt Naeima. We will not go there because we are afraid it will bite us."

A few years ago, Naeima was in the unusual position of being the only full umīya of zār in Sennar, when the last leader in burei died very suddenly. She agreed to let one of the apprentice umīya work with her, and then later presided over a girding ceremony to initiate the woman as an umīya in burei. Unfortunately this has had unexpected consequences. The new umīya is constantly troubled by tombura as well as burei spirits, which are interfering with the organization of her work. The distinctions so carefully underscored between the different zār groups in Sennar may well be breaking down. However at this stage it is too early to tell.

Not least because of the difficulties I encountered in interviewing Naeima, or even in completing a conversation with her, I was concerned that she might have reservations about helping me again. I therefore decided I should ask Shirumbay directly about this. One Wednesday in October, I went to Naeima's house with three friends, women who had expressed interest in meeting Shirumbay and learning more about zār.

Naeima had told me that she now has Shirumbay every Sunday and Wednesday from noon to 4:00 P.M. We arrived shortly after 1:00 P.M. and found four other women in the verandah chatting with Naeima, still herself. She welcomed us warmly, ushering us into Shirumbay's old room, where she brought us cold water to drink, and sugar mints. We chatted briefly and Naeima left us to rest. Some time later, when Shirumbay had already come, one of the women called us back into the verandah.

There we found Naeima squatting in the corner on a mattress, wearing only her white house-dress, with a rakish brown hat on her head. From her body language, Shirumbay was clearly in her head, carelessly throwing round cigarettes from packets of cigarettes lying nearby. As I went up to shake hands with Shirumbay, he made a big fuss of me, muttering "It's been too long," and asking, "When did you come?" Also he asked me if I remembered his room. A woman sitting nearby marveled that I understood Shirumbay's language. Next to Shirumbay, sat Hajja Asha, who tearfully remembered me and embraced me tightly. They sat surrounded by cigarette boxes and incense pots and another intriguing piece of equipment: an old toilet roll holder, a porcelain cup with the wooden roll holder still attached, clearly all meant to be attached to a wall. The women were using this as a cigarette dish—splashing the ash from their cigarettes into it. What sort of statement can this be? Perhaps a symbol of the Western, khawaja nature of Shirumbay? I am not sure.

Another woman was already assembling the unsweetened coffee and passed me a small cup. More than a dozen women had assembled. Shirumbay chatted casually with them, and then seemed to distance himself. A woman was trying to tell him about her illness, how she had been sick for a long time with fevers and pains, but he began to lose attention. My three companions became restless, anxious to talk with Shirumbay but unable to understand what was happening. One stood up, impatiently, and looked as if she was about to leave. This seemed to send a clear signal to the spirits. Shirumbay-in-Naeima also rose, awkwardly, and made his way towards the back rooms, followed by my three friends. The other women urged me to follow, clearly expecting me to have come on a mission. In the back room, Shirumbay sat in the middle of the floor and, placing the incense pot and the tin for letters firmly in front of him, looked at us expectantly. My impatient friend squatted in front of him and squeezed some money between the tins. Then she began to talk about her problems. She was married, her husband was working overseas and had not come back for the last three years. He had not sent for her and she was afraid he had taken another wife. Also her children were sick all the time. Shirumbay took a large pinch of incense, added it to the pot, and inhaled the large clouds of smoke that bellowed forth, apparently thinking deeply. Then he told her that someone had tied *(ugda)* her husband so he was unable to come. She should burn some special incense from Shirumbay, and return in a week for further consultation. Thanking him, she got up slowly and moved to one of the beds lining the room.

I was next. I took out £S5,000 pounds ($2)—a not inconsiderable sum, but I was mindful of the outstanding obligations I had in this house— and sat in the vacated space. I told Shirumbay that I had a big problem. After I met him many years ago, I had written a book about Naeima and now I wanted to reissue it, to include information on what had happened since that time. However, I had heard that Naeima had trouble with the government and had been put in prison and beaten. I did not want to bring problems to her. What should I do? Shirumbay beamed broadly and added a little incense, not too much, to the pot on my behalf. This was clearly not an issue for him. "No problem," said Shirumbay, "write your book, take your pictures, do whatever you like. There will be no difficulties for Naeima."

The next person to get up was not a local woman, but a friend visiting from another town. She spoke quietly with Shirumbay and I learned later she was asking about her marriage prospects. Shirumbay put a big pinch of incense on the pot, taking his time. The problem, he said, was that there was talk. Did she not know about this? "What talk?" she asked in surprise. People are talking about her, and that is causing the problem. What are they saying? Just talk, Shirumbay said vaguely. I could not help but recall hearing rumors that the woman is already married, perhaps divorced, and moreover has three children. Who is doing this? she demanded. Silence followed. "Is there a husband for me?" she then asked again. "Yes, yes, there will be, eventually," Shirumbay replied. She was also told to return.

And finally the last of our group sat down and said she wanted to know if she would get a proper job. She still does not have one, however hard she tries. Is there one for her? Clearly Shirumbay did not understand this, since she had come with me. Was she not working at the moment, with the foreigner, the khawajīya? "Maybe, but she needed a permanent job," she replied vaguely. Shirumbay told her to return and bring a paper and said that he would get a job for her.

And that was it. None of my friends had any intention of staying longer in the house of Shirumbay. I had not realized their visit was quite so focused. They all clearly had a reason for wanting to come, well beyond simply seeing what Shirumbay was like. While we were still seated on the ground, two more women came in to greet Shirumbay and the second looked at us very pointedly, waiting for us to leave. She already had some money out to give Shirumbay and, as I left, I heard her say, "So you are seeing foreigners now, eh, Shirumbay?" If the others had waited, I would have stayed to see what was going to happen and chat with the people in the verandah, but the other three marched resolutely out into the street, without a backward glance or farewell to anyone.

One of them later asked me what I would do if Shirumbay had told me I was not to write the book. I said that I would take his words seriously and would not add anything to the earlier chapter on Sitt al-tombura. I would take it as an indication that I should not try to get Naeima to give me more information. She said triumphantly—then you believe in Shirumbay? But surely is not that the point of this chapter?

AL-SUDANIYIN
SUDANESE WOMEN AND THEIR WORLD

Sennar, 2001

We arrived back in Sennar on September 9, 2001, on sabbatical leave from our universities in Indiana—Simon from Purdue, me from Butler University in Indianapolis. Simon planned to spend four months in the Central Veterinary Research Administration in Soba, Khartoum, revising a diagnostic manual he had completed almost twenty years earlier, but he accompanied me to Sennar to greet old friends and help me settle in. I was to stay in Sennar, starting new research at Sennar University Medical School but living with Halima and her family in al-Gul'a.

Two days later, in the late afternoon, we were all gathered in the courtyard of Halima's daughter, Miriam. We had just finished lunch and coffee was being prepared. Miriam's daughter was washing clothes, and several of the neighbors had come to welcome us, including Zachara the midwife who was in the middle of a wonderful story. Then the telephone rang. Miriam's niece, who lives a few blocks away, was calling to tell us to turn on the television. "Tell Susan there is urgent news from her country," she said, ominously.

Both channels of Sudan television had switched over to al-Jazira programming shortly after the news broke of the first attack on the World Trade Center. Certainly as people in the eastern United States were tuning in to the news at 9:30 A.M., many people in Sudan already knew that something terrible was happening in *Amreeka*. Simon and I hunched over Miriam's little black and white television, struggling to make sense of the blurred images from New York; the bewildered commentary from Arab journalists in the Gulf, Europe, and North America; the awful reality of more destruction; spreading panic; and for us, a helplessness at not knowing what this was all about or, more selfishly, how it would affect us and our friends in Sennar. The others joined us around the television, and an energetic conversation developed as more people came in and tried to add what they knew to the breaking story. It all seemed unreal, as though we were watching a horrible film. I remember thinking that we had suddenly wandered onto the wrong set . . . we were in the wrong place. Our worlds had collided in an incomprehensible way.

As dusk fell, we walked over to our old home in the veterinary compound where we knew one of Simon's colleagues had a satellite dish, hopeful that perhaps if we watched CNN we might be able to make sense of what was happening. Friends we passed on the way were quick to offer condolences to us. The news was spreading rapidly about the disaster, and to those we knew in Sennar, it was happening to our family, and in that way was of immediate import to them as well.

The men were at prayer together in front of the veterinary laboratory, but one of the women there told us, in grieving tones for the seriousness of our tragedy, that their satellite dish was down. Prayers over, the men suggested we go to a neighbor's house where we could watch CNN and BBC and assured us we could stay as long as we needed to follow the breaking news. With our friends accompanying us for support, it was a fairly large group who was welcomed into a house of (to us) total strangers. Our new hosts served us refreshments and treated us with kindness, before leaving us alone to try to understand the English account of what was happening.

Still in shock, we watched President Bush make a brief statement and heard Orrin Hatch blaming the catastrophe on Islamic *jihad,* holy war. This was really a global catastrophe being played out on a most unlikely local level as we sat in a strange bedroom in Sennar, with a group of friends and children, glued to the television. Our companions quickly rejected any suggestions that this was the work of Arab terrorists, or some sort of holy war. "How could we do anything like this?" wondered Abdullah. "We, like the Palestinians, have only stones [for weapons]." The general feeling was that only the United States possessed the technology, the knowledge, the ability to pull off something as devastating as what we were witnessing. The Oklahoma bombing was mentioned as a precedent. Suggestions that Osama bin Laden was involved were equally rejected. People talked about how he had come to the Sudan some years earlier, seen what a poor country it was, and invested in its roads and buses. However, he had not stayed long; they scoffed at the suggestion that he had been building up a network of terrorists or that he had been able to use Sudan as a training ground for terrorism.

Our discussion was interrupted by a message that Katie was trying to reach us by telephone, and she had arranged to call us back at the veterinary laboratory in ten minutes. Offering thanks to our gracious hosts, we all hurried back for the call. Katie sounded as dazed and horrified as we were. She did not have television, and in some ways we knew more about events than she did; but she was more concerned to know that we were all right. We also all have close friends in New York City, and we worried about how they were faring. She promised to call her brothers and reassure them. Meanwhile our conversation was carefully observed by our friends, who were clearly concerned for our well-being and eager for news that our family was safe.

As we hung up, we were once more back in the world of Sennar, far away from the events in the States, which still seemed unreal. Our friends beckoned us to join them outside for tea. The women had set up a circle of chairs and quietly served us tea and biscuits and beans, joining in the conversation about the tragedy, clearly made immediate for them all by our presence, by Katie's phone call, by *our* view of what had happened. Abdullah shook his head sadly as we left. "It is we, the poor, who once again will have to pay for this," he said. Several times they had recalled, very clearly, the attack on al-Shifa Pharmaceutical plant in 1998, after the U.S. embassies in east Africa had been bombed. Four people had died then.

Back at Miriam's house the television was still on, still broadcasting events from the United States, the drama of which was only matched for the women by Katie's earlier phone call and evident anxiety. Despite the language difficulties, they wanted me to know that they had told her how upset everybody was by the tragedy and shared their condolences with her.

We both slept badly. The following day Simon had to return to Khartoum and I watched him go with trepidation, worried about what more could happen, and also mindful that he would be working at a laboratory that was a potential target of U.S. retaliation. We spoke with our sons before he left and learned that the evidence pointed clearly to Arabic-speaking perpetrators. Like our local friends, we feared a swift response.

However, despite this threat, in Sennar I met only kindness and concern. Everybody was angry at what had happened and was anxious to express their sympathy to me and my family, which seemed to include the entire American nation. Our presence had localized the whole series of disasters for the town. There was concern about our children, and word that we had spoken with them spread quickly. As friends repeated the stories of how our children had been trying to contact us, to reassure us and tell us about events from their end, Sennar became a part of the larger tragedy, touched in a very immediate way by events that the attack generated. Sudanese television continued to give full coverage to the events, and within twenty-four hours, we saw Sudanese President Omar al-Bashir hold a press conference to express his and his nation's sympathy to the American people, and their outrage at what had happened. The vice president also made a lengthy statement denouncing the atrocities. Certainly, the general sentiment was one of horror, and at this stage I did not hear any ill will towards the United States. Indeed, most ordinary people seemed to hold very idealized ideas about Amreeka, to want to know more about life there and to have closer contact with American people.

It did not take long for things to settle back to normal. Within a couple of weeks, the tragic events receded from Sennar. Television in town was down for a few days, and Halima had no radio in her home, so several days went by when I had no outside news. The major concerns for most people locally were the heavy rains that year, and the dramatic increase in cases of malaria in Sennar, which affected almost everyone. Different sorts of problems were uppermost in my mind as my research assistants arrived from Khartoum and we started our work at the medical school.

However, fear of a possible war was never far from the surface, as people wondered if they would be attacked in retaliation. These were clearly turbulent times. Even as many people continued to show outrage at the attack and sympathy for the victims, there was increasingly vocal support (generated particularly by fundamentalist Muslim groups like Ansar Sunni) for Afghanistan, and calls for people to join a holy war in its defense. Even moderate men and women wondered if bin Laden was a "sign," someone who represented Muslim interests against the West. On television there were educational programs about Afghanistan, a country not particularly well known to the women of Sennar. They were surprised to see how similar the countries were, but in many ways Afghanistan appeared to be even poorer. Thus when news of the U.S.-led invasion of Afghanistan was broadcast—and once again, both Sudan television channels switched over to coverage from al-Jazira—most women were angry that so much force was being targeted against such an impoverished nation. Earlier sympathies for Amreeka and its people began to dissipate. Some students at the medical school no longer wished to work with us, or to have their name known in the United States. Rumors of heavy-handed U.S. pressure on governments like that of the Sudan began to fly. But then

Ramadān started, and within a few days fasting and prayer were the pre-occupations of the town.

Since that awful day in September we in the West have learned a great deal more about the Muslim world. Sadly, much of the information we get is not particularly helpful in terms of learning more about the lives of ordinary people. Motivated by political and economic agendas, media accounts generally fail either to account for the enormous appeal of Islam as a religion and way of life or to provide any real understanding of how individual Muslims, especially women, cope with situations of political, economic, and social challenge. As I prepare the second edition of this book, I hope that this will be one of the lasting lessons from the *Five Women of Sennar.*

Continuity and Change in Central Sudan

Dramatic and terrible as the events of 9/11 were, viewing them from Sennar serves to highlight the extent of change in Sennar. People's lives there are now lived in a global context. Vastly improved telecommunications give men and women access to world news in a very immediate way. Local television (which draws on stations throughout the Middle East) as well as the availability of satellite dishes means that

Improved transportation in Sennar (2001). This includes rickshaws (imported from India) as well as air-conditioned express buses.

even illiterate women are aware of world events and hold opinions about them. Ease of telephone communication from relatives overseas brings a second stream of information into many homes, and although again the emphasis is on parts of the Middle East, women and men are aware of events and developments outside the Sudan. The same ease of communication is breaking down the differences between rural and urban communities, for most villagers in this region also have access to television and telephone, and improved transportation further facilitates movements of ideas and people back and forth.

Change has come in many forms to this part of the Sudan, as the women's stories make clear. Not all the changes have been happy for them, as the account of the market woman clearly illustrates; and her situation is a reminder of the constant struggle for simple survival that many households in Sudan face. "Illness of money" is a common complaint, made more severe by awareness of the affluence in other countries and even in parts of Sudan itself. The decline of the women's "shadow economy," which Fatima's experience illustrates, is also seen in the commodification of many of the services that were formally provided by women for women. Increasingly these are being provided for cash (many perfumes and oils, as well as formerly handmade sheets and skull caps, are now bought in the market), by institutions, or by men (as Zachara the midwife explains in her discussion of changing birthing patterns in town). This may be paralleled by the expansion of higher education and professional opportunities for women, but many uneducated women are left with dwindling alternatives.

On the whole, however, change is greeted optimistically by women such as the five who tell their stories here. There is pride in the way the next generation is discussed, a distinctly positive feeling that their children's lives will be better than theirs. Despite the many economic and political crises they have experienced, the women are open to innovations in which they perceive advantages for themselves and their families. With their grandmothers' encouragement, several young women were anticipating professional careers: one of Bitt al-Jamīl's granddaughters is a lawyer, one of Halima's granddaughters is planning to be a doctor, while the midwife's own daughters all completed college and continue to practice their professions as they raise their own families. Their sons and grandsons, on the other hand, are less fortunate. For them the pressure is to find a position overseas to further the family fortunes. Several young men, like Halima's grandson, prefer to seek employment as a laborer than struggle to complete high school and then, because of conscription, risk being sent to fight in a civil war that few people support.

These developments in turn affect social life, particularly patterns of marriage and family. On the one hand, there have been attempts to eliminate

Commodification of services (2000): A bridal shop in Omdurman sells wedding regalia

the excesses of the traditionally arranged form of marriage, particularly exorbitant bride wealth. Men often cannot afford to marry. In the early 1990s, the government introduced the practice of group weddings, but these have not been popular in Sennar. Most young men prefer to find work overseas to meet the expenses of marriage. On the other hand, more young women are completing high school and working for a while before trying to get married, only to find that there is a shortage of marriageable men in Sudan today. This is partly because so many young men have gone overseas for economic or political reasons and not returned. Many others have been lost in the tragic war in the south. Recognizing that they need to be married, for both personal and social reasons, young women are prepared to consider alternatives. Polygyny, for example, is increasing because, despite potential problems, this can offer a woman full adult status and motherhood. Expectations of marriage are also changing. Women no longer want such large families and are more knowledgeable about contraception. Some want to continue working after their marriage and the birth of their children. They also generally want their own home, although for economic reasons they may have to share a compound with parents in the early years of marriage.

Other social changes are evident in the accounts of the five women. While a sense of tribal identity remains important for them, the tribe no longer determines where their daughters live, whom they marry, or indeed their behavior. Another form of identity, nationalism, is rapidly being fostered through radio and television, school, and politics. The Sudanese woman, al-Sudaniya, feels a distinct sense of kinship and pride in the attributes that this term conveys, encompassing as it does ideas of dress, style, traditions, and knowledge.

Changes are also evident in spiritual areas. During the six years (1979–85) I was living in and visiting Sennar, zār groups were expanding and consolidating. In many ways, zār had become a sort of exclusive club where some women went to relax in what they perceived as a cosmopolitan, if otherworldly, atmosphere. With the introduction of the Sharī'a in 1983, attitudes to zār began to change as a stricter form of orthodoxy was spread through the country. Zār spirits were denied many of their former luxuries (such as alcohol), and ceremonies became shorter and less extravagant. However, it was not until the early 1990s that political attempts were made to suppress public zār performances. Naeima's vivid account of her brush with the law illustrates the tensions of that period. Today, zār is once again practiced with apparent impunity and in the thanksgiving ceremonies of Rajab, 2001, I witnessed far more women celebrated far more lavishly than twenty years ago.

Yet, despite the often dramatic changes that have been occurring in recent years, a sense of continuity pervades each chapter. Several reasons contribute to this. Each woman was middle-aged when we first met and is now elderly; they all have a strong sense of how things should be done, of how they were done in their parents' day, and of what is proper. They are not necessarily resistant to change; rather, they are ordinary human beings who tend to believe that there is a lot of good in well-tried patterns. They are all experienced women and have found ways that work for them. Each contributor is basically illiterate and, as Zachara explains in chapter 4, their education was largely informal and verbal. They learned from the previous generation, by story or by practical example, rather than by studying in school or from books of the formal conveyance of the ideas of others. They continue to feel that there is a proper order to the way things should be.

This quest for order, in all aspects of life, is evident in each of the above chapters and continues to be important in understanding women's lives in contemporary central Sudan. With themes variously woven throughout their stories, the five women describe this quest quite clearly. We encounter it first in relation to a woman's physical appearance, in the quest for beauty and cleanliness that Halima the hairdresser describes, although her comments are particularly echoed by Zachara, the midwife. Fatima, the market woman, emphasizes the order of her work in the market, activities that reflect the daily domestic duties of all Sudanese women, writ large. In the midwife's account we see just how carefully female health and reproduction is ordered, particularly through the rituals focused on sexuality. Through Bitt al-Jamīl's work, we learn more about women's relations with formal religion and the various levels of order and comfort this provides for their lives, through answers to daily dilemmas, health concerns, and family welfare. Indeed, a casual perusal of the cases brought to Bashir Fath al-Rahman in October 1981 throws more light on the problems and faith of individuals in Sennar than a whole volume of analysis. Finally the ongoing discussion of zār, and in particular Naeima's story in chapter 6, highlights the search for ordered relations with the spirit world, a realm where the possibility of disorder is greatest. This is evident from the tension ever present in the coffee parties held for Shirumbay.

The biggest single factor of continuity, however, is the influence of Islam. The pervasive nature of religious belief is evident throughout the accounts. The main source of order in each woman's life comes from her submission to the will of God, however that is interpreted. The timeless routine of the process of prayer, the regularity of the daily prayers, of the weekly and yearly patterning of the Islamic calendar, the certainty of God's will and his expectations of each individual, all further reinforce women's sense of identity within a very organized world. When we first met, many Sudanese women had had little contact with non-Muslims and, like Zachara, experienced some difficulty in placing them in the sphere of things. The role of the non-Muslim spirits in zār epitomized the confusion such "foreigners" bring. Their behavior challenges the whole orderly basis of traditional Sudanese life, yet they also seem to be successful in breaking apparently inviolable laws and customs. Fortunately, in zār it is still possible to control those alien challenges and bring them within acceptable bounds. In real life, there is an increasing realization that this is not always so. By 2001, education, media, and easier travel were all challenging the order on which their lives were built, and by which they interpreted Islam. Indeed, several of the women were themselves contributing to the changes. Halima, Zachara, and Bitt al-Jamīl all visited Saudi Arabia more than once, both for the haj and to visit relatives. Halima and Zachara returned from the experience chastened by what they felt was their former ignorance of "true" Islam, and since that time they have struggled to practice a more "modern" submission based on what they learned overseas. Both are increasingly devout, devote time and money to their local mosque, and have renounced all interest in such "un-Islamic" activities as zār. The increasing influence of Saudi Arabia in the lives of ordinary Sudanese—on religion, their economic situation, their sense of identity—is considerable, and the recent visit of two Saudi businessmen to the house of Halima vividly illustrates how personally this can affect individuals and communities.

Final Comments

Five Women of Sennar is a study in the changing roles of women in Sudanese society. It is also a little more. It is an attempt to look at that well-defined world of women and to suggest ways of approaching and understanding that world. It is both an account of women's lives in a segregated society and a description of Sudanese society from a female perspective. The women I talked with accept the conventional ideology of a male-dominated society. Yet they are well aware of the difficulties men can make for women's lives and have found ways of dealing with them. Neither Halima nor Zachara wanted to remarry when their children were young, anticipating conflict between their second husband and their children and realizing that they would almost certainly lose custody of their children to their first husband. Now that their children are older, they have found themselves a full and independent life.

"The man is like the morning shade," commented Halima, an expression that men dislike. I was told by several Sudanese men that it could be interpreted in various ways and was easily misinterpreted. The women knew exactly what it meant. They use the saying mockingly and with gentle irony. Men are unpredictable. Their ideas tomorrow may be quite different from those of today. Therefore it is unwise to rest all one's expectations on a man, be he father, son, or husband. Women's resources, social and economic, are also with each other, and these must be protected. It is these resources that help women to see to their own special needs and that perpetuate women's distinctive culture.

The fact that men are fairly invisible in these pages is significant and perhaps one of the most important points to be made. Sudanese women are coping with recent and traditional crises in well-tried fashions, often on their own. In recent years political developments have enabled some professional women to assume more senior and responsible positions. On a public level, however, it will take some time for this to happen throughout the Sudan. Yet as more women speak out, leaders and politicians as well as teachers, hairdressers, professional women, and holy women and midwives, along with the rest of the world, will be aware of the contributions they have been making to family, society, and state in an important part of the world.

A definitive account of the changing status and roles of Sudanese women obviously cannot be compressed into a few chapters on the careers of five individuals. The Sudan is a vast country, with a great variety of environments and ethnic groups, as well as sociocultural, linguistic,

Five women in Sennar (2001): Halima and daughter Miriam (left) greet guests

and political forms. Far more than five voices need to be heard before this complexity can be fully understood. This is a study from only one town, an ordinary market town, the seventeenth largest town in the country, with its own distinctive historical and environmental characteristics. Having met five women from Sennar, however, we are in a better position to go out and talk to their sisters and daughters in other parts of the country. This study is only a start. As more information is gathered, then it is possible that the complexity and dynamics of women's roles in contemporary Sudan will be fully appreciated.

GLOSSARY OF SUDANESE ARABIC TERMS

abu	father
'adal	lit. "reconstruction"; describes the reinfibulation of circumcised women
āhal	nuclear family
'ain	lit. "eye"; it usually refers to the Evil Eye
'aiyla	extended family
akhu	brother
'amal	lit. "deed" or "practice"; it commonly refers to a form of (black) sympathetic magic and category of diagnosis used by the *fakī*
'amm	father's brother
'amma	father's sister
'aragi	local spirit distilled from dates or sorghum

'ārid
lit. "obstruction"; a category of diagnosis used by the *fakī*

'arūs (*masc.* **'arīs**)
bride (bridegroom)

'azima (*pl.* **'aza'īm**)
type of cure used by a *fakī* that involves mumbling Quranic incantations and spitting after each verse to transfer the *baraka*

bakhūr
incense made from local woods, seeds, and resins

baraka
blessing, grace, benediction; also used to describe a beneficent force or power of divine origin

basīr
bone setter; a type of traditional curer

beit
house, household

bitt (*pl.* **benāt**)
girl or daughter

burei
a type of *zār*; most popular in central Sudan. See also *tombura*

daiya
midwife

daiya al-bāladi
traditional or local midwife, often referred to as *daiya al-habl*, "rope midwife," after the preferred method of giving birth

dastūr
lit. "hinge or constitution"; a synonym for *zār* spirit

Derewish
used in *zār* to refer to the category of spirits of Sufi leaders

dilka
a highly perfumed cosmetic made from millet flour, sandalwood oil, and spices and used as a skin conditioner

dōwa
medicine or treatment; also used to refer to the herbs or spices used in cooking

dugāg
a style of hair braid

fakī
(*fem.* **fakīra**, *pl.* **fugāra**)
religious teacher and holy man; colloquial version of *fagih* or *fakir*

farasha	sweeper or cleaner
farīg	district or neighborhood
fath	lit. "opening"; it commonly refers to a revelation or divine inspiration
fātiha	lit. "opening"; it describes the first *Sura* or verse of the Quran, which is used as the Islamic salutation of condolence or sympathy
Fellata	
(*fem.* **Fellatīya,** *pl.* **Fellatīyin**)	collective term applied to immigrants of West African origin, largely irrespective of tribe
firka (*pl.* **firāk**)	woman's garment, similar to a small *tōb*, used to cover the lower part of her body. Usually striped and red in color, associated with the bedroom and smoke-bath
firka al-garmasīs	particular *firka* used at weddings, made of brightly colored silk
fironi	pharaonic, the name for the type of circumcision that entails both excision and infibulation
gabīla, (*pl.* **gabaiyal**)	tribe or ethnic group
gubba (*pl.* **gubab**)	tomb or shrine
al-Gulʻa	name of a fourth-class district on the southern edge of Sennar
Habbashi	generic term for Ethiopians, and also a category of *zār* spirits
habōba (*pl.* **habōbat**)	grandmother, a term commonly used for old women
hai	official term for urban district
haj	Islamic pilgrimage to Mecca
henna	*Lawsonia alba*, the leaves of which plant are dried, ground, and made into a paste that Sudanese women use to dye and dec-

orate their hands and feet. Commonly used throughout the Middle East and western Asia. In Sudan, is frequently used by married women, and the most elaborate *henna* painting is made for a bride. A man has *henna* only when he gets married.

hijāb — charm, amulet, or curtain

'id — religious festival. The two main *'īd* are *'īd al fitr* (immediately after Ramadān, the first day of the tenth Islamic month) and *'īd al-adha* (the tenth day of the twelfth month).

'ilba — lit. "container"; in *zār* it refers to the tin box and its contents of exotic paraphernalia owned by leaders

ishfa — a needle-like implement (bodkin) used in plaiting hair

jabana — prepared coffee; term also used for coffee pot and coffee party

jallabīya (*pl.* **jalalīb**) — men's traditional outer garment, resembling a long shirt

jidd — grandfather

jinn (*pl.* **junūn**) — a ubiquitous type of spirit

kanūn — traditional Sudanese cooking stove, a sort of brazier made from pottery or from metal boxes

karāma (*pl.* **karāmat**) — lit. "generosity"; it is the term used for a thanksgiving ceremony or offering made to God on occasions of good fortune. It has no set form, but most commonly a sheep is slaughtered and a feast held. The word also means a miracle, as performed, for instance, by a *fakī*.

khāl	mother's brother
khāla	mother's sister
khalīja	type of *jinn* or spirit; an extremely ugly supernatural being with evil or demonic associations
khalwa	Islamic or religious school
khashm al-beit	lit. "mouth of the house"; it commonly refers to a lineage or subgroup
Khawāja (*pl.* **Khawajat**)	Persian word meaning notables or merchants. In the Sudan it refers to white-skinned foreigners.
kheira	method of diagnosis used by the *fakī*
kisra	Sudanese unleavened bread made from fermented dura or millet
klubsh	eclampsia or calcium deficiency
kufāt	a style of hair-plaiting. See also *mahlab*, *simsim*, and *dugāg*
kursi	lit. "chair"; it is a term used in *zār* to refer to the seven-day ceremonies
kushuk	kiosk, shed or enclosed stall
mahlab	a style of hair braiding. The term also refers to an aromatic plant used in making local perfumes.
Mihāya	the water used for washing off Quranic verses written on a wooden board (*lawh*) by the *fakī*. It is believed to have medicinal properties.
miskīn (*fem.* **miskīna**, *pl.* **misakīn**)	lit. "poor" or "unfortunate"; the term is usually complimentary when applied to a female, and indicates a quiet and modest demeanor.
mūezzin	caller to prayer from the mosque
mulūkhīya	*Corchorus olitorius* or Jew's mallow. Annual plant either cultivated or wild;

used as a vegetable or in native medicine (El-Shahi and Moore 1978:228). In Sudan it also refers to a traditional and very popular type of stew made with meat, onions, and the *mulūkhīya* leaf, which resembles spinach.

mushāt term used for hair-plaiting and in particular the Sudanese woman's so-called traditional style

mushāta the traditional hairdresser

Pashawat term used for category of Turco-Egyptian spirits in the *zār* cult

pashdaiya associate midwife (term employed in condominium period)

rabāba type of lute

Rajabīya special annual festival of *zār* occurring in the Islamic month of Rajab

rakūba lean-to or shelter

Ramadān the ninth month of the Muslim calendar, which is the month of fasting

rīh lit. "wind"; refers to types of spirits

al-rīh al-ahmar lit. Red Wind; it is the formal (religious) term for *zār*

sandug lit. "box" or "container"; it popularly refers to a method of financial saving, a rotating credit association, which in the Sudan is particularly popular among women

sanjak male, largely ceremonial leader of *tombura zār*

sharaf lit. "honor"; it is used colloquially to refer to a virgin's hymen

Sharī'a Islamic law

simsim	lit. "sesame seed"; it also refers to a style of hair braiding
Sudan gafal	a style of hair-plaiting employed by young girls in which the hair is pulled straight back from the brow, without any fringe
Sufi	lit. "wool-clad"; it refers to Islamic mystics and mysticism
suk	market
Sunna (*adj.* **Sunni**)	tradition, saying, or act of the Prophet Muhammad; the term is used in the Sudan for the mild form of female circumcision operation.
Sura	Chapter of the Quran
Taktūk	name of one of the best older districts in Sennar
Tariga (*pl.* **Turug**)	lit. "path" or "way"; it refers to a Sufi order or brotherhood
tasbīra	three-day ceremony in *tombura zār* where no animal is sacrificed; also written *tusdīra* and *tazfiya*
tōb (*pl.* **tiyab**)	women's formal outer garment, made of a 10-metre length of fine fabric. It is also worn by some men, though is of a coarser cloth, is put on differently, and nowadays restricted to nomads. It may also be used as a sheet.
tombura	type of *zār*
tushit	large round shallow multi-purpose metal bowl
ukhut	sister
umīya	term used for the leader of *zār* in Sennar
umm	mother
umregeiga	lit. "the mother of delicacy"; a basic traditional stew made from crushed dried okra, meat, and onions

usra	nuclear family
wad (*pl.* **awlad**)	boy
wajib (*pl.* **wajba**)	lit. "duty, duties"; also refers to specific and mutual social and financial obligations
wāli (*pl.* **wilyān**)	guardian, male protector of a woman
zār	a belief in a particular type of possessing spirits; the spirits themselves; and the cult associated with the beliefs. See *burei* and *tombura*.
zikr	lit. "remembrance"; it is used in Sufism in the sense of invoking or worshipping God. ("Remember God with frequent remembrance.")

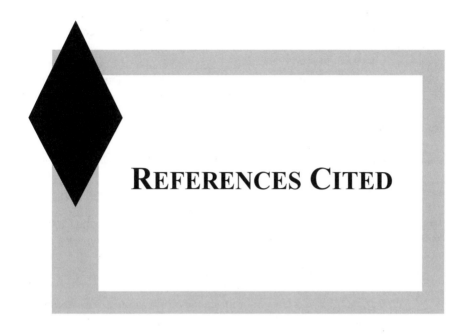

REFERENCES CITED

Ardener, S. (1964), "The Comparative Study of Rotating Credit Associations," *Journal of the Royal Anthropological Institute*, 94(2): 210–29.

El-Arifi, Salih (1980), "The Nature and Rate of Urbanization in the Sudan," in Pons 1980: 381–411.

Bernal, V. (1993), *Cultivating Workers: Peasants and Capital in a Sudanese Village.* (New York: Columbia University Press).

Boddy, J. (1989), *Tombs and Alien Spirits: Women, Men and the Zar Cult in Northern Sudan.* (Madison: University of Wisconsin Press).

Bruce, J. (1790), *Travels to Discover the Source of the Nile in the Years 1768–1773*, 5 vols. (Dublin and Edinburgh: printed for G. G. J. and J. Robinson by V. Ruthven).

Cailliaud, F. (1826), *Voyage à Méroé et au Fleuve Blanc*, 4 vols. (Paris: L'Imprimerie Royale).

Constantinides, P. M. (1972), "Sickness and the Spirits: A Study of the Zaar Spirit Possession Cult in the Northern Sudan." (Ph.D. dissertation, University of London).

Department of Statistics, Khartoum (1961), "The First Population Census of the Sudan 1955/56," 3 vols.

——— (n.d.), "The Second Population Census of the Sudan 1973."

El Dareer, A. (1982), *Women, Why Do You Weep? Circumcision and Its Consequences* (London: Zed Press).

Geertz, C. (1962), "The Rotating Credit Associations: A Middle Rung in Development," *Economic Development and Cultural Change*, 10.

Gleichen, A. E. W. (ed.) (1905), *The Anglo-Egyptian Sudan: A Compendium Prepared by Officers of the Sudan Government*, 2 vols. (London).

Gruenbaum, E. (2001), *The Female Circumcision Controversy: An Anthropological Perspective*. (Philadelphia: University of Pennsylvania Press).

Hale, S. (1996), *Gender Politics in Sudan. Islamism, Socialism and the State.* (Boulder, CO: Westview Press).

Ismail, E. T. (1982), *Social Environment and Daily Routine of Sudanese Women.* (Berlin: Dietrich Reimer Verlag).

—— and Makki, M. (1990), *Women of the Sudan..* (Koeln, Germany: Hundt Druck GmbH).

Jackson, H. C. (1954), *Sudan Days and Ways.* (London: Macmillan and Co. Ltd.).

Kenyon, S. M. (1991), *Five Women of Sennar: Culture and Change in Central Sudan.* 1st ed. (Oxford: Clarendon Press).

—— (1995), "Zar as Modernization in Contemporary Sudan," *Anthropological Quarterly,* 68(2): 107–120.

—— (2001), "Zar," *Encyclopedia of African and African-American Religions,* ed. S. T. Glazier. (London: Routledge).

—— (in press), "Rotating and Escalating Credit in the Female Domain: The Sudanese *Sandug,*" *Financial Institutions in the Political Economy in Africa,* ed. E. Stiansen (Uppsala, Sweden: Nordiska Africakinstitutet).

—— (ed.) (1987), *The Sudanese Woman*, Graduate College Publications, No. 19, University of Khartoum (London: Ithaca Press).

Makris, G. P. (2000), *Changing Masters. Spirit Possession and Identity Construction among Slave Descendents and Other Subordinates in the Sudan.* (Evanston, IL: Northwestern University Press).

El-Nagar, Samia El-Hadi (1975), "Spirit Possession and Social Change in Omdurman" (M.Sc., University of Khartoum).

—— (1987), "Women and Spirit Possession in Omdurman," in Kenyon 1987: 92–115.

Pallme, I. and Petherick, J. (1980), "Accounts of el Obeid in the 1830s and 1840s," in Pons 1980: 79–96.

Pons, V. (ed.) (1980), *Urbanization and Urban Life in the Sudan.* (Khartoum: Development Studies and Research Centre, University of Khartoum).

Rehfisch, F. (1980), "A Rotating Credit Association in the Three Towns," repr. with postscript by S. El-Nagar, in Pons 1980: 689–706.

Sanderson, L. P. (1981), *Against the Mutilation of Women.* (London: Ithaca Press).

Sennar District Commissioner's Office, minutes of the 1950–1 council meetings.

Sharafeldin, E. Abdelsalam (1983), "A Study of Contemporary Sudanese Muslim Saints: Legends in Sociocultural Contexts" (Ph.D. dissertation, Indiana University).

Stevens, E. S. (1910), *My Sudan Year.* (New York: George H. Doran, Co.).

Sudan Public Record Collection, particularly information on Condominium policy, Files CIVSEC 5/6/33, CIVSEC 57/3/C, and PUB 3/2/7.

El-Tayeb, G. (1987), "Women and Dress in Northern Sudan," in Kenyon 1987: 40–66.

Trimingham, J. S. (1949), *Islam in the Sudan.* (London: Frank Cass & Co. Ltd.; 3rd impression, 1980).